LOUISA YOUNG

You Left Early:

A True Story of Love and Alcohol

THE BOROUGH PRESS

The Borough Press
An imprint of HarperCollins*Publishers* Ltd
1 London Bridge Street
London SE1 9GF

www.harpercollins.co.uk

This paperback edition 2019
1

First published in Great Britain by HarperCollins*Publishers* 2018

This is a work of non-fiction based on author's experiences. In order to protect
privacy, names, identifying characteristcs and details have been changed.

A catalogue record for this book is available from the British Library

ISBN: 978-0-00-826520-5

Set in Minion Pro by Palimpsest Book Production Limited,
Falkirk, Stirlingshire

Printed and bound in the UK by CPI Group (UK) Ltd, Croydon CR0 4YY

MIX
Paper from
responsible sources
FSC® C007454

This book is produced from independently certified FSC™ paper
to ensure responsible forest management.

For more information visit: www.harpercollins.co.uk/green

Inversion of Intervals:

Major becomes Minor.
Perfect stays Perfect.
Augmented becomes Diminished.

from Robert Lockhart's
music theory notebook
1969

For everyone who has found themselves here

Introduction

2017

The book you hold in your hand is a memoir by me, Louisa Young, a novelist, about Robert Lockhart, a pianist, composer and alcoholic, with whom I was half in love most of my adult life and totally in love the rest of it. It's as much about me as about him, and is of necessity a difficult book to write. So why am I writing it? Why expose, so openly, chambers which are only usually displayed via the mirrors and windows with which novelists protect their privacy?

Because his life is a story worth telling.

Because our love story, while idiosyncratic, is universal.

Because alcoholism has such good taste in victims that the world is full of people half or totally in love with alcoholics – charismatic, infuriating, adorable, repellent, self-sabotaging, impossible alcoholics – and this is hard, lonely, baffling, and not talked about enough.

Because although there are a million and a half alcoholics in Britain, many people don't really know what alcoholism is.

Because alcoholics also love.

1

Because I don't want to write a novel about an alcoholic and a woman; I want to write specifically about that alcoholic, Robert, and this woman, me.

Because everything I have ever written has been indirectly about Robert, and the time has come for me to address him directly.

Because the last time I tried to address it directly I told him, and he said, 'You won't be able to finish this until I'm dead.'

Because I have realised that for me, quite the opposite: he won't be properly dead until I've finished it.

Four months after he died, I wrote this:

It can't be surprising that I can't write now. All I can think about is Robert and death, so that is all I could write about, but I can't. To write Robert would be to seal him. I, who can rationalise my life into any corner of the room and out again and rewrite my every reality in any version I like, and back, twice before lunch, I cannot pin that man to the specimen paper. I cannot claim to have all of him in view at one time. I cannot slip him into aspic, drown him in Perspex, formalise him – look, there he is in that frame, that's how he was, that's him. No, that is *not* him. *He* is an alive thing. His subtleties and frailties are living things. I cannot bind to myself or any other place the joy that he was. It makes no sense to me for him to be dead. And when it does make sense to me, as no doubt it must at some stage, then – well then he is even deader, because I will have accepted it. And I do not accept it. I do not want to accept it. I reject it. I say to death: Fuck off.

But I am a writer, and without writing I was bereft. And God knows I was bereft enough already. I have so much and yet these have been years of loss. Each loss lost me something else as well. Losing Robert lost me writing. I wanted to talk to him about it. Instead there I was, writing about not being able to write: If I write this book, am I preventing other versions? Will making this our conversation disbar me from remembering other things we said?

Am I bruising my memories by handling them? If I file them, will I ever find them again? Will their bloom be intact?

I was always terrified of losing him; I lost him a hundred times and had him back. I wanted him back yet again. His nine lives, the nadirs he specialised in. I thought: he wouldn't really be dead. It's so unlike him.

This is my version. Anyone who knew him will have their own version. I understand that. I've done my best to balance open honesty about this illness with sensitivity.

Part One

1959–2002

Chapter One

Beirutsbridge Road, he called it. This neighbourhood! Between charming Holland Park and its neighbour Shepherd's Bush there is a difference in life-expectancy of eight years. A six-foot woman pushing a buggy yells 'I've got my child wiv me 'ave some fuckin' respect' at me for no reason I can imagine, unless it's that I'm wearing only one blue paper flipflop following a pedicure-related broken-blue-paper-flipflop incident. Then a big West Indian man comes towards me, with a tiny Thai man trying to pat his – the big man's – back and wipe something off his – the big man's – front at the same time, both of them giggling. A scrawny pasty-faced undertaker in his frock coat walks by, swigging Diet Coke from a bottle. A tiny pregnant person who says she's Greek but I'm not sure she is wants some money, so I give her some and direct her to the Greek church, but I don't think she understands. An old Spanish man informs me that he's seventy-one; I say Happy Birthday, he howls with laughter and says 'Happy New Year!' There are giant yellow tubes piled up all down the middle of the road. A barefoot man goes by on crutches, his feet swollen and dry and

7

sad; he gives me a glance of barefoot complicity, but mine are bare out of vanity, not need. I wanted to get home, but I didn't want the nail polish to smudge. It's Dickensian. A barefoot man on crutches.

Always, walking down this road, heading west from the Tube station to the street where I have lived for twenty-five years, to the house where he had so often pitched up over the decades, and kind of lived with me for ten years, I look for Robert: leaning in the doorway of Paolo's cafe, beaky nose, skinny legs, having a cigarette; coming out of Jay's newsagent, hobbling across the road from the Nepalese restaurant popularly known as the Office, in the brown velvet-collared tweed coat I gave him after he left the dark blue one on the train to Wigan; or the old leather jacket, or the new old leather jacket, in his jazz-cat hat, hunched like a grey heron at the edge of the city street, being liminal, looking about him, in the rain, or the sunshine, perhaps sitting outside a cafe, newspaper, cigarettes, espresso, pencil, sketches of a melody in the margins of the sports section. In later days, glasses, and crutches, or the two ugly black walking sticks with ergonomic handles shaped like bones.

In his youth he was beautiful like an off-duty Bowie – skinny, pale, romantic-looking, naughty, with something fugitive about him; he was always about to leave. In maturity, a craggy battered face, Northern, a big bent nose, a small chin, no eyebrows to speak of, cheekbones, a broad brow, small scar to the left, brown to grey hair tending to the fine and fluffy unless smoothed back, from which it benefitted, plenty of it, usually either too long or too short, always badly cut, because I did it, because he wouldn't go to the barber. Widow's peak. A bashed pale mouth, thin lips, curled in some sardonic look often enough. Big flat English ears. Beardwise, kind of bald on one side, a bit goatee-ish on the other; a wiry moustache which could have been elegant with the slightest bit of care. The odd pockmark. Glasses – whoever's, it didn't matter much. A bit Ted Hughes, a bit Samuel Beckett. All crag and stoop. Eyes? Yes, he had eyes. They were blue, and much clearer than they had

8

a right to be. I may come back to them. Right now they are staring at me from various photographs, and, writing this, I see him looking at me, and my tears come up again and I need to go and rail against horrid fortune which made him as he was and not just a tiny bit different.

I see him, sometimes, in the criss-crossing currents of people. But he is not there.

Chapter Two

Primrose Hill, Wigan, Oxford, Battersea, 1982

I know for a fact which balcony it was. It has grown mythical in my mind: the balcony on to which he invited me, where he first kissed me, though I can't actually remember the first kiss. But I remember the thrill of him wanting me to go out there with him. First floor, overlooking the park, leaves – plane trees? A very London balcony, as seen on the first floors of many handsome white stucco London houses of the mid nineteenth century.

It was our mutual friend Emma's party, in a first-floor sitting room with long windows. We were twenty-two, twenty-three, at the stage where you go to parties in flocks, losing and gaining companions in the course of the night. I recall it being crowded, glamorous, noisy. I recall my little thrill at the sight of him.

I'd met him before. The first time was on a staircase in an Oxford college in 1976. We were going in and he was coming out. ('We' was me, my childhood friend Tallulah and her calm, amiable law-student boyfriend Simon, who we were visiting, and whose new friend Robert was.) I, a born, bred and dedicated Londoner, had never met a Northerner before, never heard gravelly basso profundo Wigan profanities coming out of a skinny whiplash chips-and-lemonade body. An old cricket blazer of some kind hung off him; clearly not his. He had that romantic demeanour of consumptive turn-of-the-century sleeplessness and intense energy – what my father called 'pale and interesting' (I was more pink and interested). He was gorgeous, incandescent. And leaving. He may return. *Please return* was my only thought.

He did return. He was at an upright piano between two windows, playing – Chopin? Debussy? People piped down. Girls were leaning over him. With my usual instinct to avoid what was attracting me, I went to the other end of the room and stood looking cross with my back to the wall. Oh, I knew how to let a chap know I liked the cut of his jib. And I listened. As someone said years later, 'It was different when Robert played.' It was. He was mesmerising. And he knew it, and he used it, and he was not comfortable with it.

People talked about him. He'd won his place to read music at Magdalen from Wigan Comprehensive (formerly Wigan Grammar) at the age of sixteen. (I, a day older than him, had only just passed my O-levels.) By seventeen he was a demy, a half-Fellow – this is a form of scholarship for 'poor scholars of good morals and dispositions fully equipped for study'. Previous incumbents included Oscar Wilde and Lawrence of Arabia. By his third year he was teaching the first years, and he graduated at nineteen with a double first, twice as good as the normal and tragically insubstantial single first, which was clearly not good enough for him. He'd got Ds in his two other A-levels, French and German, and had massive streaks of ignorance about everyday subjects. Two highly knowledgeable musicians recently – and separately mistook a tape of the young Robert playing for Arthur Rubinstein.

Child prodigy? Massive over-achiever? Cultural cliché? Chippy Northerner? Workaholic artist? All of the above?

'There's no fuckin' *frites* on my *épaule*,' he said.

There was a song he used to sing:

11

'We're dirty and we're smelly,
We come from Scholes and Whelley,
We can't afford a telly,
We're Wigan Rugby League, diddley de dum OI OI.'

He would do it in broad Wigan – 'We coom fro Scerls'n'Welli'
– or, for variety, in a posh, southern, actor-y manner: 'We *come*
from Scales, end Welleh, we *carn't*, aff*ord*, a *te*lleh . . .' Alongside
his exceptional ability on the piano, it made an amusingly ambig-
uous impression. No Brit is left untouched by the terrible four
– class, geography, money, education – and there was an assumption among Oxbridge undergraduates at that time that Northern
= working class. The niceties of 'Rough' v 'Respectable' working
class, or respectable working class v lower middle class, were pretty
irrelevant in that world. It all counted as Not Posh. Sometimes
when posh people realised Robert wasn't entirely working class
they would say he pretended to be, and resent him for it, when in
fact it had been their own presumption in the first place. Once,
for a week, he made a conscious effort to get rid of his accent.
Then he realised people noticed him because of it, and that as long
as he could put up with the mockery it was actually an advantage.
People whose class is unexpected can get away with things. They
can be seen by the class they are arriving in as somehow superior,
gifted with knowledge from the other side. It can work well for
intelligent, socially mobile working-class boys: their strangeness
confers a powerful status – which in turn contributes to the anxiety
of the uprooted, those who by being socially mobile become psychologically divided.

In his uncomfortable, nervy move south and up, Robert did
sacrifice pronouncing book to rhyme with fluke. In Wigan once, a
cabbie taking him home from the station wouldn't believe he was
from there, saying 'Ner, yer not' as Robert, upset, insisted. Meanwhile
in Oxford and London he remained the most Northern thing anyone
had ever seen. He never rescinded his Northern passport, preached

the gospel of rugby league daily (and interminably), and replaced bath-to-rhyme-with-hath not with bath-to-rhyme-with-hearth but with, every time he used the word, a piss-takingly long, self-aware and scornful *barrrrth*. He couldn't use the word 'dinner' without either a sarcastic accent or a short monologue on why he wasn't saying 'tea'. People were often accused of mitherin' and maulin' him. Checking there was enough cash for an outing, he'd say 'As geet caio?', a usage so arcane I doubt there's a Wiganer alive now who'd use it other than in nostalgia and irony. But then those two never quite sorted out their differences in Robert's first-in-the-family-to-go-to-university heart.

His was not a childhood of clogs and tinned food – they had a piano, records, laminated recipe cards – but he was familiar with factory sirens and rough lads and the River Douglas – the Dougie – running a different colour on different days of the week because of the dyes. He loved Les Dawson and explained to me the source of his silent exaggerated mouthing: the 'mee-maw' that women working the mills would use to make themselves understood over the sound of the machinery. And he reserved a lifelong interest in people who, like him, made the risky, lonely leap of class: David Hockney, Alan Bennett, Jeanette Winterson, Keith Waterhouse, Victoria Wood, Dennis Potter. Especially if they were drinkers: Dudley Moore, Richard Burton, George Best, Gazza.

At Oxford, with people he didn't know well, who all seemed to sound like the BBC and wear Eton ties, he felt he had to assert himself to be noticed. He didn't like to be ignored. He wanted to experience everything at once, to lead a life as intense as it could be, to go to bed with as many women as possible, see everything, do everything. 'It's what you do in these sorts of moods that gets you a bad reputation,' he said to a friend who wrote a profile of him for a student magazine. 'And when I'm in one of them I really revel in my reputation.' But he also wanted an introverted life, writing music, reading, with a real relationship, warm and secure and emotional. Then, he said, he despised his other self for sleeping anywhere, and putting up a huge facade. He was really a romantic. 'Just one note,' he said, 'a particular chord, can give me an incredible sense of, well, it can't be nostalgia, because it's not for anything in the past. I suppose it's more like nostalgia for another world . . .'

Robert was *very* popular. His legends abounded: the time his tutor popped in to see him, and a naked girl was playing his piano. The occasion when a scorned admirer – male – dropped an empty champagne bottle from a high window, just missing Robert's head – Robert was convinced it was a murder attempt. The pissing in the sink so often it had to be removed, whereupon he just pissed out of the window. The Dean of Music calling in to wake him every day around noon. The dancing naked on the lawns; the streak across the river during an Eights Week boat race, pursued by loud-hailing patrol boats. And, as a female friend said years later: 'He slept with everyone except me and Benazir Bhutto.'

People mooned over him. *I'm not bloody mooning over you*, I thought. So proud! I *longed* to moon over him. I was SO romantic, and the only thing I was more so than romantic was proud. And of course I found *him* SO romantic, and so of course, because I was seventeen, He Must Never Know. Also, I was narked about him being two years ahead of me academically, though a day younger, and fully state-educated where I was only half, which to my mind gave him a cracking moral advantage. I went from a posh Lefty West London home – 'don't say pardon, say what' – to a state primary – 'don't say what, say pardon' – and then to the kind of highly academic girls' private school which told us that we were better than everybody else. Some of my coevals took this as read, and are currently running the world; those who knew it not to be true tended to slump to the polar opposite and believe themselves to be worse than everybody else, and certainly Not Good Enough, hence the prevalence of drugs and eating disorders among pupils at those places; or, in my case, a mildly dysmorphic conviction of my own fatness, and cider. I grew up drenched in all that should have made me feel at home when I went to university at Cambridge, from accents to architecture, yet found myself bemused, class- and location-wise. Three thick card invitations in the same envelope, to a 'dinner party', a 'dance' and a 'house party', all from names I didn't recognise, on the same night, at different addresses, in Hampshire where I had never been – what was this? I quietly asked a country-gentry type I knew. He sneered at me, for 'faux naivety' and 'inverted snobbery', for, as he saw it, pretending not to know. But I *didn't* know. In London, at nineteen, dinner was a doner kebab on the night bus; if you stayed over after a party it was because you fell asleep on someone's sofa. Being sneered at by someone who considered himself my social superior was . . . educative.

*

At Emma's, I remember a long sofa against the wall; sitting on it with him being, as we later called it, Lockharted – being tested and chauved (a Wigan verb, meaning to wind someone up), regaled and assaulted with a barrage of combative and contrary wit, filthy flirtation and intense, wilfully polysyllabic musical erudition which made strong men weak and weak girls melt – and some people, of course, sidle off in bemusement and/or disgust. Gesualdo's duel, Schubert's syphilis, my bra strap, Bill Evans, more wine, Red Garland, Singapore laksa, Argerich's rubato . . . He was a centre towards which things spun. So when you're on the sofa with him, the focus of him, getting all of it, the intensity, immediacy, challenging, drinking, smoking, the *you – here – now. I want yer* – there was a tendency to go 'Whoa!' and fall into the tidal wave.

Seeing myself as fat and not what boys wanted, I drank too much and had had my heart severely broken at university. I wasn't stupid, but I was dismally blind when it came to reading men's intentions towards me: I got into situations. It was still, just, the era of 'men' and 'girls'. I did agency work (security guard, catering, tea-lady in a parking meter factory) and lived in a squat and wanted to be a writer but I had nothing to say on paper and I knew it. I was frustrated and not good at going after what I wanted. I knew exactly how lucky I was, and I suffered the paralysis which can affect intelligent posh girls, saying to them 'You have been given so much; you with your education and your stable family and your prosperity and your accent, seriously, you're asking for more?' I thought to be loved you just lived your life until someone turned up and loved you. I did actually think, like Shakespeare's Helena, that *we cannot fight for love, as men may do; we should be woo'd, and were not made to woo.* It didn't occur to me to go out and get them. Quite often I stayed in bed reading because it was easier. Looking back at me, I might say I was depressed. Emotions were extreme.

That night, he made me laugh so much. The cutting through the crap – he wouldn't just cut to the chase, he would cut to three chases at once, going too far too fast in all directions and assuming that everyone else wanted to go there too. Which I did. He seemed to carry a kind of truth within him, an honesty beyond that of less intense people. This he never lost. Anyway, we went on to the balcony, and later we went back in a cab to the cheerful little house I lived in. A cab! I was the posh one, but I couldn't afford cabs. We stopped on the way at a kebab shop on Queenstown Road, and Robert kept the taxi waiting. There was a group of skinheads at the back: Ben Shermans, Doc Martens, overhead strip lighting. They made Robert nervous, but it was me they laughed at, with my very long hair – 'Oi, skin'ead!' they yelled at me.

I remember that the wall between my bedroom and the back room was half dismantled; I'd taken down the plasterboard and the strips of lath, leaving only the wooden struts, which I used as a kind of tiny unsatisfactory shelving system. I had a single bed. I remember he was very thin, and the sex was revelatory.

He left the next afternoon, and vanished off the face of my earth. I remember I was hurt and mortified. For months. I did not understand – and still don't – how a brilliant night with someone could possibly *not* lead to wanting another brilliant night with them, and another, and another. Seriously, why? I didn't understand how you could do all that together, and then – nothing. It made me a fool and him a bastard. I hated being a fool and I *hated* him being a bastard.

Many years later, we discussed it. He said, 'You could have rung me. You're a feminist.' But girls didn't ring men in those days. Even educated feminist London girls. Politics was all very well, fear of rejection was something else. And there were none of the modern alternatives – a Facebook friending or a witty little tagged snap on Instagram of something of mutual interest. The telephone was all you had. Or a letter, but Christ, a letter! The permanence! No, it was the telephone or nothing, and that meant the possibility of having to talk to his mother, or his flatmate, or, if you did get hold of him, of the embarrassed silence. Boys, of course, had to face this great compounding pyramid of potential embarrassment all the time. (There was a sub-clause whereby if a girl was more attractive than the man she was allowed to ring, as long as she was prepared to take the risk that as the man was less attractive, he might be over-awed, or as we called it, 'scared of you'. But this never worked in practice, because then as now most girls thought themselves unattractive, and even if they didn't they weren't allowed to admit it, for fear of being labelled 'full of herself'. No, ringing a man you fancied meant you were desperate.)

We – girls – well, I – believed that the boys knew what they were doing. I believed they had thought about it, and were doing it on purpose. I assumed they had all the power. By assuming that, I actually gave them all the power. I didn't learn that for another twenty-odd years. I wish I had rung him. Everything might have been different. But no. I sentenced myself to a ludicrous punishment: burn with desire, and keep quiet about it.

'What would you have done if I'd rung you?' I asked.

'I'd've loved it,' he said. 'I'd've been flattered.'

'But why didn't you ring me?'

'Because I was a little twat.'

*

Many years later, in Primrose Hill with Emma, she pointed out the flat where she used to live. It was on a different street. It didn't look out over Primrose Hill. It had no balcony.

I pointed out the balcony I remembered, a few streets away. She had never been in that building.

But I remember. There had been a brightly patterned rug hanging on the wall on the left as you went in; reds and oranges.

'Hm.' She looked doubtful. Neither of us knew if we remembered or not.

And then in November 2015, poking around in my own past for structure for this book, I found this. (The previous entry ended: 'I'm going celibate'.)

From my notebook: 20 December 1982:

Friday night to a party full of precious hunch-shouldered Oxford boys working on modern TV channels.

'Oh goody,' Emma cries, 'my pianist has arrived. Such a shame we don't have a piano.'

'Who is your pianist?' I enquire.

'Oh he's wonderful, he comes from Wigan and he's . . .' Rob Lockhart, of course. Who was being his usual sweet dirty charming self, uttering his usual friendly lascivious greetings. 'One of these days someone is going to take you seriously,' I say.

'I wish you would,' he replies.

'OK, I do.'

'What, now?' he says.

'Perhaps a little later,' I suggest.

'Excellent!' he says.

And so we check up on each other periodically and then run off up Primrose Hill in the frost and kiss in a most fourteen-year-old haze of clothes and cold and party smells. He slips one shoulder out of my clothes and kisses my throat, and we run down the hill and into a taxi and take the piss out of each other all the way to the Queenstown Road.

'I've changed my mind,' he says. 'You see I went off the pill last week and I've got my period.' (True of me, but not of him.) 'And I've just broken up with someone and I'm still very depressed about it . . .' We bought kebabs and chocolate among the skinheads. 'But could you bear to wake up to this face on the pillow tomorrow morning, or will it be just one of the worst figments of your hangover?' And all through, the feeling that we don't *have* to do anything, we're just mucking about together.

At home he played and I sang Cole Porter, drank tea, I went to the loo, he hopped into bed. I grew a little shy as we sobered up, towards three. 'Are you going to sit there and read me a bedtime story and then creep off somewhere else?' he asked. Nope.

I rang Tallulah today as I felt she ought to know. 'Well one of us had to before he lost his looks,' she said. 'Was he good?'

'Yes.'

'I thought he would be.'

He was. It was. Complete and revitalising and full and bloody nice. Literally, actually – 'I've bled all over everything, oh dear,' I say.

'Sooner you than me,' he says. 'You're meant to. I don't mind if you don't.'

In the morning he said, 'Well, what do you reckon to the face then – weedy, anaemic, pathetic . . .'

The house, including Claude looking for socks, Rory looking for Kevin, Kevin looking for gas fittings to build the bathroom with, came and went about their business. We got up around five, knowing that as a one-night-stand we couldn't push it to the second night, but could make the first last as long as possible. He slept very very deep, very long, very quiet. Hardworking boy. Talking about music, first and last. 'What's the point of music? I'll tell yer. Order from chaos. You don't know where you're being taken. But when you get there, it's all all right. Of course it's not so effective if there's not an interesting route taken, enough chaos on the way, and that's why Mozart is so fucking dull, it's all order, nothing but fucking order . . .' And food. 'I'll take you there,' he says, of a Thai restaurant. I quite wish he would. I quite want more, of course, but

i) I'm celibate
ii) I don't want a boyfriend I want love
iii) If I did it wouldn't be Lockhart
iv) You don't get love from one-night stands
v) (iii) and (iv) vice versa.

So we parted on the corner with a friendly peck and a see-ya, and that's it. It has cheered me up no end, so much I did two dance classes on Sunday.'

The notebook continues with seeing my friend off to Hong Kong, having breakfast in bed with my housemates Claude and Berny, band rehearsal, washing the sheets, a long talk with Tallulah where she says that he wasn't actually planned as the father of my kids but that evidently a good time was had by all. 'I have the obvious leaning towards Lockhart but the head says no' – and then: 'Lockhart called to say don't cash the cheque yet and he'll be in touch when he's back from Christmas in Wigan'.

He called?

All that resentment about not ringing was about *nothing*? What, I somehow made that *up*?

And then, a few weeks into the New Year: 'Tonight I had dinner with Lockhart. Nice. We took a taxi to Queensway because he is so thin that he couldn't take the cold.'

I had been totally maligning him as a discourteous Lothario, for decades. He was a courteous Lothario, and by this evidence so was

I. In this contemporary account I am giving every impression of not particularly wanting to continue our liaison. I have rewritten history. Hmm. Thank you, memory.

And I'm wondering – why was there a cheque? My mind leaps in to assist: perhaps the cabbie wouldn't have taken a cheque, so I paid cash and Robert, insisting on paying the fare, gave me a cheque. That makes sense. It must have been that.

Dangerous phrases, 'that makes sense. It must have been that'. Armed with those phrases a passing thought can march off into the back of your head and set up in its pomp as memory, as truth even, claiming through the passing years all the rights and privileges of those titles, to which it is not, actually, entitled. It can permeate a person's overall idea of what their life has been.

So, practically the only thing my memory got right was that it was Emma's party, it was Primrose Hill, there was a taxi and skinheads. I'm really sorry not to have looked at the notebook for thirty-five years, not to have had the chance to read it to him, and have that 'I wasn't a bastard! You weren't a fool!' conversation, in which he would have got to say it was all *my* fault. How he would have laughed.

And then I think again. Well. When, exactly, did I rewrite this history? Was I, perhaps, lying to my notebook, with all that cavalier one-night-stand stuff? Was that my pride? The 'I know he won't want me so I'll not want him first' approach?

I have no idea. But yes, of course that is possible. Probable, even.

Perhaps it was after the *dinner* that he didn't ring.

And now I'm rewriting it all over again; anecdotalising, shifting perspectives on long ago, making excuses, looking for reasons, searching for meaning, wishing.

They say you don't remember what people said, or what they did, but you remember how they made you feel. I would adjust that a little. You remember *that* they made you feel.

*

There's his phone number in the back of a notebook: 720 5399. But I didn't see him for a few years. Tallulah broke up with Simon and moved to New York; I was half in love with loads of other people.

There's another party I do remember: Oscar Moore's, in a snooker club in King's Cross: very dim and low-ceilinged, smoky and so forth as things were then. Robert was wearing a Wigan Rugby League rosette: cherry red, though I was not familiar with the term then. In a move of pure attention-seeking, I stole it off him. He was quite drunk in a cheerful way and didn't really notice, until he saw that I had it pinned to the back pocket of my jeans, where-upon he chased me all round the room demanding to know why I had never told him of my passion for rugby league, and Wigan in particular, with not the foggiest that it was *his* rosette I was sporting, and that I was trying, with considerable lack of either clarity or effect, to express thereby my deep attraction to him.

Anyway, he left, with a group of others, and I stood on a rainy corner in King's Cross with the rosette. I think that's what happened.

Chapter Three

London and Wigan, 1970s

A grand piano's feet take up only a tiny area: three indentations in the carpet, each the size of a conker, cradling a brass ball clad in a brass foreskin attached at an unlikely angle, like a stallion's ankle, to a rising pillar of polished hardwood. Very small, to hold so much weight, and cover so much area: a superior crate the shape of Africa, hollow yet full. With the solid wing raised it shows the heartstrings within, laid in green felt across swirls of miniature golden architecture, and the internal teeth, the hammers coming up from below, sharks from the darkness to bite and bump the strings; dampers above swooping down to see them off every time.

Robert's Bechstein, as long as Rachmaninoff was tall, his father's before him, lives with me now. (I smile as I write that. To Robert, saying a thing 'lived' somewhere was an unforgivable anthropomorphic poncey fuckin' southern bourgeois affec*ta*tion.) Underneath it are boxes and suitcases containing the entire history of Robert's family. It has been my job to poke around in them, sorting things out. I find a brown paper-covered booklet, costing 30p, 15p if sold on Saturday only: the programme of the Wigan and District

Competitive Music Festival, 1972, affiliated to the British Federation of Music Festivals, of which Her Majesty the Queen is patron. It smells of coal-dust and rain, and opens with a message from the mayor, who with the mayoress hopes to see the festival well supported. It lists the patrons, the areas which count as 'local' – Abram, Aspull, Billinge, Ince, Orrell, Standish, Skelmersdale, Holland, Chorley. Perhaps it is in fact these place names which smell of coal-dust and rain. It lists the scale of marks (for piano: accuracy of notes and time, technique, fluency, pace, touch, expression, interpretation); the trophies and medals available and who they are in memory of, the general regulations, appreciations, thanks, and the policy for receiving suggestions. There are ninety-nine classes, with up to twenty-five entrants in each. Choirs, recorder solo, folksong, violin, instrumental ensemble, organ, sight-reading, girls' vocal duet. Thirty-six ten- and eleven-year-olds play 'Ship Ahoy!' by Arthur Pickles on the piano.

In Pianoforte Solo (ages thirteen–fifteen), Robert Lockhart, turned thirteen a week earlier, plays Debussy's 2nd Arabesque, and comes first with 91 points. He wins £1.65, and a stiff certificate with a gold, red and green coat of arms. The following night he comes back to hear Pianoforte Solo (open), and marks what he hears. His marks are a little harsher than the adjudicators' and his observations, in tiny blue biro, are precise. Betty Wilson was slightly too temperamental in her Dohnányi; Richard Eastham lost all movement in his *La Fille aux Cheveux de Lin*. Alison Cratchley's rubato was not up to scratch, though otherwise her Bartók was superb. 'Not delicate,' he writes. 'Dotted notes not clear'; and 'Too much Chopin style for Bach'.

I have Robert's little red Letts diary for 1969, when he was ten: lists of rugby players in pencil, and a few entries in splatty blue fountain pen: 'Grandpa just out of bed been ill. Grandma in bed now.' 'Play with train practise putting hippy wig on.' I have photographs: tiny 1960s black-and-white ones with scalloped edges, carrying all the freight of the out-of-focus faded technology of the past. There he is: a fat baby in incredibly tidy clothes with smocking across the front, chortling. With an ice cream, in Blackpool. Aged about seven on Coniston Avenue in Wigan, with a cricket bat and knobbly knees under baggy shorts. Hurtling towards a finishing line, when he was the second fastest boy in Wigan. With his four plastic horses hitched up to the *Bonanza* covered-wagon playset. There at the piano with his father, John.

'My parents, John and Pat, were deemed to be a glamorous couple in their lower middle class (for want of a better term) milieu,' Robert wrote, much later, in his rehab papers. 'He a travelling salesman with a souped-up Ford Anglia, she a hairdresser.' John, charismatic, grumpy, lovable and extremely musical, developed a form of agoraphobia which rendered him incapable of leaving his home town. If he drove ten miles from the town centre he would start shaking, and have to turn around. It happened once during an outing to Manchester to see a special railway yard, for which permission had had to be sought. Robert and his friends were very excited to go, but by the time they got to Longsight Depot John had what we would now call a panic attack; Robert was embarrassed, his pals in the car didn't know what to say.

John had been a choirboy at Wigan Parish Church and knew everybody in the town. He was once seen weeping in uniform – National Service – at Wigan Casino, in the early fifties, out of unrequited love. As a young man he'd made a record in Norman Leather's record-yourself studio. 'Johnny Lockhart' plays a jazzy, elegant piano and sings in a lustrous baritone the smooth Eddie Fisher song 'When I Was Young'. He must have recorded it for Pat; they married in 1954, the year after the song came out: elegant, beautiful, a satin dress, a dress suit. It's from another world, a Terence Davies world of face-powder and Ford Anglias, a Northern world that I never knew, with a lingering G at the end of my own surname, Young, a way I never heard it pronounced before I met Robert. It's the voice of a man I knew and loved. Not that we pronounced the word love the same either.

John, young, looked like Alain Delon in a raincoat, on a bridge; older, like Michael Caine in the heavy glasses. He stopped drinking overnight in his early forties, but smoked tremendously. Robert called him the Owl of Ormskirk, because of the specs on the very tip of his big nose, always just about to fall off. Or, Pop Lockers. Pat, Robert's mother, had the maiden name North which was already funny because she was from the South. She was blonde and pretty and ran a hairdressing salon in their front room in Coniston Avenue, where Robert was dandled by the ladies, played at their stocking-clad, high-heeled 1960s feet, listening as they chatted, absorbing their affection and glamour. Later Pat worked on the beauty counter at Boots. 'Not quite Elizabeth Taylor and Richard Burton, but never mind,' Robert observed. I never met Pat; cancer got her before I made it north. Robert could be dismissive about her, which made me want to talk to her all the more. It must have been quite something being the woman in a household made up of John and Robert. They all played the piano, but Pat, who was not a bad player either, never got near it because Robert or John was always on it.

'I was a relatively happy child,' Robert wrote, 'successful academically and at sport, plenty friends . . . I didn't think it odd that my dad often got home from "work" at ten p.m. '

John had a girlfriend called Lily Glinka, an anorexic Russian secretary who was afraid of the wind. John took her out on to Southport Sands to try to cure her. Later there was another, Jenny, who loved horses. Robert knew about these things. He and John always talked. And he was woken by the arguments in his parents' bedroom late into the night. His mother was protective but eventually she too 'succumbed to an affair'.

Robert was twelve or thirteen when the family fell apart. John lost his job. He came up to Robert's room and said, 'Are you staying with her or coming with me?' So Robert got up out of bed, put some things in a bag and went with John on their bicycles to John's mother Granny Annie's house. There they shared a single bed.

Robert was horrified by John's toenails, which looked to him like nicotine-stained elephant tusks. He and his mother became 'somewhat estranged'. He said it was not because he loved her less, just that he had more in common with his father. Then Pat's boyfriend died, of diabetes. The trauma ping-pong started, as Robert shuttled from one unhappy home to the other.

John was playing Tchaikovsky in a public place – a hotel? – one evening, and a woman called Kath Griffin sat next to him, saying, 'I prefer the slow movement'. It turned out all she knew about classical music was that she preferred the slow movements, but that wasn't an impediment.

I say all this. I don't know if it's true. It's hard enough getting sense out of your own memories, let alone somebody else's. Robert told me his versions. His parents fighting one Christmas because John had given Pat a bottle of Elizabeth Arden Blue Grass which wasn't what she liked, it was what Lily Glinka liked. Another Christmas when Robert was in the back of the car and he threw up on Granny Annie – or her best hat? – having drunk half a bottle of repulsive sweet sherry because he didn't want to go to Kath's family – or indeed his mother's place, but he hadn't been invited. Pat had met another man. John married Kath, Pat married Mike. Robert was in no mood to like step-parents, but acknowledged later that it must have been 'very difficult . . . to deal with a precocious, wilful teenager'.

He had made the under-13s 100-metre and triple jump teams and went to the Royal Northern College of Music junior school in Manchester on Saturday mornings. This coincided with an influx of 'rough lads who beat the shit out of us supposedly posh grammar-school boys'. He escaped punishment despite being a prime target as a classical pianist – 'automatically a puffter' – because he had played for Wigan Rugby League schoolboys, which even at that age was 'a sport for hard lads'. He loved rugby league with a passion all his life, but because he was studying the piano, due to the high risk of breaking fingers, he had to stop. He had obsessions, often masochistic: 'I would force myself to practise a difficult passage 100 times, having to start again from scratch if a mistake was made. By the 99th rendition, I'd have hot sweats, shaky legs. I assumed I was doing this to harden myself against concert nerves – to develop the ability to switch into robotic. It worked, sort of – but it made arguably the most beautiful language – both to "speak" and to listen to – awkward, dry, an academic, technical exercise.' And, 'having to hold my hand under a boiling hot tap for ten minutes. If not, my mother would die. She did. Admittedly not until eight years after I stopped the habit.' I still wonder what, of the things young children are diagnosed with now, Robert might have been diagnosed with when he was small: Asperger's? Obsessive-Compulsive Disorder? He thought so. Depression? Certainly. Autistic spectrum?

I asked Robert's cousin Diane, who's a few years older than Robert, what he was like when he was little. She said, 'Always on the naughty stool', with a smile.

So there in the north, the boy Robert is beside his father on the yellow brocade duet stool; or on it alone, perfecting his left-hand trills, making certain his *Fille aux Cheveux de Lin* maintains its structure and momentum.

Meanwhile in the south, though I had lessons for years, I had no talent and did no work. I remember locking myself in the loo in a futile attempt not to have to go to a piano lesson. Even now I read music like a six-year-old, counting up and down the notes, naming them under my breath. Robert was repeatedly amazed by the fact that I am, as he put it, 'illiterate.' It was not that I didn't love the piano. I adored it. I spent hours beneath my dad's Blüthner while he played. My companions there were a French horn in its battered leather case lined in blue velvet; an old silver trombone, ditto; a curious stringed thing our grandfather brought from Iraq in the 1920s in a heavy wooden box with a price label in Arabic inside the lid; a schoolchild's violin with a soft lemony cloth and a little round of rosin; my brother's trumpet, yellow and bright compared to the older horns, and a moth-eaten concertina in an octagonal box like a gothic chapter-house. Usually I was eating almonds and sultanas from my jeans pocket, and reading. I couldn't put my book down even for a moment (Narnia, Moomins, *Swallows and Amazons*, the myths of Greece and Rome – it wouldn't cross my mind to put the book down. I used to read walking down the street, and bump into *nothing*) and it was tricky for me to get my hand into my pocket when piled in among instruments, so sometimes I'd kick the pedal column. My father, Wayland, who would be playing Bach, or Schubert ländlers: 'Homage to the fair ladies of Vienna', didn't mind. Our double stool is the kind that opens, full of children's music books and collections of carols published in the 1950s. It is covered in worn *petit point* done by my grandmother. Over that is a sheepskin, put there to cover the wear in the *petit point*, now worn itself. On that, Wayland, who I loved more than life. The music came down through the belly of the piano. It sounds quite different under there. He was careful not to play too loud. For decades I didn't know he did that. Across the room my mother would sit on a sofa in a pool of light, reading about defence policy and sea-use planning.

Before the Second World War, before he went into the Navy, Wayland studied music at Cambridge. When he went back to university after the war, he switched to history. His youthful compositions are still in that *petit point* piano seat. Instead of being a composer, his first dream, he became a journalist, a writer, and ultimately a politician, a Labour member of the House of Lords. My mother, Liz (Oxford and the Wrens) was his partner in politics, his backroom intellectual powerhouse. Their subjects were foreign policy, conservation, peace, the sea, the environment. Wayland's mother was a sculptor, Captain Scott of the Antarctic's widow.

These are the composers Wayland rated: Bach. Then Mozart, who added characters, then Beethoven, who became one great huge character, then Brahms and Schubert, who were just beautifully lyrical. Wagner? 'A bicycle pump,' he said. I liked Chopin and César Franck and Verdi: I knew they weren't officially as good as the ones Wayland liked, but I could run around to them and be fleeing through the forest, hiding from bears, clambering mountains, rescuing and being rescued, riding unlikely beasts. I thumped and pirouetted up and down the sitting room (I did ballet classes – the plump one in a class of music-box fairies). Nobody minded the thumping but if I wriggled too much when sitting near my mother she would say: 'You're making me seasick.' Liz's mother drowned at the age of twenty-nine; six-year-old Liz, playing with her in Lake Geneva, was rescued. This shaped everything, but that is another story.

I'm seeing myself here aged about seven, when my parents were about forty. My brother and sisters are older than me. In the way of elder siblings, they went out more, and further, and in a different way: Beatles concerts, boarding schools, festivals, university, California, Afghanistan. Later, I had a baby sister. Robert always rather yearned for a sister – he thought if he had one he could look after her. He wondered if he could borrow one of mine, I had so many.

The Blüthner had been in that room for forty years, and was there another forty afterwards. My nephew has it now. My family was large, individually adventurous, but overall, steady.

Robert came on a school trip to London when he was eleven, and stayed in a hotel in Lancaster Gate – a hundred yards from where I lived. (He went on another school trip a few years later, an exchange to Amiens. He ran away to Paris and got into trouble.) We might have passed on the pavement as I set off for school, and he crocodiled off to the Tube station to go to the Planetarium. We were born one day apart at different ends of the country, but you could get a direct train from where I was born – Euston in London – to where he was, in Wigan. We were both conceived on holiday. One day a year – my birthday – I was his older woman.

The first time he came to my childhood home, he didn't come

in. It was 1978: after our encounter in Oxford, before Primrose Hill. I was recently back from my post-school year off adventures in India with a small array of revolting digestive illnesses, and had to spend the traditional few weeks in the Hospital for Tropical Diseases at St Pancras, and some time at home recuperating. Tallulah came to visit.

'I can't stay long, the boys are in the car.'

Which boys?

'Simon and Robert.'

My bedroom was on the ground floor. I thought of the yellow line outside, and Simon's little Renault 4, the only car owned by anyone we knew of our age.

Which Robert?

'Lockhart.'

'Oh, they can come in,' I say, nonchalantly.

'You're not well enough,' she said.

'I am well enough,' I said.

'No you're not.'

'Yes I am.'

'No,' she said.

'Yes,' I said.

She didn't bring them in. This occasion was one of the moments when the slippery crystal polyhedron of missed opportunities slips sideways and could, just might, have landed on a different surface. Robert didn't know the details at the time, but later it became for him a moment when we might have got together. 'You'd have been irresistible,' he'd say. 'In bed, all skinny from your illness, too knackered to give me any grief – we could have got together then. We'd have got married – and you'd have divorced me, of course, but then we'd've got married again and been happy and I never would've become an alcoholic . . .' Our non-existent children were to be named after composers: Claudette, Frederica, Cesar and Sergei, for Debussy, Chopin, Franck and Rachmaninoff. Much as he loved Satie and Ravel, we drew the line at Eric and Maurice.

Tallulah doesn't like this story, because it suggests he would only have wanted me then because I was thin and brown. I don't see it that way. At her fiftieth birthday party, we formally forgave her for not bringing him in to see me. She said, 'Actually, you do make rather a good couple', and I felt it as a blessing. I thrilled like a seventeen-year-old to see our names written together on the invitation, even when we were well middle-aged. Public acknowledgement of coupledom. I was never the marrying kind and anyway Louisa Lockhart would be a terrible name – I can see Louisa Lockhart in a third-rate novel, scurrying over the storm-lashed moors, sodden shawl clutched round her after the Young Master done her wrong. Or writing light erotica. Or being an eighteenth-century fishing boat.

According to my diary, I went to his twenty-first birthday party, on 27 March 1980. 'Jolly flirt with L', I wrote in my diary. I have no memory of it whatsoever. And there is his name on the list for my twenty-first birthday party, a few days later. All the names are crossed out, in an 'invitation sent' or 'def coming' way, in a single straight line. His is crossed out in a cloud-formation zigzag of circling pencil, which continues into an arrow pointing to the top of the page. I remember that I cooked dinner for about ten people and then everyone else came afterwards. I made a veal thing where you rolled it up with an omelette inside, and ham, so when you sliced it it was striped pink and yellow, and I added lots of parsley so it could be green as well, deckchair stripes like my favourite trousers of that period. And a pile of meringues and cream. I had friends old and new from different areas of my disparate twenty-one-year-old life, and none of the dinner people, my nearest and dearest at the time, knew each other. I remember we had two bands – Sore Throat and The Arials – and Sore Throat's roadie took all his clothes off and chased round the house trying to apologise to me for being naked, and Shane McSweeney hid the clothes up a tree. But I can't remember if Robert came. So I can't have loved him much then. The following year, only one sighting: ' . . . in the foyer of the Wigmore Hall, listening to the pleasant strains of the first half of the programme, and the whispers and rustlings of the latecomers and ushers. The second half is Rob Lockhart . . .'

I had recently graduated, and was working as a lowest-of-the-low on the making of *Britannia Hospital*, the third of Lindsay Anderson's trilogy of films which started with *If . . .* and *O Lucky Man!* It was filmed in the still-active mental hospital at Friern Barnet, where actors and mental patients mixed perhaps more than had been planned. One chap followed me about to give me ginger cake in a brown paper bag. I had a weakness for talented men with beautiful accents: Glaswegian Robbie Coltrane who slid across the floor of the cast bar on his knees and collided with my bum, which he bit; another of the actors, Welsh Bob Pugh, who read me Gerard Manley 'Opkins and played Van Morrison songs on the piano; history professor Norman Stone (also Glaswegian) who had taught me at Cambridge. I'd had it, forever, with Cambridge, with posh English chaps, dinner jackets, repression, arrogance, misogyny and fear faintly concealed behind perfect manners. The establishment. I was moving into my squat, busking, working as a barmaid, running round with deep-sea divers, Jamaican musicians, despatch riders; saving for New York, wanting to work in films, anything, anyone, but not that Chelsea banker quacking entitled educated ignorant money-making narrow-minded posh ungrateful world . . . It was in that mood that I ran into Robert at Emma's party.

*

Tallulah came back from New York in 1986, and moved in with my friend Swift. We all, in our late twenties, became pals again. We were working hard. I got a mortgage on a one-room flat; I was a freelance journalist now, travelling the world for *Marie Claire*, correcting the spelling on *The Sunday Times*, riding motor-cycles for *Bike* magazine, doing columns in the *Guardian*. Tallulah was running a publishing house. Swift was moving from magazines into the literary end of film. Robert had meanwhile come to London to study piano as a postgraduate, teach at Oxford, and play cocktail jazz in wine-bars to support himself as well as concerts on Radio 3, at Wigmore Hall and the South Bank. He had a girlfriend: kind, pretty, mickey-taking Lisette, who everybody liked. And his mother died. 'Seeing her dying,' he wrote, 'aged 52, looking aged 80, deaf, blind, incontinent, was probably the most disturbing moment of my life.' He retired from professional piano around then, unsure if it was because of his mother's death or not, and started writing music for radio and TV, theatre, films and advertising. He was a musical director at the National Theatre, he triumphed in the West End and New York. He had his little thespian habits and nicknames: Serena McKellen for fellow Wiganer Sir Ian McKellen; Pierre Vestibule for Peter Hall; Pierre Ruisseau for Peter Brook. In 1986 he did the musical arrangements for a production of Arthur Miller's *The American Clock*, and was extremely excited after meeting the author – mostly because of shaking his hand, and Marilyn Monroe. 'I know where it's been,' he said, staring lovingly and disbelievingly at his own hand that had shaken the hand that had made love to the goddess. There was big pressure and scary deadlines, but he didn't have to be on stage, and could therefore drink. That world brimmed with drink.

Being Terence Davies' music director, on *The Long Day Closes* (1988) and *Distant Voices, Still Lives* (1992) and *The Neon Bible* (1995) drew him back to the North, and to his father. He had to conduct a choir of Liverpool schoolboys, singing in Latin. When he corrected their pronunciation one of them said to him, 'Sir, sir, are you Latin?' Oh the joy. As a Wiganer – or Cocchiite, he preferred, because it was both Latin and rude – he liked nothing better than mocking Liverpudlians (unless it was mocking people from Skelmersdale, or his default position in the south, *épater*-ing *les* fuckin' *bourgeois*). He orchestrated the gorgeous version of 'Love Is a Many Splendored Thing', in the scene where they're all in the cinema, crying. Years later I sat in the cinema, crying. I looked at those 1950s Northern people, so beautifully turned out, quoting lines from *The Philadelphia Story*, and thought, is that where he's from?

When he told me how he had fallen out of someone called Nina's window, I thought he and Lisette must have broken up (which they did several times) and felt, God help me, a little pang of jealousy. I wanted him to be falling out of *my* window, or at least trying to climb in it – and it wouldn't have been nearly so perilous, as I was on the ground floor with a window directly on to the street, Jesus, there'd have been no risk at all, he certainly wouldn't have impaled his arse on the railings.

*

His past is in boxes under his piano in my sitting room, for me to deal with, to rationalise or romanticise (which sometimes seem to be the same thing); to put in order, any order that can pass as orderly, so that thereafter it can be put away. I am in charge of his sheet music, his music manuscripts, his CDs, his cassettes, his dad's LPs, his rehab papers, medical notes, autopsy report, boots, books, love letters from his girlfriends, letters to them that he never sent. 'Dear Buttock', he wrote, in 1981; 'Dear Rectangle'. They break my heart. The older ones from Manchester and Nottingham, biro and lined paper; fountain pens and Basildon Bond like a granny, then brown Rotring ink and cartoon sunsets, speech bubbles coming from the picture of the queen on the stamp, or the cherub on the front. Postcards from Siena and San Gimignano, airmails from Ohio and California. Letters starting, 'I've just put down the phone from our conversation but I can't bear not to be talking to you still . . .' Letters which stop and start over days: 'I'm on the train now; sorry about the writing . . . I'm home now, it's so cold . . . Just scribbling this at the bus stop . . .' Funny letters, love letters. Haunting letters: 'WHERE IS YOUR WARM BODY

35

NOW?' A lipstick kiss. A postcard showing a naked lady from behind, waist down, long legs in high heels crossed at the ankle to make a very elongated heart-shape, and on the back, in thick black felt pen: ROBERT JE VOUS ATTENDS AVEC IMPATIENCE. Incomprehensible letters: 'Arms and legs! Arms and legs!' And: '. . . I have written endless letters to you, but have abandoned all due to distress and muddle. There isn't much to say anyway, other than what a fantastic and unforgettable adventure we had, despite our differences . . . If love isn't worth fighting for it was probably not love in the first place but a mutual passion driven by intensity (of a volatile nature). Because to me love is about understanding and security as well as the sex and excitement which always features in the beginning . . .'

One from him, giving his phone number as 999. A photo of a girl with a teddy bear, aged about twenty, and on the back written: 'Only one of these is your girlfriend': she's a film star now. Several have filled me with jealousy appropriate to the age I was at the time they were written: *But I knew you then, why didn't you want me?* wept the ghost of me aged seventeen.

I don't want to read them. They're not mine. Yet here I am in charge of them, which is a damned odd sort of victory over time and the ghosts of love rivals who have long been living other lives.

And there's something addressed to me: a printed invitation to a production of *Woyzeck*, which as it is in 'the Newman Rooms' and gives the date 'Tues–Sat 4th Week' must be to do with Oxford, which exists in its own chronological universe. I do look at that and think –1978? 1979? What if I'd gone?

I could identify about 80 per cent of the letters' senders. I recognise their handwriting; I know the stories, the places, the timings. Tough, sympathetic curly-haired Beth who was my pal at school; Emma who I knew a bit at Cambridge; Jackie the violinist. I put them back in the boxes. All that love, all that youth. I take them out again. Put them back again.

It adds up to a chaotic record of a life which might have been lived differently; a map across which he might have traced a different, better, route. A map I was going to have to look at.

And, for a while, it was like getting a dose of him, after he was gone.

Chapter Four

I am invited for dinner at Robert's flat; the top half of a Victorian house in Shepherd's Bush. He has cooked – late, delicious, pans all over everywhere, as usual. Everyone is clever and funny and affectionate, relaxed verging on chaotic, and it turns into one of those magical evenings. There's a string of fairy lights around the kitchen window frame; we drink lots of cheap wine sitting at the wooden table. Robert plays – Liszt, Debussy's *La Fille aux Cheveux de Lin*, which has become my song, as I have *cheveux de lin* – on his new piano, a Yamaha Boston, black and very sleek. I am surprised by the piano. He doesn't usually like new things. I don't like his new carpet either. It's purple and shiny – the kind you think you'd get electric shocks from. Lisette goes to bed early – perhaps midnight? – as she has work in the morning, and we all agree this is a terrible waste. I'm actually thinking 'how can she bear to?'

As the small hours start to get bigger again people fall away and it ends up with Robert, me and Alastair – a very tall, handsome builder, nicknamed Truncheon for his apparently prodigious dong – lying about smoking and talking rubbish. Nobody in Lockhart-land was allowed their actual name. I was FCB – Flat-Chested Brunette (which I am not). Patrick (who is tall) was The Giraffe. The other Patrick, large of chin with a regal manner, was the 'Crown Jowls'. His adored Jackie, middle name Ruth, a very kind, ferociously talented and focused red-haired violinist, was known as 'Ruthless'. His best friend Graham from Wigan was a simple 'GFW'. Martha Argerich, the pianist he most admired, was 'That gap-toothed Jewish Argentine Lesbian', spoken in tones of awe and wonder. The soprano Elisabeth Schwarzkopf was Betty Blackhead. Phil, who has a mole on his forehead and played Subbuteo, was Centre Forewart. One woman who always got up to dance, no matter the circumstances, was Pan's Person. An employer called Charles, who didn't always pay reliably, was Cheque-bounce Charlie. A Wigan pub, the Swan and Railway, could be the *Cygne et Chemin de Fer*, the Duck and Tram, the Albatross and Cyclepath. An acquaintance who was born without feet, on an occasion of infidelity became 'Foot-Free and Fancy Loose'. Only composers were allowed their real names – their first names, usually used thus, while listening to their music: 'Maurice, you fucker . . .' with a shake of the head and a smile of delight, at some particularly beautiful turn of musical phrase. When I told him about the church that Satie set up in Paris – the Metropolitan Church of Christ Conductor – he was just so happy. 'Eric,' he said, with such fondness in his voice. 'Oh, Eric, you bastard.' That Debussy changed his name from Achille-Claude Debussy to Claude-Achille Debussy was a source of perpetual and unresolved fascination.

Mostly that night we are listening to Chopin.

'I hate them,' Robert says. 'Arseholes. They know nothing.'

'Who?' we enquire.

'Those arseholes.'

'What arseholes?' we say, concerned.

'Critics.'

'Who? Where?' We think he must be referring to something in the paper, or recent. Certainly neither Truncheon nor I have said a word against Chopin. We don't want Robert thinking we are against Chopin.

It becomes apparent that nobody has called Chopin second rate for some years, when somebody, it wasn't apparent who, did.

It comes up that I have never knowingly heard Puccini's opera *La Bohème*. Robert is appalled by this state of affairs, and cannot let it continue. He rumbles about in a pile of cassettes, throwing unwanted ones aside till he finds it, and puts it on. We are to listen to it. It is essential. We refill our glasses and subside, swoonily.

'The thing is,' he says, lounging back in a zigzag of skinny torso and crossed legs on the sofa – 'there is no orgasm. Listen – all build up, and build up – but no orgasm.'

Soon enough Rodolfo – it's José Carreras singing – is catching hold of Mimi's hand on the floor, because they have dropped the key in the dark, and telling her in his heartbreaking bravura romantic tenor that it doesn't matter because they have the moon, and he's a poet, he writes, he lives! I am blown away like Cher in *Moonstruck*: the singing, the beauty, the emotion – I'm lying on my back on the horrid new carpet in a state of considerable ecstatic delight – *the piling up of the music, oh my God, this is SO BEAUTIFUL*—

'No orgasm!' Robert cries. 'See? The bastard's doing it again!'

'SHUT UP,' shout Truncheon and I. We're busy being blown away. Mimi is responding, telling Rodolfo who she is: '*Mi chiamano Mimi, ma il mio nome è Lucia*' – they call me Mimi, but my name is Lucia – how she embroiders roses and lilies in her little white room under the rooftops, where she lives alone and the first kiss of April is hers, how sweet is the scent of a flower—

And then just when she is reaching the peak of this gorgeous spiralling climactic moment, Robert shouts, 'There! Did you hear it?'

'WHAT!?' we snap, wrenched from our reveries.

'Talk about no orgasms,' Truncheon says. 'You keep pulling out.' But Robert is up again and over to the stereo, rewinding the tape, fag between his teeth. Replay. Mimi – Barbara Hendricks – takes up her magnificent song again, in mid-bar, heading for, whatever he says about orgasms, some kind of climax—

'Wait . . .' he says. 'It's coming . . .'

'*Foglia a foglia la spio!*' she sings. '*Cosi gentile il profumo d'un fior—*'

'THERE!' he shouts.

'What?' Truncheon and I cry. 'For God's sake, man.'

'Oh fuck sake,' he grumbles. 'You've no fucking idea . . .' Rewind, again. 'Pay attention,' he says. 'Sit up.' He presses play. 'OK,' he says, 'now – listen – OK – OK – NOW!'

What? We are genuinely uncomprehending, and bewildered. What is he hearing that we are not hearing? What is he so desperate to share?

'Dear God,' he says. 'Fuckin' hellfire. I don't know. Fuckin' southern philistines . . . What you just heard *three times* is no less than the finest use of the triangle in Western Civilisation.'

We listen again. It was impossible to determine, if you didn't know what you were looking for. Once you knew it was there, it was sublime.

Towards dawn Robert declares that we must all go to Barn Elms Reservoirs, not far away, by the river. I have a brief Bruce Springsteen moment – though to be honest there was little chance of anybody's body being tan and wet down at that reservoir in the middle of the night . . .

I was at that time a biker, riding a Harley Davidson 1200 Sportster, its left foot-peg welded into place with a metal plate by a rural blacksmith after an unfortunate incident on an Italian backroad earlier in the year. Robert normally would not go near it – he didn't drive, would hire a moped on a Greek holiday if he had to, but thought the taxi the only civilised form of transport. Motorbikes were to him alien beasts, totally incomprehensible. Nevertheless – I think because he realises he'll get to put his arms round my waist – he decides he will ride pillion. I have a spare helmet with me, which he puts on, but he won't change from what he is wearing, so when we are pulled over by the police on Shepherd's Bush Roundabout ten minutes later (in convoy with Truncheon in his Morris Clubman) Robert is barefoot in a pink towelling dressing gown given to him by Dustin Hoffman as cast and crew gift at the end of the West End run of Peter Hall's production of *The Merchant of Venice*, with something to that effect embroidered on the back. It is an unlikely set of biker's colours.

The police car circles up behind us, makes itself known, and pulls us over.

Where are we going? they wonder.

'Barn Elms,' I say.

Why?

I am at a loss. Well – I know why I am going. Because Robert wanted to go. But that probably isn't the answer they want.

Behind me, Robert is struggling with the visor. 'It's the migration season,' he says, from the depths of the helmet.

The officer looks unconvinced.

'We're hopin' to see a black-tailed godwit.'

I assume Robert is joking and bite my lip. But the copper accepts the explanation.

'Oh, all right,' he says. 'Take it easy', and waves us on.

Robert isn't joking. He does want to see a black-tailed godwit. That is in fact the purpose of the expedition. When we get down there to the broad damp common, bordered with thick undergrowth, wet and fragrant, and after a degree of ornithological patience no black-tailed godwit is forthcoming, he decides instead to educate us in the ways of rugby league, so we run up and down alongside the reservoir, throwing the crash helmets backwards to each other as the mist rises.

In the end, after a greasy spoon breakfast, we go back, and go to bed – well, Robert goes to bed, Lisette goes to work, and Truncheon and I fall asleep on the sofa. That afternoon when we wake, Robert wants to know if it is true about the legendary penis.

'I don't know,' I say.

He is bemused. 'What do you mean?' he asks. 'You must know.'

He is quite bewildered – amazed – by the news that Truncheon and I shared a sofa without any sexual goings-on. It seems impossible to him.

Why? we ask. People often don't engage in sexual goings-on.

'It's such a waste!' he cries, in the end. 'I mean, look at you! The pair of you!'

Chapter Five

London, Washington, Henderson Tennessee, 1990
In May 1990 Swift (Baroness Alacrity; Alassitude when asleep) married David (Flussie) by the golden pagoda in Battersea Park. She wore a tiny top hat; he a riverboat gambler coat. Lisette and Robert danced. This is the only time I ever saw him on a dance-floor. She was wearing a red dress. Later she was dancing with someone else, and he said: 'Look at her, isn't she lovely?' Later still he was conducting some kind of athletics competition in the shrubbery. Later still, a bunch of us filled a minicab with the wedding flowers – armfuls of fresh bouncy lilac – and went back to my flat. Robert fell asleep in my bed and was narked when I turfed him out so I could get in there with the best man. Tallulah married that year as well; but I had my Harley and purported not to care, in slightly too bravura a fashion, that my two best friends had achieved this state of romantic glory – as I saw it – whereas my most recent triumphs were getting off with a nineteen-year-old, and refusing a freebie offered by a Leeds gigolo I was interviewing for *Marie Claire*. And then Robert and Lisette broke up, and that changed things.

I was at my grandfather's house in Wiltshire, a place of moss, wellingtons and woodsmoke, with Swift and David. I had a cold, and had retired to bed. Robert arrived by taxi from Chichester (some eighty miles) where he was a musical director at the Festival. (I knew him for thirty-four years and I never saw him on London Transport. He'd take cabs from London to Wigan, until he was on his sticks, when his pride made him take the train. Another time he came by cab to Wiltshire from London, and we offered the driver a cup of tea and the bathroom. He had arrived from Afghanistan three months before, and had not been outside London. At the sight of the Marlborough Downs, he had tears in his eyes. He said he would bring his wife and children to live here because it was the most beautiful green.)

Robert didn't like people going to bed without him, and when Swift and David retired at around 2 a.m., he appeared in my bare bedroom, lonely. 'I'm being good,' he said, 'and quiet.' So I woke up. After a bit he went downstairs and came back up carrying the Dulcitone, singlehanded. A Dulcitone is the size and shape of a child's coffin, on four spindly legs. My grandfather had acquired it to fit on a boat. Its mechanism is made of tuning forks, and it sounds like the arthritic ghost of a music box.

'No, no, don't help,' he said. 'You're ill. It's a treat for you.' He set it up by my sickbed, with a candle on the one side and his glass of whatever it was on the other, and he played for me: Ravel's 'Pavane for a Dead Infanta', *La Fille aux Cheveux de Lin,* a nocturne or two, and other pieces appropriate to a sick blonde, including excerpts from the Fauré requiem, and a small lecture on why Mozart is crap: 'It's these highly symmetrical structures which appeal to people who like their lives to be very ordered – he puts his mannered and predictable material into a preconceived struc-ture – first movement sonata form, relying far too much on the tonic/dominant axis – you know, C to G – structurally and harmonically – it's all SQUARE – there's an announcement of what's coming up, and a pompous phrase saying something's finished – he never allows his material to grow organically because the sheer SQUARENESS cannot accommodate organic growth. Inflexibility appeals to a certain type of person, class even. OK he wrote some truly great music – *Don Giovanni*, the Requiem – the late concerti slow movements, that intimate interplay between the piano and the orchestra – listen to Murray Perahia – and the clarinet development in the slow movement of the quintet – but why is *every* boring note of *every* boring piece adored by these boring people? I'll tell you – Fear. Security and predictability gets those smiles of approval because it makes them feel comfortable and secure, i.e. fuckin' smug . . .'

The next day he brought the Dulcitone into the garden, and taught me a bit of Ravel's *Mother Goose Suite*, a duet for ten-year-olds which I could just manage, sitting in the sun on the lawn. In the evening we were in front of the fire: his tormented genius, his broken heart and me, him telling me how Brahms was raised in a brothel, what he'd cook me for lunch the next day (scallop salad with coriander and ginger, or salmon with sorrel sauce, or lamb and black-eyed peas) and watching me fix the fire, which I'm rather good at. 'Fuckin' hellfire,' he said, getting enthusiastic. He took the bellows from me and held them nose into the fire, and let the top drop very slowly down, a slow breath to the embers. And again. And again, not quite so slowly. A tiny flame rose, and he slowed down, then sped up, and a little more, making faces at me while performing a tumultuous and deep-rooted fake orgasm, on the bellows. The fire blazed like merry hell. Then he honoured me with his Schubertian theory of the death of genius: 'So, has there been *any* uncontested genius in any field since 1945? No there hasn't – and not just because genius needs to be proven by time – no, it's because, listen, since penicillin, nobody has syphilis any more. Well, they do, but not tertiary syphilis, which is when the angels start serenading you, or if you're Schumann stood in a river it's Schubert,

46

and then your wife puts you in the loony bin and runs off with fuckin' Brahms – so, putting the interests of art above the interests of health, and bearing in mind that it's not just Schubert, Schumann, Beethoven, Scriabin, Donizetti, Delius, Smetana, Scott Joplin, Wolf, Ivor Gurney and Henry the Eighth but also Toulouse Lautrec, Van Gogh, Maupassant, Flaubert, Rochester, Monet, Oscar Wilde . . . and probably a few others . . . is the loss of syphilis actually a benefit to civilisation? Or does the truly dedicated ar*tiste* in fact have a creative fuckin' responsibility to ac*quire* the poxy disease, so as to honour his muse? What d'you think?'

Then he burnt our socks, because they were wet, before getting hold of my foot so as to demonstrate his ideal blowjob on it.

I was very afraid of the effect he had on me. I could never remember, when he was kissing me, what I knew fifteen minutes before, and the following morning: i.e., why I didn't want to sleep with him. I told him this; he stroked my head. I burst into tears and wouldn't have him. Looking at him, I saw my enemy. I saw what I could lose myself in; what could take me from myself, enthrall and imprison me, keep me from my own free life. I feared it, and I desired it.

The following morning I went and curled up with my book on the end of his single spare-room bed, and that was that really. Sex to oblivion, and that night he dragged me out barefooted on to the frosty lawn, and there was a shooting star.

That weekend became the mainstay of the opening (or the middle, or the end) of the novel I tried to write about him. 'He's much gentler out of town,' I wrote. 'He points out fieldfares. His mother has died. Lisette has left him. He's given up performing, and won't compose except for money. I believe he thinks that because geniuses are tormented, and because he is not as much a genius as Debussy, he must therefore torment himself. We his all-knowing friends think he should take his talent back to his heart and face its responsibilities. We believe that he is frightened to do so. We think this is the root of his sadness, the demon which he seems to be trying to

47

drown. He wonders why everybody is always doing down his fucking work, which we are not, we respect his hard work and success, but we know that he wants and needs something else. He knows this too. We all find this hard to talk about. It is easy to be simplistic.'

None of us blamed Lisette for leaving him. We all knew that he drank twice his share in half the time. She said, he didn't know why he loved her; that it was just because she was pretty, and there. That wasn't enough for her. And every now and then some other girl was pretty, and there. He provoked emotion: envy, lust, admiration, resentment – many people felt seduced by him. But how enviable is it to live constantly surrounded by those emotions? How could he possibly satisfy them all? They were there and often the easiest way out was just to give people what they so wanted. How was he to know what they meant by wanting that? It wasn't just girls. If there was food he'd eat it; if there was drink he'd drink it. Everything existed to be flirted with or consumed. His considerable self-discipline was occupied elsewhere.

Lisette also said, 'It's amazing how boring he is when you're not in love with him.' I flinched at the truth in this: drunk, he could be boring.

On the Monday night I gave him a lift back to London and said, not for the first time, that I didn't think we should. But I did think we would. He and Lisette having broken up, that line of defence was gone, and I was stuck with my own dichotomy: I wanted what I did not want. And he said things like, 'You don't want a boyfriend who drinks and smokes all the time and keeps you up all night.' Not unless he loves me, I thought. I didn't say it.

*

A few days after we came back, I went to the US to write some articles: Washington, Williamsburg Virginia, Nashville, San Diego to a Swingers' Convention – a repellent episode full of repellent men trailing their surrendered wives round arid ballrooms full of stands selling fluffy handcuffs and writing-paper with pictures of sex positions on it in mauve. Crossing the parking lot, I was invited to an orgy; in the spirit of journalistic integrity I thought I ought to go, but the sight, among the many bodies writhing on nylon sheets in an executive suite, of a fungus-coloured middle-aged dentist patting the hair of a woman with pink plastic beads dangling on a clip from her clitoris who was sucking him off while being unconvincingly fucked from behind by what could have been his twin – this tad of humanity so revolted me that for the first and last time in my life as a journalist I made my excuses and left. My old school-friend Boots (male – from the boys' school I went to after I deserted the horrid girls' school) came down from LA and we went to Tijuana together and decided, in a jokey and merry mood of exasperation with the world, that to get married would be a splendid idea, but fortunately we couldn't find the wedding chapel. And then I went north! To Alaska, to interview single men who advertised themselves for love in a special magazine, full-page shots of them in their plaid shirts with their dogs and pick-up trucks and hopeful expressions, and sometimes a bit of pipeline or a chainsaw. I slept in a log cabin with antlers above the door; I had blueberry pancakes for breakfast and spent a day on a horse in the wilderness, and it really was wild – there were no fences and the sky was huge and the air was sweet. I sang 'Don't Fence Me In', and have never had a happier day. Back at the hotel in Washington I picked up one of the foot-long dark and white chocolate grand pianos with the lid up full of chocolate-dipped strawberries that they used as the little chocolate on the pillow. They packed it for me beautifully, and I brought it as hand baggage home across the Atlantic to Robert. He was not nearly appreciative enough, and left it at my flat.

We were *not* boyfriend and girlfriend – as I told everybody who asked, or assumed. I had seen enough of him as a boyfriend to accept the truth of what he said: 'You don't want a boyfriend like me. You just want a shag. That's all right, it's a common mistake.

But I'm very easy, you can have me without, you know, signing up.' However, we were talking, all the time; making each other laugh, a lot; sleeping together, kind of regularly; he worried and annoyed me, much of the time. But we weren't going out together, oh no.

I wrote: 'He professes "virtue". Climbs into bed with me long after I'm asleep, and I murmur "Is it six o'clock then?" because it had been the night before, and he says "No, one thirty. I'm learning. Civilised." I love the way he says "civilised" – you can almost see what he calls mono-lateral northern erectile nostril – but I don't know if he really thinks civilised has anything to do with it. It. The big business of letting Robert live, opening the shutters on Robert's soul and flooding him with sunlight. Emptying out the ashtrays of his heart. It's all starting to look wrong but he remains our designated roué.'

He said he had tried not drinking.

'How long?' I said.

'Three days,' he said, 'Staring at a bottle of Poire William and drinking only beer.' He believed that counted. He thought it proved he had a balanced attitude. Robert wouldn't know a balanced attitude if it kicked him.

He said he didn't feel well. I said, 'Do your nails no longer fit your fingers and does your flesh feel like over-ripe fruit?' He said, 'Yes.' 'It's a hangover,' I said. 'You coming to the pub?' he said.

He read things I was writing, and picked up on aspects that nobody else did. I wrote: 'He is wrapped in a veil of misconception, a curious blindness rent with insight but cut off from us and his true self. Anyway, he's gone off to Wigan with his drink and his fags and his *weldschmerz*, if that's what I mean, and if that's how you spell it.'

What an utter fool I was. But everyone knows the romantic hero has to be flawed – how else can the heroine save him? And even if you are quite convinced that's not what you're doing, you probably are. Even knowing you are can't protect you. My rational history-graduate self says knowledge should protect you. My hindsight, meanwhile, quotes from *O Brother Where Art Thou?*: 'It's a fool looks for logic in the chambers of the human heart'.

*

Robert made a recording with Steve Parr, his mate/recording engineer/producer, of the Dmitri Tiomkin song 'Wild Is the Wind', famous for versions by Nina Simone and David Bowie. On it, Robert sings like Tom Waits, plays the piano like Red Garland, and undermines the whole thing with fart noises and stupid bleeps. It opens with the sound of a match striking and a cigarette being lit, ice cubes clinking into a glass, and closes with the sound of two hands clapping. It is a precise portrait of him: musically sublime, funny, seductive, naughty, self-sabotaging, vulgar, beautiful, ridiculous.

My memory is that Robert sent a cassette of it to a girl he was flirting with who took it as a love declaration; it caused some confusion. My memory is, I was sad he hadn't sent it to me. But you know, we weren't going out together. It would have been during one of our off periods. Steve's memory is that late one evening, after they had finished recording Robert's piano overdubs for a film soundtrack, they were about to drop into the Lily Langtry when Robert asked if he could run in to the studio and record something extra. The piano was still set up and Steve had some sound effects running live in the S1000 sampler. He popped in a tape and hit record; Robert started to play and sing. It was all very ad hoc and they only did one take. 'And then,' Steve told me, 'if I remember correctly he asked me to run off a cassette so that he could give it to you.'

I like this incorrect memory very much. I could have this one for myself – look, I have a witness that says it wasn't for her, it was for me. Perhaps I remembered incorrectly! Perhaps it *was* for me! Certainly, it is for me now: the tenderness with which he sings; the slight echo of laughter as you-hoo-hoo kiss me, the fart noises bubbling up when he hears the sound of mandolins; the clink of the ice cubes as he wonders whether we know we're life itself.

Tiomkin was second only to Bernard Hermann in Robert's pantheon of film composers. He revelled in tales of the great Russians and Germans who went to Hollywood in the 1930s and 40s; Schoenberg writing his *Accompaniment to a Cinematographic Scene* without there actually being any film; and on being complimented on his 'lovely music' snarling 'I don't write lovely music'. And Stravinsky – or was it Shostakovich? Or Schoenberg again? – could be all of them – who when invited to write a score wrote it and sent it in, and when told no, he needed to see the film and write the music to go with it, suggested that the director cut the film to go with the music.

Steve emailed 'Wild Is the Wind' to me in 2012, with the message 'I know he wanted you to have this. No one who didn't know him can understand what we have lost.'

*

In London Robert's regime was to work all night, sleep till 3 p.m., wake up and get a cab to his preferred curry house. It was beautiful to see him working. It remained unchanged all his life: manuscript paper, pencil, sharpener, rubber, pack of fags, lighter, ashtray. Seven items denoting concentration. Initial work could be done anywhere – in the margin of the newspaper often – the five lines of the stave sketched, the phrase or chord that struck him jotted down over a coffee (double/triple/quadruple espresso, lots of sugar, several cigarettes, a brandy or calvados or two) in the sun somewhere, on a paper napkin over lunch, in a pub. But for concentration he preferred an actual table, and silence. In his flat, this was regularly assaulted by his neighbours' building work. Hence his frequent presence in my house, or in Wiltshire. I can see the curve of his back now. His terrible posture.

'Don't you need a piano?' I asked. He was working on the

soundtrack for *Distant Voices, Still Lives*: full orchestra, serried ranks of gorgeous strings, muted brass, moody woodwind, crashing percussion, the whole shebang. No, he didn't need a piano. He needed to Sellotape leaf after leaf of music manuscript into a great accordion of folds, and to rule and label the staves and the bars and the keys and the time-signature for every part of the orchestra. Then he needed to write down all the music that was in his head, individual parts, a line for each instrument, twenty or thirty parts. Occasionally he'd go and check something on the Dulcitone – that least dulcet of instruments, its tuning forks well out of tune after seventy years in a Wiltshire cottage – but otherwise the orchestra flowed direct from his mind to the paper. When Daniel Barenboim was on *Desert Island Discs*, he said he'd rather take the scores than any recordings of music, because when he read the scores he could recall and enjoy every performance he'd ever heard.

I am a puddle of admiration for this kind of capacity. This admiration makes it difficult for me to talk about Robert's music. I fall at the first hurdle: I love it. I loved things he said were crap; I was bedazzled by his skill, by the ease with which he created pure beauty, by the delicacy with which he could shift a mood, by his versatility. He'd produce a piece of cracking 1920s flapper jazz; a haunting scrap of electronica with chanting sopranos; a lush nineteenth-century orchestral waltz; a fair imitation of 1959 Miles Davis; a driving hard rock piece with electric guitars; a sprightly yet somehow corrupt carousel melody; something feral and Celtic that seemed to be made entirely of cloud and a girl's voice, a hackneyed 1980s-style TV crime theme. 'They want hackneyed,' he said. 'I give them what they want.' De-composing, he'd call it. But even if he tried, he couldn't write bad music. Everything had something in it which stopped you, or moved you. God knows he was articulate in English but music was his first language. It was a language I could understand but not myself speak, though I devoutly wished I could. It meant, to me, blood and love and beauty. It meant my father at home.

And then I was sent to interview Johnny Cash, at home in

Tennessee. At that time, he was almost a has-been; his rebirth as Patriarch of Americana was many years in the future. We got talking about the evils of the world. I mentioned a song he recorded, 'Here Comes that Rainbow Again' by Kris Kristofferson. It's a small drama, based on an intensely touching scene from John Steinbeck's *The Grapes of Wrath*.

'You know that book?' Johnny said, his face lighting up.

'I love that book,' I said. 'And *you* know that book!'

'I *was* that book.' He smiled at me. It was like being smiled at by Monument Valley, or the Hoover Dam.

'You like that song?' he said, and pulled over his guitar. He tuned up, and played, and sang – all my favourites, all afternoon, in that shadowy room with the sun hot outside, and it was one of the finest afternoons I've ever spent, and definitely the worst interview I've ever done. We hardly talked, because this music was his way of communicating. He did say one thing I remember: 'You have to be what you are. Whatever you are, you gotta be it.'

I came away realising that I didn't want to be a journalist any more. Although it was journalism that had given me this extra-ordinary day, I didn't want to be the person oohing and aahing on paper about Kris Kristofferson, John Steinbeck and Johnny Cash. I wanted to be the person writing and making the stuff that makes people ooh and ahh. Cash loving Kristofferson's song; Kristofferson loving the way Cash sang it, both of them loving Steinbeck's book. I wanted to be one of them. I might as well admit it.

Somebody took a photo with my camera of Johnny Cash and me in the low spring sun. He has his arm round my waist. He picked me a daffodil from his front garden, gave me a kiss, and then I went home to start trying to be what I was: someone who wanted to create. I had the daffodil on my desk while I wrote my first book, a biography of my father's mother, Kathleen, the sculptor. I still have it – a little dried-up papery ghost of a thing, reminding me that that's what integrity means: being what you are. It's some-where in a pile of significant flowers (a rose from a May Ball, jasmine and marigold from the Taj Mahal, a tuber-rose from Graz, a tuft of the last cotton Tammy Wynette ever picked). I kept it in a bowl by my bed, until Robert set fire to it – rather unsuccessfully – with a cigarette end.

Chapter Six

London, Wiltshire, Paris, 1992–3

Well, I was only half in love with him, and just as well, as I had every reason to tell myself. Imagine the chaos if I had been fully in love with him! He was trouble. Not nothing but trouble – he was plenty else, but all that just added to the trouble. And anyway, I had other fish to fry.

In early summer 1992, I found I was pregnant, and not by Robert. This was a massive surprise, a great adventure, and, strictly, another story. Briefly, it was the only night Louis (kind, handsome, self-contained, Ghanaian) and I spent together, and, as the agony aunts warn the teenagers, it is possible to get pregnant without actually having sex. He and I both knew that we had done nothing that would normally result in conception. Tell that to most people though (they did ask . . .) and eyebrows screech into hairlines because all of a sudden everyone knows much more than me about what I got up to in bed on a particular occasion. Also, I had been told I would find it hard to conceive, for medical reasons. It was rather surreal. But there it was. Piss-on-a-stick proof.

I told Robert on the day of the pregnancy test. He, who never wanted to be left out of anything, was very keen that the baby should be his. I would have had to be three months pregnant already, which I wasn't, but he was not interested in details, unless they were musical. I told him about Louis. 'It'll be an entertaining nine months,' Robert said, 'waiting to see if it's white or black. I'll babysit! There's going to be a massive rallying round.' It had a curious effect on him: he developed a kind of want/don't want attitude. He was very keen to help. I went to Wiltshire to be with my sisters; he wanted to come. It was May and lush, with six little children for me to look at in a new light. Robert cooked, played Frisbee with my nephews, played Debussy on the Dulcitone, and reduced one sister to near hysteria by smoking while brushing his teeth. He understood that we couldn't sleep together any more – found it absurd on one level, but understood. His presence was a massive comfort to me. We all lay about on lawns in the sun and I revealed my secret to my nephew Joe.

From my notebook:

Joe (4): Louisa's going to have a baby

Louis (8): No she's not

Sisters (43 and 39): !

Joe: But you're not married

Louis: Yeah you need a sperm

Joe: Where will you get a sperm from?

Louis: Will you get it from a sperm bank?

Me: I've already got one

Louis: Where did you get it! Did you sex? Who with?

Sisters: !!

Theo (6): Person with a baby in her tummy, how did it get there?

Louis: You were being naughty!

Joe: Is your baby already in you?

Louis: It's a joke

Sisters: Is it?

Me: No

Louis: 'Well you'll need to know what children want so I'll tell you – sweets and wrestling stickers and a wrestling magazine

Joe: What's its daddy called?

Me: Louis, like Louis

Louis: Isn't Robert its daddy?

Me: Nope.

Robert: (shaking with silent laughter)

Joe: Is it going to see its daddy if you're not married?

Me: Yes I hope so

All childish faces crease in horror. *Hope so?*

Me: Yes! Yes of course!

Louis: Is he going to sleep all the time like Tom?

Tom (a baby): snuffle

Me: Not when he's bigger

Lily (2½, coming to sit beside me, very quietly): I'm glad you've got a baby in your tummy

Sisters and Alice (12): (unbridled delight)

Robert had told me how some months ago he had declared love to someone and been heartbroken because she rejected him. And that a glamorous Middle Eastern woman, a single mother who was engaged to a man she didn't love, had become obsessed with him and now the fiancé wanted to kill him. I dropped him off at the BBC just as 'Papa Was a Rolling Stone' finished on the car radio. That night I was suddenly, irrationally and oddly joyously certain that the baby was Robert's, though I knew perfectly well it couldn't be. I sat by an open window with Tallulah and she told me all the ways in which Louis was perfect.

The next day I had a painful conversation with Robert. I found myself being snide, protective, defensive. He was upset, I was upset – chucking out what I half wanted in order to protect myself against wanting it more and it not wanting me. I explained that if he helped me I'd come to rely on his help. 'Look, shall I come over?' he said, and I said no, I'd want you to come and stay and be here. And of course I wouldn't really. He'd just be smoking, drinking, requiring instructions, taking no responsibility. That phrase want/ don't want applied to us both. I cried a lot, after I'd hung up.

Two days later I sat Louis down, gave him a vodka, and told him. He straightened his shoulders, looked me in the eye, and said, 'Well it must be mine then.' I knew in that movement that everything was going to be OK, and I was right. Everything I wrote in my notebook about him at the time – he's sunny, he's private, he's reliable, he's mysterious – turned out to be true. I was unbelievably lucky in who I got accidentally pregnant with. We both were.

The following day I had the first scan: there it was, a tiny little thing having a kip. An ammonite, a croissant, a coracle. Eight weeks, they said. Louis had rung to give me all his phone numbers and ask if he could come to the next scan. Sometimes you can feel reassurance running through your veins.

I had to drop a tape off at Robert's. He answered the door shirtless, and for a strange moment there on the steps in the London sun it was as exactly as if we were in love. I told him about the scan, and the dates.

'So there's no chance it's Lockhartian in origin?' he said sadly.

'No.'

'Have you told Louis?'

'Yes.'

'So you've fucked him now?'

'No!'

'Fuckin' hellfire, why not?'

'Because I don't love him,' I said.

*

My father was in hospital having heart surgery again, which terrified us all. ('News like yours would give him another heart attack,' Robert said.) My sister-in-law was about to give birth. My Harley had been stolen, and the insurance cheque arrived the week I found out I was pregnant – well *there's* a message from Fate. No more leathers for me, for the duration. Everyone expressed their fears and concerns about my situation in the best and worst ways: I have never had so much advice in my life. I should marry him, I should have an abortion, I should be aware I'll never make any money now, my career is over, no one will want to marry me, Louis will be sad if he thinks I'm waiting for someone better, we should live together, if I won't move in with him I should move in with Robert. Shotguns were polished, voices were raised, true natures revealed. Relatives arrived from Ghana. My dad said to Louis, 'I suppose I should take you into the library for a chat about your intentions, but I don't have a library. How about the dining room?' Louis and I sat in the middle of all this getting to know each other, saying to each other: 'It's going to be fine.' To everybody else, we said: 'One thing at a time, you know.' The phrase 'no, we're just good parents' emerged. 'Semi-detached' was another. We went around together, happy, fond, pregnant, proud, planning to stick by each other, but we weren't a couple, nor planning to be.

My old friend Cynthia, the perfect embodiment of Jewish humour, was over from New York. She sat us down. 'Could you have made it weirder if you tried?' she asked.

'He could have been gay?' I suggested.

'No, that would have been easier. No jealousy,' she said.

'OK, one-legged?'

Louis offered to cut his leg off.

Cynthia pointed out, later, that I couldn't fall in love with Louis if I wasn't sleeping with him.

It was so confusing for others that we had to make it clear for ourselves, and we did.

I didn't stop to think of it being confusing for Robert. I wrote down a conversation we had in my notebook:

Robert: 'There's love between us, and we fancy each other.'

Louisa: 'So why aren't we going out together?'

R: 'I was just wondering that.'

L: 'Well, it's because you love another' (the one who had rejected him)

R: 'I gangrene another – you said so.'

L: 'Yeah, you gangrene lots of things.'

Silence

R: 'Well we kept that moment of melodrama up for a good ten seconds.'

Later he was talking about friends having sex. I said, you're not my friend, and he was hurt. I explained: that he was my friend of course, but not only: he was my lover and always would be. He told me a friend had said he should marry me; I agreed, but didn't mention that I of course shouldn't marry him. He said, again – Jesus, doesn't it get repetitive? – 'Anyway you don't want to go out with an alcoholic.' And again, it wasn't about who I wanted to go out with, it's about who I wanted him to be – or rather, not to be.

I didn't want him to be an alcoholic (not that either of us knew what alcoholic actually meant). I didn't want him smoking sixty fags a day. I wanted him to stop drinking himself stupid and smoking himself dead. I described Dad's bypasses to him blow by blow and told him about the writer Dee Wells having half her leg amputated because of smoking. 'But why?' he asked, and I explained about the blood system, and clots, atherosclerosis and nicotine, the hardening of arteries, the risk of embolism.

Ten days later we had another argument, explained by a letter I wrote from Paris but didn't post:

30.6.92

Dear Robert

Here I am on the steps of Chopin's tomb, so of course you cross my mind.

Yes I hope we are on speaking terms. Foolish not to be. But when at one a.m. a fellow has a choice between being with a woman who is crazy about him or going for another drink, and he chooses to go for another drink, the woman would be foolish not to hear what she is being told. And when he defends himself by saying 'But this is how I am' she would be foolish not to defend herself against him. When I invite you in it is because my feelings for you are uppermost in my heart. When I hold you off it is because your lack of feelings for me are uppermost in my mind. Meanwhile I have a pregnancy to look after and a life to try to make sense of after it has been turned upside down and I have to go to bed early and no doubt alone. None of this means I don't wish you well.

xx L

Back in London his messages went from 'Give us a call' to 'Still not in . . . hm' to 'Lou, *please* ring me, I hope you're OK' to 'Give me a fucking call'. In the end we spoke. He thought I was giving him an ultimatum. I said yes I was, but it wasn't about our relationship, it was about him. It was, Grow Up.

There now. Was that a moment? The polyhedron of missed opportunities flashes me another possibility as it whirls slowly by. He saw an ultimatum. What if I'd let him define his own ultimatum, and respond to it as he wished? What then?

A month's silence followed. Then he was there at a party: for the first three hours I avoided him, but he needed to talk me through Ravel's string quartet in F, quoting Debussy and Stravinsky ('bespectacled little gay Russian dwarf' – was that sardonic or reverent?). I was to notice the pizzicato in the basses. Later he curled up asleep around a candle in the garden. We shared a cab, stopped for a curry. I got to bed at 1.45; he wanted to sleep on my sofa. I pointed out it is cruel to want to sleep on the sofa of a woman who is crazy about you. I said, what if I sneak out in the middle of the night and make passionate love to you in your sleep? He had the grace to leave. I felt that his needs were so big in his eyes that he saw no others. I thought I knew his feelings. But I thought I knew everything, and if I didn't I'd decide, just to keep things under control. Now I'm not so sure. I gave him the chocolate piano again. I said, take it away, any way I dispose of it will be too symbolic. I was four months pregnant, and my embryo was growing eyelashes.

There was a screening of an unforgiving, bleak, heartbreaking documentary he had scored, *The Execution Protocol*, about death row. Robert's music pierced through it; a blade of cold light, desperation in the sound of a muted trumpet. I wanted to drink a whisky afterwards, but couldn't. I gave it to him. Robert's music has always, whatever else is going on, had the capacity to unravel me, or to rebuild me, or both at once.

The following week we had lunch. He picked me up, and kissed me, and took me to Alastair Little's where he told me how gorgeous I was and got a stiffy during the fish soup and changed the subject eighteen times a minute. He said, 'What are you going to live on?', offered me money 'you know, if you need some', and started referring to me as 'my wife and child'. He wanted to kick off the child's musical education, and sang to it. We went to hear *Katya Kabanova* at Sadler's Wells. He argued with the doorman, fed me early enough ('by ten thirty or I will scream, it's not princessy, it's physical') and came home with me. He wouldn't let me go to bed; wouldn't leave me alone. He was drinking neat Campari and mauling me (in the Northern sense of not leaving someone alone); then holding me. I cried. He mocked me for crying – or I felt he did – and I cursed him. He said, 'What did I do?' At 4 a.m. he was still banging on about Jánaček's atonality and smoking in my bedroom. I left him there passed out when I went to work four hours later, and came back at the end of the day to find a tune written on the back of an envelope, dedicated and directed to me, a little swoopy arrow pointing to my address on the front. And an apology. 'I'm sorry I upset you. I don't know what I said but I'm sorry.'

I spent half my time wanting to know where I stood, and the other half running away from it.

Meanwhile Louis came to baby preparation classes with me and pretended to have contractions. I'd met his slow-moving, smiling mother – she was a midwife! – and she'd come to dinner with my parents. The first thing she said to me, in her deep, honeyed Ghanaian voice, was, 'A baby is a blessing from God. How are you feeling, my darling?' The new nephew was born and christened; Louis came, and wore a suit. Everybody was in love with Louis by now, except for me.

And then one day Robert had a new girlfriend. He called her Lacrimosa Clark because she wept easily, and also Clarkapart, because she was short like Napoleon Bonaparte, which developed into Wellaparte, because her profile was like the Duke of Wellington's. When I heard, I cried so hard that Baroness Alacrity sent me flowers at work. My colleagues assumed they were from Robert, cheering me up about whatever it was I was so sad about. What a great guy, they said.

*

My daughter – let's call her Lola – was born in the evening. She was the most strange and glorious little thing that ever existed. It took forty-eight hours, two inductions and an emergency caesarean. Did I care? Did I hell. I was listening to *La Bohème*, eating satsumas and translating the libretto for the nurses, as if they were interested, high as a satellite on gas and air. Louis was wearing surgical greens and talking Twi with the midwives. The babe was finally pulled out to the strains of Aretha Franklin singing 'Dr Feelgood', and I was fully, fully in love (apart from during the two-hour attack of post-natal depression three days later, when I decided to send her back, as clearly I would never be good enough for her).

Robert came to visit the next morning. He pulled the pleated curtains shut behind him and said 'Fancy a fuck?' Then he sat and held her and got that look of amazement, and said, 'She's not *that* black. She could be mine?'

I moved house. I didn't want my baby to live in a one-room flat. I extended the mortgage and got a place in Shepherd's Bush, natural home of those who can no longer afford Notting Hill. Home also of Louis. And of Robert. The new place had a little garden to put the pram in. That's what babies need.

Robert *really* liked her. I hadn't expected that. I'd assumed that as a roué he would find babies dull, but far from it. He thought she was just great, called her 'your pulchritudinous semi-negritu-dinous offspring' and would attempt to come and sit smoking in the bathroom with us while I washed her, saying useful things like 'She'll need a nappy now, won't she? Don't babies need a nappy?' It became apparent that he was to be my disreputable friend still, companion of nights off, keeper of misbehaviour and preserver of my wild young soul now that I was a clean and decent mother. He and Louis took to each other, and Louis was honoured with a nickname: Enigmus Africanus. Louis babysat when I went out with Robert; Robert babysat when I went out with Louis. But more often, in practice, it meant that when I finally collapsed with exhaustion after a long day's mothering followed by him keeping me up all hours, he would go and talk to her. One dawn I found him lounging in a chair with an unlit fag and his feet up on the cot, explaining counterpoint. She was fast asleep.

Chapter Seven

London, 1994

I bought piano #3, a weird little square late nineteenth-century thing, in a junk shop for £15. It looked like no piano I had ever seen: much smaller than an upright, more like a low-level cabinet made of walnut or cherry. Inside the strings were rusted and it had moss growing on the swollen dampers. I thought of restoring it somehow, but one visit from Art put paid to that. Art is a soft-spoken, shaven-headed, polo-necked LA jazzer who learnt to tune pianos as apprentice to the ancient blind Jewish man who tuned the instruments in Hugh Hefner's bunny mansion. His patience is considerable, but it was clear the little piano was, musically speaking, going nowhere. Meanwhile Robert tried to play '*La Cathédrale Engloutie*' on it, in honour of its internal dampness, and burnt a hole in the top with a neglected cigarette. (This sort of thing happened frequently. I've seen him with three on the go.) In the end I gave it to a theatrical props company. It would look good at the back of someone's parlour in a period drama. Why did I buy it in the first place? Because it was pretty, and £15, and, because I didn't like having Robert around without a piano for him to play.

When he was at the piano, I was happy. And because a proper home, one with a baby in it, needed a piano. Clearly, a Dad thing.

Robert's work took him to Dublin, so I was able to get some kip. He'd broken up with Lacrimosa Clark. There was an Irish friend, Emer, who he brought round to meet me, which was unusual. She was, like every girlfriend of his I ever met, clever, funny, gorgeous, self-deprecating, warm-hearted, hardworking and very worried about him. They are an excellent array of women. Some – Jackie, Nina (nicknamed Sequin-Smythe, for her double-barrelled surname) whose window he fell out of, Beth from school, Antipodean Cath – have become, or always were, good friends of mine. I met Lacrimosa Clark years later. We spent the whole evening saying to each other 'I so see what he saw in you'. She said she'd never met anyone since who uses words like 'detritus' and 'homo-sapient' but could only get three-letter words on the Scrabble board; that she adored Rob but wasn't an intellectual match for him, that he would be up all night composing and muttering about directors who pissed him off – all of them – and occasionally bursting into the room (usually naked) to holler 'you know NOTHING about fucking Chopin' – 'and sadly he was right'. She told me she had been jealous of how moved he was by my daughter's birth. Something in me likes the same women he does.

*

I went to Peru, where I chummed up with Centre Forewart's sister Anna. I was writing the biography of my grandmother. Robert and I spent New Year's Day up to our elbows in Szechuan crab at Poons in Whiteley's. He bought me a pair of pink velvet Indian pyjamas for a late Christmas present, only his credit card failed and the shop assistant was instructed to chop it up, physically, with scissors, so I paid instead. John Schlesinger's *Cold Comfort Farm*, for which Robert had written the soundtrack, was on at the cinema there. His name was on the poster.

On Thursday nights Lola went to her father's, and it became a habit to spend Thursday evenings with Robert. We went to concerts, watched videos of what he was writing the score for so I could explain the plot to him, played pool at the Carlton Club on the corner of my street. This was a late Victorian dance hall, one of four built by an Irish navvy magnate, one for each of his four daughters, in the north, south, east and west of London. Only this western one survives. (For some years now it has been the music venue Bush Hall.) The ceiling was high and dim, the lights low, the plasterwork ornamental and the company mainly off-duty police. You could order a cheese toastie via the little phone on the wall beside each vast green baize table. Andy who ran it played golf and lived on milk because of his ulcers; he would never let a lady pay for a drink, and gave both me and my child lifetime membership. At least, he never let me pay for membership and he always let her pop in for a pee if during potty training she was taken short up the road.

Phone numbers Robert uses are in the back of my diaries from these years; his gas and electricity bills fall from between their leaves. He came round three or four times a week; brought me food, took me to lunch. One pub he liked was just round the corner from Lola's nursery school. There had been builders next door to his house for a year now. During those noisy days he would work or sleep in my quiet house, only going home to work all night. He didn't sleep with me though. No, he wasn't my boyfriend. But he came and went as he pleased.

For a year or two I was seeing an Argentine musician, Julio, when he came from Rome for his concerts and recording. I recall a morning: Julio was there because we had spent the night together. Louis was there because I was going to work, and he had come to look after the baby. And Robert turned up, wild-eyed and hair on end, up-all-night-with-a-deadline written all over him, looking for coffee and company. I recall a knife with which I had been buttering toast flying out of my hand in a great curve across the kitchen, and the three of them looking at it, and me, and each other, each knowing who the other two were, laughing in their various ways, and the baby thumping on the tray of her high-chair.

I felt safe in those days. Louis was great; family life was steady, my friend Clare was living in the back bedroom, Julio was a pleasure; Robert was a friend. I had finished the biography, it was to be published; I was writing a novel. I got rid of the tragic little mossy mouldy piano. If there was to be a piano for Robert to play at my house it should be a decent one. He helped me choose it: a little Pleyel boudoir grand with red felt inside and gleaming gold-painted beams, a right showgirl of a piano, with its curly music-stand and tooled legs.

In March we had a joint birthday party; I did all the work but he turned up on time, sober, in a clean shirt with clean hair, champagne and a CD player for my present. He played three complete nocturnes, didn't try to get off with any of my friends and left – not the last to go – at one thirty. He said he got me the CD player because he needed something decent to listen to music on at my house. Then Emer was about, and I hardly saw him.

*

The birth-related gap ended like this. I'm not pretending to remember what we said, or rewriting. I wrote this down at the time.

I saw Robert tonight leaning on a cherry tree – the wrong man for this clean, child-speckled street. The angles of his body were wrong, leaning and twisted, and he was grubby. He was staring at the sky and for a moment I nearly walked past him, not looking at him as you don't look at those men, in case they look back, but then he muttered 'Fuck of a fucking moon' – and I realised it was him. Unshaven. Smell of vodka and fags. He stared at me and there was something bovine in his look: guarded, resentful, passive, out-of-focus.

'Robert?' I said. He frightened me.

'I'm dead,' he replied. 'I'm dead, don't talk to me,' and he turned and tried to walk down the street.

I called his name and followed him, and went round in front of him, walking backwards, talking to him, and he tried to dodge me, but he was unsteady and ended up propped against a wall, leaning in to its old red bricks, his face hidden. 'Go away,' he said. 'I'm dead.'

'The bollocks you're dead,' I said. 'You're dead drunk.'

'Not drunk,' he said.

I thought: *It's my golden boy. This is terrible.*

'Robert,' I said.

He gave a lurch, and straightened up.

'You can't be out here like this. Come home.'

He looked me in the face. His head was doing the drunk head's dance of minuscule movements.

'Not now,' he said, quite clearly. 'I'll come round later.'

He flung himself off the wall and down the road, scrabbling in his pocket for a cigarette. His feet seemed magnetised to the ground, heavy. He paused a moment to light the cigarette. His shoulders were hunched over and he had too many clothes on for the golden evening. Pianist posture, I thought, and I wanted to run after him.

He turned up the next day, clean, shaved, fragrant, bearing a bunch of tatty corner-shop chrysanthemums.

'God you're gorgeous,' he said. 'You are extremely bloody pulchritudinous. You've improved. Well done,' he said, looking round. 'Sorry about yesterday. I wasn't drunk actually but there's this rather evil weed about. I made the mistake of having a drag or two of a friend's and it completely did me in . . .'

'You said you were dead,' I observed.

'Well I'm not,' he said, slightly pettishly. 'Can I come in? How are you?'

'I'm all right,' I said. 'You should've said you were coming, I'd've . . .'

'I did,' he said. 'I told you.'

71

'You didn't say when, I'm worki—'

'I didn't know when,' he said, 'so how could I tell you?'

He walked through into the sitting room, shaking out a cigarette, heading for the piano. He trailed his fingers across the keyboard, and said, 'Bet it's out of tune.' His hands landed lightly as blossom falling on to a lake, and the notes rippled out. After a dozen bars he stopped and looked at me, expectantly.

'Don't stop,' I said.

'Yes but this is where you come in,' he explained.

'Me?' I said. 'I don't believe I do.'

'Yes,' he said, and played the last few bars again, counting over them, 'two three', with an exaggerated movement with his head, and a big encouraging smile.

I looked at him blankly.

'I'll do it,' he said. Played the few bars again, and then at the point in question began to sing: '*Votre âme est un paysage choisi . . .*' He smiled up at me.

'I can't sing that, Robert.'

'Course you can. Can't you? You have to. This is the most beautiful song. Fauré. You know it. It's not easy, I know. How about this one? "*Après un Rêve*"?' He played a few bars.

'Robert, I don't know them. I've no voice. Don't be such a dork.'

'Dork,' he said, and smiled. 'That's nice. Dork. I've not heard that in years. What do you want to sing then?'

'I don't want to sing. I . . .'

'Have you had lunch?' he said. 'Come to lunch.'

I hadn't had lunch.

We went and ate fish and drank two bottles of Pouilly-Fumé and were very attractive to each other in the afternoon sun. We went home to my house and did things we hadn't done in a while, with the window open and the scent of the wisteria wafting in on the breeze.

So, unannounced, undeclared, unofficial, it became, again, kind of, me and Robert. On and off. Friends and lovers. Sometimes more, sometimes less. Sometimes he'd go away for a week or two. We weren't going out together. It went on for a couple of years, and became domestic. Robert and Louis would watch the rugby together. My lodger Clare's mother came to visit, and Clare wondered if I could ask Robert to tone down his language. I felt not, as he was, kind of, part of the household.

'Where's Robert going?' Lola asks.

'He's going to Wigan,' I say.

'No, to the off licence,' she says. She's three.

My notebook tells me, 'Robert was a pig'. Perhaps it was this, also written down at the time:

'Darling,' he calls from the other room. 'Come in here and listen to this. It's Bill Evans.' I like Bill Evans and am grateful to Robert for having introduced me to his work. However I have a headache. A thumper.

'No, sweetheart, I'm going to bed.'

'Come and listen – just this one.'

'No, I've a headache, I'm going upstairs.'

'Oh come on, don't be a spoilsport.'

Is it sport for him to try to make me listen to jazz when my head is thumping?

I start up the stairs, wondering where the paracetamol are.

'Come on!' he yells cheerfully. 'I'll start it again.'

I turn back down the stairs, and poke my head through the doorway. I don't want to shout. I don't like shouting, emotionally or physically. He's sitting on the floor by the stereo; volume turned up loud.

'I have a headache and I'm going to bed,' I say clearly.

'Ah, come on, Lou – just the first track . . .'

Wouldn't a nice lover say 'Oh, darling' and turn it down, and try to find a painkiller?

'No, sit down,' he says. 'You have to hear the sax on this . . .'

'I've said it three times!' I shout. 'I HAVE A HEADACHE AND

I'M GOING TO BED. What do you mean, "No"? It's not "no". It's true – whether you like it or not. Why are you insisting – I don't want to! I'm not your toy for you to play with whenever you feel like it! Jesus Christ will you leave me alone!'

He stares at me in amazement. Why am I shouting at him? 'Barrage!' he says, mildly.

I stomp out. Upstairs. Painkillers. Into bed, teeth beginning to ache now, pulling the duvet tight. The music comes up from the room below. When it finishes, he starts practising his jazz decorations, his Red Garland twirls. Very bloody restful. Perhaps, I think, rather than fighting about it, I should move my bed to the back room.

I'm too hot, in my red and gold Chinese pyjamas. I'm damned if I'm going to take them off. He'll come up at three and murmur in my ear: 'It's a civilised hour –– not dawn yet' and be all over me. How I used to laugh at that – before I had to get up in the morning. Why doesn't he notice that there are all kinds of times when children are absent or sleeping *and* I am awake and available? Why does he come to me when I am murderously, suicidally desperate for sleep as only a mother of young can be? She has asthma and eczema. She doesn't sleep well. Since her birth I have never had an undisturbed night.

He comes up at three, making no attempt to be quiet. 'Ah,' he says. 'I see you've got your Mongolian don't-fuck-me trousers on. OK. Message received.' He goes down again to the front doorstep, his counter-asthmatic smoking spot, rattling the door I locked earlier. After a moment or two I smell tobacco smoke.

I don't know what time it is when he comes up again. I roll away from him as he whispers in my ear how much he loves, how he adores me, how I have the best arse on the planet, how he longs to insert his . . .

At that I laugh.

'Insert?' I say. 'In*sert*?'

'Yeah,' he says, sensing advantage, and I am laughing, and have

74

had a few hours' kip, and after all it's not as if I'd have to do anything.

My daughter wakes at six, and I go to her, accepting without complaint from the child what is so hard to take from the man: your time is not your own, woman. We go down to the kitchen, her bouncing with early morning child glee, me banging into walls with exhaustion. I put her in her high chair with a pile of slices of peeled apple, and fall asleep with my head on the kitchen table.

When I get in from work he's at the piano in sunglasses with a towel round his waist. He's just got up. 'I love your bed,' he says. 'I slept really well.'

Chapter Eight

London, Greece, Accra, Cairo, 1995–97
He wanted a holiday, a change, something new. He had been working incredibly hard and drinking to match. He was going to go to Australia. But first we went to Greece together, for ten days. I had to be back in time for the publication of my first ever book.

I remember: Buying a Femidom at Heathrow, and finding it hilarious. The tall stone towers of the Mani. Kardamili, Vathia. Being woken by a nuthatch, and Robert almost weeping with joy about it. Swimming. Tiny domed ruined churches, their frescoes open to the sky. Playing pool, drinking Amstel, him getting annoyed at a fisherman eyeing me up. Him getting brown, putting on some weight, playing with a lobster outside a taverna, making me photograph cats to send to his stepmother, putting jasmine behind his ear and making a peace sign, looking so much better every day. Us at a peaceful, solitary bay, an all-day lunch, so quiet, so beautiful, and two hideously loud military planes flew over incredibly fast and the noise of it was such a shock I burst into tears, and Robert looked at me strangely and said, 'I didn't know you had it in you', and I said 'What?' and he said, 'Such sensitivity'. Me reading Louis de Bernières endlessly on the beach while Robert slept. Me pouring the remains of a bottle of Ouzo out of the window at Vathia so Robert wouldn't drink it. Me wanting to go to bed, with him, on our last night, and him wanting to stay up drinking alone. Us having a terrible fight about that; me unable to sleep unless we made up, and him refusing to make up. Me reading again all my last morning, on the beach, thinking I bet Louis de Bernières would be a nice boyfriend. Robert finally bothering to get up around lunchtime, saying, 'I'm sorry, I get prickly when I feel attacked.' Me saying, 'Yeah, don't you just.' Me leaving; suntanned Robert framed in bougainvillea against the whitewashed wall. Me pursued as far as Kalamata airport by a lunatic pervert trying to drive my car off the road.

And as it turned out, Robert's ex, Lisette, arrived the next day, with *her* hired car, *her* camera to take photos of cats for Kath, etc. I didn't know that till much later. He said, 'Oh yeah, it was just an idea, I didn't know she was actually going to come.' She said, 'Bollocks, I had my ticket and everything.' But at least she wasn't sleeping with him. I remembered her comment from long before: 'I was pretty and I was there.'

But I was in London publishing my book: *A Great Task of Happiness: the Life of Kathleen Scott.* I went on *Woman's Hour.* I got nice reviews. A book and a baby. Thirty-four years old. Yes.

In the meantime, a friend of mine, Charlotte, had moved to Italy. Her family had bought a ruin and she was planting vineyards to make wine. I had spent time with her there and another life, an Italian life, had started to develop. (That too was a Dad thing. Wayland was the *Observer* correspondent in Rome in the 1950s and I had never got over the fact that though I was conceived in Italy I had never, unlike my big sisters, lived there. Such injustice.) I went to Charlotte's, and Robert was in Australia; then Louis, Lola and I went to Ghana for a family wedding. By the time Robert and I were both back in London it was October. I was missing him badly, and he was avoiding me. I knew why. The entire grapevine, including my own housemate who shared an office with the woman in question, knew why, and told me. *He* didn't. In the end I told *him*.

'Isn't there anything you want to tell me?'

'No,' he said, looking puzzled and innocent.

'Not about Victoria, the woman who works in the same office as Clare, who you met at Nina's party, and who you've been seeing for three months, and who's generally regarded to be your girl-friend?'

'Oh, that,' he said.

That week we met every day. Why couldn't he just be honest about what was going on, given that I never gave him a hard time about anything except drink and lying?

He said: 'I lie to myself all the time. How can I be honest with you?'

I said: 'Exactly.' And, 'Are you honest with her?'

I had a sense of him then, as a grenade with the pin out. But I was very angry. I told him, we can't break up because we're not together, but whatever we have going on, whatever all this has been, it's over.

Swift and I had it all worked out. He wanted to carry on being his old self with a new person who didn't know him well, when what he needed was to become a new him.

*

I wrote three novels about an English belly dancer in love with Cairo. Something of Robert crept into the policeman character. The first, *Baby Love*, was listed for the Orange Prize; I went to the party and spent it with Nina Sequin-Smythe. We picked up Claire Rayner, the agony aunt, and talked about Robert all evening.

I spent time in Cairo, researching. Julio was around. I didn't see

78

much of Robert, though he'd pitch up sometimes when he was lonely, and I would be polite.

*

In June 1997 I dreamed I had to cut my foot off. It was an epic dream, full of adventure and difficulty in labyrinthine mansions with hanging bridges and invisible enemies. I was sitting panting on a low ledge, having escaped something, and had to cut my foot off. I used a bread knife. Then Lola had a drama, and when that was done we sighed with relief – then remembered the foot. It was sitting there on its own, waxy, yellowish, but not bloody, its surface at the ankle healed over into a slightly flaccid stump.

'But what about your leg!' she cried. We turned our attention to my bereft ankle, only to find that it had grown another foot, a perfectly good one. I wriggled the toes, and turned it this way and that, and it was fine. Healthy, plump, pink and operative. I was wearing the black sandals that I had bought to go to Greece with Robert.

We looked back at the forlorn, dismembered foot. We were sorry for it, and picked it up to cuddle it. 'What should we do with it?' I wondered.

'Take it to your mum,' Lola said.

The next morning I told Lola about the dream. She was fascinated. 'I know who made you cut it off,' she said, rather importantly. 'It was a robber.'

'Robert?' I said.

'Not Robert. Robber. But Robert is a robber,' she said.

Well of course, to the infant, Robert was a robber. Stole the mother's time and affections, stole into her mother's bed, stole peace of mind, stole sleep, stole the heart from the mother and the mother from the child.

'Why's Robert a robber?' I asked.

'Oh you know,' she said, going back to her colouring book.

I told my friends about the dream, and what she had said. One suggested a Viking burial – put the foot on a model ship and set fire to it, launched out on the Round Pond in Kensington Gardens. Or put it away in a box? No, it would moulder, and smell.

They all knew that Robert was getting married.

Yeah, he was getting married.

I knew the foot was the love I still carried for Robert. I wondered why I was denigrating it. Because I had denigrated it all along. If I could make it small enough and non enough, then it wasn't even happening, and then no one could mock me for loving such an unfaithful man (There was nothing to be faithful to! It wasn't like that!) and I wouldn't be sad when it ended.

The foot floated around behind me all day, as if tied by a string. Of course I was glad not to marry him. The night he came to tell me he was engaged he drank half a bottle of gin, neat, and smoked up a storm; he put on John Coltrane and talked rubbish of the highest order. He was holding my feet, and clutching at me; and the ex-lover in me was saying get off, get off, and the friend was thinking, *Jesus*. It was a bravura presentation of pre-wedding nerves. I got him as far as the door three times but he stood facing me, still talking, and I couldn't shut the door in his face. Three times he came back in the house. I said no. Please, he said. No. Please. He leaned against the kitchen door, propped up, his head back, looking about seventeen.

'You deserve,' he said, 'to love and be loved on a regular basis.' I thought, So do you. Go on. Do it.

The next day I was due to sit for a painter friend who was trying to do an oil-sketch portrait every day for six weeks. I thought I looked OK, despite having cried all night. He painted me wild-haired, bleak-eyed, mad.

'Jesus,' I said. 'How could you tell?'

'It's my job,' he said kindly.

I thought: 'Some men look at women, and understand us.'

Robert used to. But he'd lost it. He was losing himself. I'd lost him.

*

I went round to my mother's and told her about the dream and the foot.

'Well,' she said, 'you can leave it with me if that would help.'

'Thank you,' I said. 'I think it would.'

That evening my father rang. 'Your mother told me about the foot,' he said. 'We're looking after it. We thought we might plant it in the garden, see if it might grow?'

The child thought that was a good idea. 'It could grow a tree with little new feet on it. Then we'd have lots of feet if we needed them.'

*

The wedding was in August. He invited me the night before; I didn't go. The wedding albums are under the piano. I don't look at them. I've been told it started well and they were happy. At the time, of course he didn't confide in me. He was busy elsewhere.

I went to dinner once. Robert showed me round: his music room, his family grandfather clock in the hall. I felt like a pair of sticks walking, dry and pointless and about to snap. In 1998 their son was born. Robert brought him over sometimes, in his buggy. He adored his child; absolutely adored him. He'd be jiggling the buggy with his foot, chatting and joking with him while trying to smoke in the opposite direction. He was working hard and, the times I did see him, drinking a lot. His wife always looked great.

Once I went into our local Nepalese restaurant to pick up a takeaway. It was known as the Office, for the time Robert spent working in there – and there he was, working, at a back table. I hadn't seen him for perhaps a year or more. He looked up, gestured to a beer on the table, and said: 'You took yer time. That's for you—'

If I don't say much about the marriage, I mean no disrespect – quite the contrary. I'm not ignoring it, denigrating it, or writing it out of history. But I wasn't there. I don't know about it, and it's not my business. They married; they had a child. This story jumps three years while they are doing that.

Chapter Nine

London, Wiltshire, 2000

He arrived on the front doorstep on a Sunday afternoon, while I was having lunch in the back garden with Swift and David.

'How are you?' I said. He looked terrible: distraught, humbled, sarcastic, confused, angry.

'Not great,' he said. 'She's kicked me out.'

'God,' I said. 'When?'

'Ten minutes ago,' he said. His house was ten minutes from mine.

'Where will you stay?' I asked.

'Well,' he said.

So he moved in.

'Don't you need stuff from, um, home?' I asked, that night.

'Have you got a razor?' he said.

'Yeah.'

'Pelléas and Mélisande?'

'Er – Debussy or Schoenberg?'

'That's my girl,' he said. 'Debussy.'

'Yes.'

'OK then,' he said.

'Clothes?' I wondered.

'No,' he said. And looked at me.

'Fuck sake,' I said.

'Oh come on,' he said. 'I'm not married any more. Hardly, anyway.'

So his capacity for entirely inappropriate jokes was intact within his distress.

'Certainly not,' I said – a phrase of his. God, I'd already picked it up.

The following week I came back from work to find him in the kitchen with all kinds of fancy mushrooms, talking quickly about a risotto he wanted to make for me. I wasn't hungry but I let him make it. The chopping and the smells soothed him. Garlic and warm olive oil, the crunch of salt, the chicken bones boiling up into broth, the dim musk of the bay leaf, the warmth. I left him to it; and went to read.

He brought me a glass of wine. White, smoky, just cold enough.

'It's beautiful, isn't it?' he said. 'I'm not going to have one. Like you asked.'

When I smelt burning I went into the kitchen.

'I've fucked it up,' he said. 'I'll go and get an Indian.' He left – swiftly, windily, before I could take in the situation. I turned off the flame under the pan, and went back to my book. It was nice to read without him coming in for a chat, ignoring the fact I was actually doing something.

I read two chapters. Three. Peace and quiet. Lovely.

It doesn't take that long to get a curry.

Even as I thought 'Should I worry?' I realised that yes, of course I should.

He didn't come back that night.

He was nocturnal. He could be at any one of a dozen regular haunts. Many of them I had haunted with him, in days gone by. Was I meant to go out and trawl them, asking barmen whether he'd been in, finding him and dragging him out by his ear, demanding that he get in the house and eat his supper, like some fishwife?

Or ring hospitals?

Or police stations?

I couldn't sleep, overslept the next day, was late to work (I was writing a book about the cultural history of the human heart), rang my landline every hour. He didn't answer my phone anyway. One of his little acts of respect – unnecessary, often unhelpful, but somehow sweet. One of the many ways in which he gave what he wanted to give, not what you wanted to be given. He didn't answer any phone, basically. He felt powerless not knowing who was there, and what they might want.

The following evening, when I came in, he was smoking a cigarette in the back yard, staring through the kitchen door at a pan of risotto.

'What time do you call this?' he cried, throwing down the cigarette. 'Dinner's ready. Sorry about the slight delay. You just need to stir it and add the parmesan.' He was stone sober, pale, clean. He looked exceptionally Northern, like a piece of granite. 'Get the plates,' he said.

Seeing that he was all right, I was angry.

'A word,' I said. 'Where were you? While you're staying here, don't walk out and just stay out overnight. And don't throw your fag ends in my garden. And don't tell me what to do.'

'That's about twenty-five words,' he said.

'Is that the important bit of what I just said? Or a fatuous diversion? I'm leading a normal life here. Courtesy, and kindness.'

'Normal,' he said.

'I know you're quite a peculiar person,' I said. 'That's fine. You can be peculiar. But don't be rude and don't be unkind.'

'Unkind!'

'I was worried about you. When you didn't come back. You don't drink if you stay here. You don't stay here if you drink. Simple choice.'

He grunted.

'And no, I'm not making your risotto for you.'

'It's not for me. It's for you.'

Left to myself, I'd have had four apples for dinner, and no washing up.

'It's for both of us,' he said.

He's trying to help, I thought.

The risotto was delicious.

It was me who cleared up.

He had a bath. He called me in; standing with the towel round his waist, wet hair pushed back, shaving, the bathroom half flooded. He'd aged. The snakey young torso had metamorphosed into a bit of an egg on legs. He was oblivious to the decline.

'You know that bit I never reach under my chin and it always pisses you off,' he said – a memory from many years ago, which staggered me. 'You do it,' he said. 'Do it the way you like it. Oh, whoops, unfortunate double entendre,' he said. 'Sorry, darling.'

Later he said, 'Let me sleep in your bed tonight at least.'

'No no no,' I said.

'But I'm so sad and lonely,' he said.

'Jesus Christ,' I said, 'just shut up, would you.'

He rather fixatedly bought a white suit, and lived in the back room for a few months. He was booked to start a home detox the day he got the divorce papers. I watched him carefully, delicately, wondering.

Often when I think about how things might have been, I search in a kind of orgy of ungratifiable hindsight for the many occasions when I could have said, 'Don't do that. Come with me instead.' I was thinking of saying it now. But before he was strong enough to be told it, towards the end of that summer, he headed off with Anna who I'd met in Peru, a fine woman, and one who wasn't saying, 'You can stay here if you're sober and you're serious about recovery.' And that became another year.

When Anna lost patience with him, he rolled up again from time to time, the white suit forgotten, the T-shirts grubby again. Antipodean Cath, another ex-girlfriend (or old girlfriend – what's the precise difference here? An ex-girlfriend is someone you were meant to be faithful to and broke up with; an old girlfriend is someone you used to sleep with on an informal arrangement, and may yet do so again, who knows?) had given him tickets to something at the Albert Hall – *Carmen*, I think. Did I want to go? Sure. Afterwards we went to a Lebanese cafe on Gloucester Road. On the way there I tripped on a kerb in my heels while we were getting into a taxi and he made some cheap crack to the driver about me being drunk.

I hadn't been drunk since 1992. I had a vision of a headline about something terrible happening to a child, and the subhead saying 'The Mother Was Drunk', and that I could not abide. God I was angry.

At the Lebanese place we sat in the window. I can see him now, ordering *imam bayildi* and some huge kebab, arguing. In the end he seemed to understand that for me being so drunk you fall over is shameful and undignified, and that though I liked drinking I was not and never would be a woman who fell down drunk in the street, and, also, he was an absolute hypocrite to throw that at me, and try to make a fool of me to the cab driver. In other words, I was well up on my high horse, and after a while I had stirred myself into such a tottering tower of outrage that I was able to say: 'The point is, actually, that you *have* to not drink.'

He said, 'Christ, why does everyone keep saying this?'

I said, 'Because it's true.'

He didn't drink that evening. He drummed his fingers and smoked.

Back at my house later, he said, 'What, so, I should break up with Anna and be with you?'

I said, 'She thinks you're broken up anyway.'

And I did say, that night: 'If you want to do this, and if the love of a good woman is going to help you with it, then yes, I'm on.'

This was a massive thing for me to say. Why had I never said it before? Because I wanted it to be his idea. Because I was embarrassed to describe myself as a good woman. Because I assumed he'd say no, or mock me, say, What, *you! As if!*

Where did it come from, this disbelief in myself? Why do women apologise all the time? Where do we mislay our strength and faith? I was unbeatable when I was eight – Queen of the World. Now I hardly knew how to love or be loved. I wish to God I'd picked him up five, ten, twenty years earlier.

A few days later I had a sudden, very strong urge to be with him. Physical. An absolute magnetic pull. I'd been out for dinner, and coming back up the Uxbridge Road I glanced through the windows of his regular hang-outs – the Office, the Thai – and then followed the invisible urge into Bush Hall, formerly the Carlton Snooker Club, where we'd wasted so much time back in the day. He was there at a round table, a cold open beer in front of him.

'Ah there you are,' he said. 'This is for you' – and he held it out to me. The familiar greeting, made more poignant by the not-drinking campaign that had been started.

'How are you?' I asked.

'Miserable, fucked up, insecure, immature, motherless, neurotic, troubled, tragic, raging,' he said. 'All the usual.'

'You're drinking too much,' I said.

'Of course,' he said. 'But not in front of you. And I'm going to stop.'

'Are you?'

He'd just moved flat, and wanted me to see it. It was just after our birthdays, nineteen years after our first night together. It was our third first kiss, suddenly and completely irresistible. I don't remember this one either. I just remember being on the floor with him, with a cliff-jumping, home-coming sense of this, this, this is who I love, and being unbelievably happy.

He said, 'So are we going out together now?'

I said, 'Our being together is for if you want to stop drinking.'

'Yes,' he said. 'Yes. That's what I want.'

I said to myself, Oh God.

After that I ran away to the country. He left most of a Liszt Sonata as a message, upset, inchoate and incoherent. I stood on a prehistoric earthwork high on the Marlborough Downs, Liszt and the wind competing in my ears. He rang at seven in the morning and said: 'I've been awake all night, come and see me.' He rang at three in the afternoon and said: 'I'm in Le Suquet, I've ordered lobster, are you coming?' He rang at nine when I was in the bath, and wouldn't get off the phone so I was standing in my towel, dripping and getting cold. He rang at two in the morning and said: 'What are you wearing? Take it off.' A stranger rang, saying 'Hello? Is that Miss Louisa? Mr Robert is here; he would like to talk to you please.' He rang at tea-time and said: 'I am aware this is a little odd but I love you and we need to talk about this.'

I love you?

I stared out at swaying piles of wet roses and sodden lawns, tunnels and frothy mounds of cow parsley blocking off all but the sky, heavy branches drooping down to moss and frogs, and I thought about it. There are things you are honour-bound to honour, above and beyond your common sense. Now, you say you love me, I thought – and started laughing at my inadvertent quote from 'Cry Me a River', alarming some crows, who rose in an upward swoop, chorusing doom. It had always been incredibly easy to describe my relationship with Robert in lyrics. Every damn Motown song. Plenty of country and western. A rather embarrassing amount of Rod Stewart. Robert said we were more like enharmonics. Did I know enharmonics?

'Yes, I know the word.'

'What is it then?'

'It's when the same note has two different names and roles, depending which scale you're thinking about: hence it might be D flat in one key, but in another it's C sharp.'

'It's a good image that, isn't it?' he said. 'How it can look and sound exactly the same, but it can mean, and be, something else entirely. The last note of one scale could be the first note of a completely different scale.'

When the rain stopped, I walked out into the brilliance of sudden English sun after rain, raindrop-spattered cobwebs glittering all around, the wooden garden fence steaming lightly, and I sang 'Cry Me a River' softly to the sheep who stood with tiny rainbows in their oily wool, as the wet grass soaked through my shoes and drenched my jeans up to the knee.

Tenderness crept through me. I could feel it. I imagined a future: him at the piano, playing; me on a sofa, reading. A fire. French windows, maybe. A touching end to a long saga.

Would I make him cry me a river?

No. I would follow Johnny Cash's advice. I would be what I was – in love with him. With him, finally. To turn my back on this would go against nature. All I could do now was be honest. See where love would take us. Because love can take you anywhere.

*

On my return to London I had a little speech semi-prepared, and waited for the moment, which occurred across a bowl of tom yung koong.

'I must try and make this,' he said. 'You like it, don't you?'

'So, Robert,' I said.

'Yes, Louisa,' he said, with a demeanour of self-aware ironic obedience. He was wearing a clean white shirt, and was sober, though over-shaved.

I hadn't smoked for years, but I rather wanted one now. It felt so charmingly youthful to be here with Robert. Like being twenty-five again. I took a fag from his packet.

'Bloody amateur,' he grumbled, and didn't light it for me.

'So, Robert,' I said.

'You're looking gorgeous,' he said. 'Let's skip dinner. Come under the table with me. I've had a *demi-maître* all week at the thought of you.' (*Demi-maître* = half-master = semi-erection.)

'Robert,' I said.

'Don't brush me off,' he said.

'No!' I said – and realised suddenly his vulnerability.

'No?' he said.

'Do you want me for your girlfriend?' I asked. The seventeen-year-old ghost me shivered. The nerve! To ask Robert that!

'Well it seems a bit of a juvenile way to put it,' he said, 'but partner is a dreadful term, sounds like I want you to set up in a law firm or play squash, and it's probably a little early to ask you to marry me, though I could start quite soon with the veiled hints . . .'

'I'll be your girlfriend,' I said. 'What I said – if you're looking for a good woman so you can be saved by her love, I'll do that. I can't not. Two things though.'

He was smiling.

'You stop drinking, and you get a shrink.'

My seventeen-year-old gaped. To ask Robert, straight out, and to set requirements!

He was taking a long drag, cigarette held between finger and thumb. He smiled down at the cigarette. 'Drink and smoke till the day I die,' he murmured.

'Smoking is a detail,' I said. 'Of course you smoke too much, but it doesn't make you a cunt.'

'Does drinking make me a cunt?' he asked.

'You should know. You're there every time it happens.'

'I do drink too much,' he said. 'Far too much. You're right, I should cut down.'

'You must stop,' I said.

'Completely?'

'Yes.'

'Is that a requirement?'

91

'Yes.'

'Well,' he said. 'Doesn't ask much, does she.'

'It's not for me.'

'Yes it is,' he said. 'OK. I'll do it.' (Air of doing a great favour.) 'I won't drink when I'm with you.' He announced it as if it were in his gift.

'At all,' I said gently.

'And I won't be POA,' he said. 'All right?' A little aggressively. (POA is Pissed On Arrival.)

'At all,' I said.

He avoided understanding.

'OK,' he said.

'At all, ever, whether I am there or not,' I said, very clearly. 'Ever again.'

'But I can't have a steak without a glass or two of nice fat red wine,' he said. 'It's a cultural thing, it's . . .'

'At all,' I said.

Silence. Then: 'I went to the doctor,' he said.

'Oh?'

'A few weeks ago.'

'And what did the doctor say?'

'That I shouldn't stop drinking.'

'Really?'

'Yes. He said it was dangerous.'

'Dangerous to stop drinking.'

'Yes. When you've been drinking as much as I have, it's dangerous to stop.'

'So explain to me that thing where people stop drinking because they have to for their health. That whole alcoholic business – AA, and addiction, and all that?'

'I don't know about that,' he said.

'Yes, you do. You did a detox and had to be talked to every day. What did they talk about? Perhaps,' I said, 'the doctor meant it would be dangerous to stop drinking just like that. Presumably you're meant to cut down bit by bit, or do it under supervision, with the librium, like you did before. Perhaps you might go to the doctor again.'

'I hate going to the doctor.'

'I'll come with you.' I really wasn't going to mother him. But you might go to the doctor with your boyfriend anyway, mightn't you? Isn't that what people do? Couples? If they want?

'What's the cunt like?' he asked. 'The cunt I become?'

'Incoherent and rude,' I said. 'Leaps from topic to topic, so you can't follow a conversation. Interrupts, talks over people, to repeat himself. Same stories over and over. Gets into provocative situations with strangers. Rings up at four in the morning. Asks the same question a hundred times and doesn't listen to the answer.'

'Not a hundred. How you exaggerate.'

Sober, I thought, *he won't need to be defensive. Is he sober now? Maybe not entirely.*

'And doesn't listen to the answer,' I said again. 'Obsessive. Bullying.'

'Bullying!'

'Yes. Won't let people leave, for example. Insist they stay with you, stay awake, and listen to whatever it is that you desperately want to listen to . . .'

'I want to share my passions . . .'

'At one in the morning when they want to go home?'

'Yes! People have no passion. Fucking bourgeois . . .'

'They have work the next day. They have baby sitters. They have a right to go home when they want.'

He grunted. 'What else?'

'You don't notice what they want or need. They might say – I'm just going to the loo; and you'll take their arm, hold on to them, keep talking, so they feel it's rude to leave. They could piss their pants before you'd notice. You don't notice when people hate you swearing. You lose your sense of proportion. You swear to old ladies. You take out a fag and light it and someone else could be standing there with a fag and you wouldn't see it to light it for them. You say stupid things, then you get hit. You get stuck on transmit. You're never on receive.'

'Never!' he exclaimed softly.

'Not when you're drunk.'

'And when I'm not drunk?'

'You're my true love,' I said.

'What?' he said.

'You heard,' I said.

The evening had moved on. By now he was leaning in the kitchen doorway, forgetting to blow his smoke out into the back yard.

'You were never in love with me,' he said.

There was a pause while the idiocy of his statement hit me.

'Were you?' he asked.

And I howled with laughter.

'*Were* you?'

'Robert,' I said. 'I've been half in love with you my entire adult life.'

'Half?'

'I slept with you for years and years.'

'Yeah, but you weren't my girlfriend or anything.'

'Exactly!'

'So . . .'

'I slept with you whenever you wanted, no matter what.'

'Yeah, but—'

'What – you slept with loads of people? Yes, I know!'

'So did you!'

'I seem to remember last time we discussed this I was on ten and you were on a hundred and fifty, including about thirty with names like "that girl on the flight to San Francisco" and "the Australian with the tits".'

'A hundred and forty,' he said, as if that were the point.

'Robert, men do often sleep with women just because they have the horn and no standards; but usually when a woman sleeps with

94

a man, and carries on sleeping with him, it's because it means something to her.'

'I thought you just liked shagging me.'

'Oh I did,' I said, and he smiled. 'Stop that,' I said. 'We're talking. Where was I. Yes. Shagging.' Laughing again. 'Yes.' Thinking: *and I liked your jokes and your conversation and your kindness and your magnificent intellect and your pale blue eyes and the fact you were quite nice to my mum and all sorts of things about you which added up to me being kind of crazy about you.*

'Bloody hellfire,' he said. Then he got cross. 'Why didn't you say so?'

'Because you never asked. You should have noticed. Instead of always saying I didn't want to go out with a chain-smoking drunk who shags everyone. Anyway. I was sleeping with you! That should've told you!'

'You should have told me! Properly!'

'I couldn't possibly have told you. You were off with every bloody girl you could get your hands on and you were horribly unfaithful to everybody – who'd want to be your girlfriend, the way you behaved? Who wants to go out with someone who either didn't notice or didn't value that they were half in love with them? And you might have rejected me.'

'Never!' he declared. For a moment I was hugely, enormously gratified.

'You might have,' I said. 'You rejected loads of people. After you'd shagged them usually.'

'I wasn't like that,' he complained.

'Everyone except Lucy and Benazir Bhutto?' I said. 'The woman you'd never met before, at dinner, and you lured her to the bathroom before the main course? The one you sat next to on a plane and moved in with her and her mother for three months? The Russian woman? Four violinists in a row, I seem to remember. And me? Did you ring me? Or did I not hear from you for a year and a half?'

'God, if I'd known,' he said. 'It would have been so different. We could have got together fifteen years ago.'

'Well,' I said. 'We didn't. You were too drunk and I was too proud.' Pride, the well-known B-side of low self-esteem . . . my fear-and-pride-fuelled passivity. Now, sod pride. Sod fear of rejection.

'I wasn't that drunk,' he said.

'Nina's window?'

'Obviously I've drunk quite a lot . . .'

'You've been drunk for years, and you've got into a habit of misery . . .'

'I can be positive,' he said. 'I can believe that a modicum of contentment might be available.'

'A modicum of contentment!' I laughed a lot. God, how sweet that would be.

'So if I stop drinking and get a shrink, I get to fuck you whenever I want?'

'More or less,' I said.

'Hmm,' he said, and took a hard but leisurely drag on his cigarette. 'OK, deal,' he said. 'And now what?'

'Now you give up drinking and we live happily ever after,' I said. 'And see where we are in a year.'

'Modicum of contentment here we come,' he said. 'Get yer coat.'

'We're home.'

'Oh. So we are.'

Later, he said: 'And what about fidelity and all that?

I said, 'If you so much as look at another woman I'll kill you.'

He said, "Thank Christ for that. What a relief.'

I was a balloon in a high and beautiful wind. I thought, *We can do this. He wants to. We can.* I was daffodils in April. I was Shirley MacLaine at the end of *Sweet Charity*. It was all going to be all right.

Part Two

2003–05

Chapter Ten

Home, 2003

I had the habits of regular life.

'I envy you,' he said. 'How do you know how to do that?' – as I had a bath, or sat down with a little salad at one o'clock, or fell asleep.

'God, that must be a record,' he said once, standing above me, waking me.

'What?'

'Seven seconds, head on pillow to fast asleep. God, I envy you that.'

The first morning he leapt out of bed at eight, dolloped yogurt into a big bowl with honey and sliced banana, and had a shower before getting dressed.

'See?' he said. 'I can do it. Good habits, healthy life. I know just what needs to be done.'

He came home with flowers – nice ones, not newsagent ones. 'I did slightly notice – you see, I do notice things, I'm not a cunt – that's a really bad thing to call someone, you know, you shouldn't say things like that – I did notice that you didn't really like the ones I brought before. But these are nice, aren't they?' He sounded a little anxious. 'The girl in the shop said they were . . . I thought they looked a bit skinny, but she said you'd like them. I told her you were very stylish and knew about stuff like that . . .'

They were skinny: twenty long tuber-roses, coloured like green ivory and smelling like the Elysian Fields, in thick cellophane and cream ribbons. I liked them very much. I put them in the bedroom but could hardly breathe with the scent, so I distributed them round the house, and the smell made me feel like a chorus girl in her dressing room.

He was sweet to me day and night. He played for me endlessly; my personal piano jukebox. He looked vaguely healthy.

'I'll go swimming,' he said, and he did, but the pool was so revolting that it was only the once. 'Well, nonce, actually,' he said. 'I didn't go in.'

It's astonishing how many alcoholics are charismatic, witty and attractive people.

'I'm going up the road,' he says, one sunny morning. He always goes up the road in the morning: fags, paper, coffee at Paolo's. 'Do you need anything?'

'Bog roll,' I say.

Half an hour later he is in the front garden, chuckling. He has bought twenty-four rolls, and has unwrapped them all, and is building a pyramid for me on the grass.

I go to lunch with an editor to talk about a new book, about roses and the people they are named after. During the meal a waiter brings a massive bunch of roses to the table, to me. They are addressed to 'the most beautiful woman in the room'. (Later I learned he had tracked through the entire publishers on the phone to find the editor, to get the name of the restaurant. He charmed her, asked her if the gesture would be naff (she said no). On a later occasion she recognised him in the street by his voice; they spoke and made friends.)

On my birthday, he is unwell and unable to take me out to Locanda Locatelli for lunch as planned. He says: Take Baroness Alacrity in my place, I'll pay. During the meal, again a waiter brings a massive bunch of roses to the table, addressed this time to 'The two most beautiful women in the room', signed Roberto Lockhartelli.

Robert and Wayland (in his mid-eighties, half blind and playing from memory) are playing duets. 'It's amazing how much better I am, playing with him,' Dad says, as Robert plays three and a half hands' worth, the pair of them with their blue eyes and their twinkling.

He leaves me a note on the back of half a photocopied map of Lola's new school. (The words in roman are what I wrote to him; the italics are his annotations.)

L: Good morning

R: (*On this he has drawn a traditional cock-and-balls, using the tail of the final g as one of the testicles. This was his preferred sign off, an affectionate scribble, often with a few dots for sperm, used universally, including to his father.*)

L: Here are my keys – when you go out PLEASE LEAVE THEM IN THE GARDEN LETTERBOX so I can get in later.

R: (*With an arrow pointing to the capitals*)
could you possibly print this larger? I can't quite read it. In addition, I can't find a letterbox in the garden. [There is one, actually.] *I think, worryingly, you might be embarking on succumbation to the evils of a distortedly surrealist malaise. Salvatore Tarka Dahli will be turning in his wooden hammock. As Apollinaire would have said:* "Je ne veux pas laisser les clefs dans la boi(s)te de lettres dans le jardin . . . je veux ronfler." [This, God help us, is a complex reference to the song 'Hotel',

101

a setting by Poulenc of a poem by Apollinaire, of which the final line is '*Je ne veux pas travailler, je veux fumer*' – 'I don't want to work, I want to smoke'. He's made it 'I don't want to leave the keys in the wood/box (French pun here) of letters in the garden, I want to snore'.]

L: Also there is a chocolate croissant in the gym. [I have no idea what I meant by this.]

R: *and a baguette in the brothel. Sadly I will be visiting neither today* xx

One possible explanation for this charm among alcoholics is that, like criminals and the insane and other wild people, they need it. If they didn't make others happy at least some of the time, nobody would look after them. It's Darwinian. Only the most irresistible alcoholics survive at all. Of course, there are also many many alcoholics who make everyone around them unhappy all the time, who are aggressive, vicious, malevolently calculating, boring, ungifted and unattractive, who keep their abusive relationships going by sheer wretched force: *Take care of me or I'll beat you up. Take care of me or I'll discard you, and all the other people in our community will regard you as damaged goods. Take care of me or you will lose my portion of our meagre earning potential and we'll both starve and so will our kids. Anyway you're so stupid and ugly no one else would have you.*

As with any other type of person, some alcoholics are in themselves kind and thoughtful people; some are just narcissistic bastards anyway. Similarly some are solvent/lucky/educated/ employed, with independent-minded and healthy partners, well-equipped to be strong; others live with all the burdens of poverty and dependence. Alcoholism apart, Robert and I lived in a pretty nice world. But addiction doesn't give a toss about background. It feeds off whatever weakness there is. A solvent alcoholic can just afford more booze, more easily. Money and a safe home can themselves be enablers.

*

He was writing music for the TV series *The Inspector Lynley Mysteries*. As usual his music was much better than it needed to be, but he took the piss out of the entire enterprise, undermining both himself and the show. Film and TV composers are often divided into two types, the brilliant talents who write brilliant music which the filmmakers work with and are inspired by, and the box-ticking 'paint-by-numbers' type whose every predictable note or snatch of melody is pre-assigned to a mood or a character. Robert, predictably, could be either and both. He was very reliable, from the point of view both of quality and of deadlines, to such a degree that he gained early on a reputation as someone you could call on when the score you commissioned turned out not to serve, and you needed a new one in two weeks. He had considerable respect for his own talent, and got in a fury about the socio-professional aspects of that world – the requirement to get on with people, be civil, and produce what you are asked to produce. He saw lesser talents overtake him, 'operators and retro-heroes who camouflage their small talent with charm and mere technical competence', as he put it – but he admitted he was a massive self-plagiariser, and declaimed on the pointlessness of writing modern classical music for its own sake, because you slog for a year, it gets played once if you're lucky, in a tiny studio behind an opera house where they do Mozart all the time, they can't afford an actual orchestra anyway, and nobody would come.

Lola (now ten) and I had been writing a novel together: *Lionboy*, about Charlie Ashanti, who can talk cat and runs away with a floating circus. Robert amused himself and us by writing a suite of piano pieces based on the book for Lola, who was learning – and hating – the piano: a pretty waltz for zebras; a stalking habanera for Pirouette, the Girl on the Flying Trapeze, a tragic eerie melody for the tight-rope-walking violinist. The Lionboy books took off, and suddenly we were being hailed as The New J. K. Rowling, doorstepped by the *Evening Standard*, published in thirty-six languages and proud purveyors of the film rights to Stephen Spielberg. We went to New York, Buenos Aires, Amsterdam, Bangkok and LA. Robert recorded the tunes he had written, and they became the soundtrack of the audiobook.

Robert was seeing his son every other week, for pizzas, trips to the park, lunch at my house. This involved not just the delight of seeing him but also the torture of having to say goodbye. I cheerfully thought that seeing Jim would be a simple good thing, but Robert suffered monumental shame and self-punishment in this area – for the pain he must be giving Jim; for having allowed this situation to arise; for not handling it better – as well as the visceral pain he felt at the end of the visits. He'd say, 'I need to be alone after I see him, calm myself down.' At times he sabotaged these meetings, made himself ill to put them off because he feared he would be unable to resist the urge to drink afterwards.

'I want a new flat,' he said. 'I'm fed up with these basements. Fresh air will be good for me. First floor, south facing. Nice big windows. I love a first-floor sitting room.'

I helped him move in. Some furniture came out of post-marriage storage. There were some boxes that he had never unpacked: books and old stuff from before he was married. Concert posters, piles and piles of music, photos.

'Didn't you sort out your things?' I asked.

'Nope,' he said. 'I just said to her to put in whatever she didn't want. I'll unpack them,' he said. 'That'd be good. Let's go for lunch.'

I hung his pictures and drew a heart on his mirror in lipstick, and we went and ate sushi.

'That'll build me up,' he said. 'Fish oils. I talked to Ingrid. She's a nutritionist. She says to eat fish, apparently.'

His ignorance was still touching: the way he brought up basics of common knowledge as if they were jewels of important new information.

He wore clean clothes, and was careful about Lola's feelings. He bought me a painting. I bought him shoes. He lent me £1,000 when my tax bill was alarming. We talked of moving to the country. I celebrated when he got to the doctor to see about pain in his legs, and his terrible insomnia, both of which kept both of us awake at night (along with horrific post-apocalyptic nightmares that made him shout aloud, in which he was watching through the window of a fast-moving sealed train as awful things were being done outside to those he loved. As a metaphor for addiction it's unfault-able.)

I had already lost contact with the fact that these things I was celebrating should be normal (tricky words, should and normal) and that celebrating them suggested a low standard of expectations. He said 'I'm fine, I'll be fine', because he wanted to be; I believed him, because believing was my default. I was ignorant, but not naive. He apologised for not being at his best, but I wanted him to do, not say; to be, not to promise to be. How could I show him how to do things – to get the doctor to pay attention, for example? He didn't even know what kind of specialist it was he had seen, or what he'd been tested for. Timing became an issue: when does patience become indulgence; support become enabling? When does 'being taken for a ride' begin? Not by him. By the addiction which had already taken him.

I assumed he was both serious in his intention not to drink and capable of delivering on it. A counsellor *was* in the pipeline. He did a second detox: librium, to ease the potential side-effects. I didn't know what the side-effects might be. I didn't know how long 'coming off' went on for. I thought he had already come off. He told me he was tempted, and needed help. I didn't know if he was taking the pills. I didn't know what the specialist actually said. I didn't know anything. He wasn't going to AA meetings. He just went to the doctor and got some pills. That was his idea of medicine – a cure, some tablets provided by a third party, rather than any kind of prevention that involved him doing anything. I was leaving him to it because they have to do it themselves, right? After hitting rock bottom? I knew that much. And being divorced, that's quite rock-bottomy, isn't it? The bitter end of your rope, as someone once said.

I feared that my loving care would make him happier and healthier and more attractive, and by then I would be properly in love with him, and then he'd go and fall in love with somebody else. I feared that my loving care wouldn't make him happier and healthier and he'd get ill and I'd have to push his wheelchair while he vented his frustrations on me. Though he was trying hard to limit himself, and though I didn't know it, he was drinking.

Truth was, I didn't know detox from rehab, rehab from recovery, alcoholism from a hole in the head. He and I had been using the word alcoholic for years, but we knew sweet nothing, and never bothered to find out because we were young, and still immortal. Now that I do know, I want more people to know; to say whatever I can say to improve the chances of nobody ever having to go through what he and I went through. I want to make clear that alcoholism – addiction – is not a racy lifestyle choice, not a decision, but an insidious and baffling condition which kills people. I'm not telling anybody what to do. I'm just telling how it was, for him, and for me.

So: detox is a set of pills to take in order to safely come off alcohol after an extended period of heavy drinking. Rehab is an extended set of therapies dealing with the physical, mental and emotional results of long-term heavy drinking, and the obstacles to giving up. Recovery is where you want to end up: a long-term state of carefully nurtured sobriety.

And alcoholism? The simplest and most useful account I ever heard is this: It's not what you drink or how much you drink, it's why you drink and what it does to you. You might drink every day and not be alcoholic; you might have been sober for twenty years and still be alcoholic.

Technically, it's a primary chronic disease of unknown cause and a slow onset, with genetic, psychosocial, cultural and environmental factors influencing its development and manifestations. (It's worth mentioning here that genes work in complex relation to each other, and concern risk and possibility, not destiny. Research shows that genes are responsible for about half of the risk for alcoholism. Epigenetics – how different factors can alter the expression of our genes – also affect the risk for developing alcoholism.) It is the compulsive consumption of and psychophysiological dependence on alcohol. It's associated with a cumulative pattern of deviant behaviours, impairments of social and behavioural function that interfere with the person's health, relationships, and/or means of livelihood. It is progressive and pathological, mainly affecting the nervous and digestive systems, including the brain, pancreas and liver. It may occur at any age. Families of alcoholics have a higher incidence of the disease. It is characterised by distortions in thinking, most notably denial. It's often fatal.

It isn't a moral failing; an act of aggression; lack of willpower; personal. Nobody fills in a form saying 'I'd like to be an alcoholic please so I can destroy myself and ruin the lives of everyone who loves me.'

Here is an explanation I was given by a specialist, which makes most sense to me. If a person has (1): the genetic predisposition to physical addiction, and also (2): the psychological predisposition to using chemicals to change the mood when they are suffering mental or emotional pain, and also (3): things happening in their life which cause them that mental and emotional pain, then it is likely that enough of that pain will provoke them to use enough of those chemicals for the physical addiction to kick in.

And then they are in trouble. Two out of three, one out of three, won't do it.

Perhaps because it is not a straightforward physical condition, and perhaps because it makes its sufferers behave so badly, people say that they don't think addiction is an illness – although illness is the usual term for something that gives a person life-threatening physical and/or mental symptoms which need medical attention. Illnesses have been ascribed moral character ever since the gods first threw plagues on misbehaving Ancient Greeks: poetic tuberculosis, for those too sensitive to bear the vulgar everyday world; mad syphilis for the uncontrolled and lustful; dirty leprosy, attention-seeking anorexia. (A good guideline to an illness's moral status is the use of a noun to describe its sufferers – a leper, an alcoholic, an anorexic – rather than using the illness as a qualifier, which allows the inclusion of other qualifiers and thus preserves the patients' humanity: a child with flu, a woman with gastro-enteritis, a man with cancer. The use of a noun also re-iterates the illnesses' chronic nature. These are conditions which must be managed but cannot be cured.) This approach lingers, including among alcoholics themselves, who often see themselves as bad people who should be ashamed of themselves, rather than sick people who are having trouble getting their head around this complex and murky condition. This maintains the illusion that they personally are in control, which leads them either to forced periods of 'dry-drunkenness' – white-knuckle trying to stay sober without help – or to further drinking, further shame at their failure to stop, and a feeling that they deserve the problems drinking brings precisely *because* they have been weak in failing to give up. The moral reality I recognise is this: addicts are not to blame for the genes/circumstances which contribute to their illness. But they are responsible for what they do about it. They have choices. Only when they recognise this can they start to deal with their condition. And recognition takes time.

When your boyfriend is sick with alcoholism, there can be a tightening of the lips, a small raising of a judgemental eyebrow, a 'Well what do you expect/God, not again'; and for you, his companion, a low-lying murmur of 'poor fool'. This is a natural impatience, for your and/or his own good. Courtesy, embarrassment and shyness keep it just far enough out of range that one cannot quite respond to it. But it is there. How could it not be? People get fed up. God knows I got fed up, and by the end he was beyond fed up – even without Christian morality and the 'just fuckin' sort it out' post-Victorian Northern working-class ethics he was born into, and to which he half subscribed himself. Clearly it's hard to live with an addict. Imagine how it feels when the addict lives in your head.

I wonder whether as a society we will make a leap of understanding about addiction that will cause people to look back and be ashamed for describing (as I heard all yesterday on the news) a murder victim as 'an alcoholic' rather than 'a woman'; for pursuing Amy Winehouse to her death; for all the mockery and ignorance. In a documentary I hear the blotchy, sick, swollen, desperate alcoholics, dying of this physical and mental disease which though it is their responsibility is not their fault, saying: 'I must just be strong'; 'I've been naughty all my life but I'll be good now', 'You get what you deserve'. Nobody deserves it.

I know a doctor – an alcoholic doctor, as it happens – who doesn't think alcoholism is an illness, displaying with wonderful irony the first easily identifiable symptom of alcoholism in everyday life: denial. That's the thing about denial: you don't know you're doing it. Because – as Robert told me later – and I didn't hear – your own self is the first person you deny everything to. It shows up not just in individuals, but also in a mass of institutionalised semi-alcoholic social habits and terms (Happy Hour, pre-loading, prinking, lady-petrol); in jokes: 'I don't have a drink problem; I drink, no problem!' 'Giving up drink doesn't make you live longer, it just makes it seem that way!' 'I'd rather live a shorter life to the full and go out on a high . . . ' as if liver disease and cancer were some kind of easy way out, Thelma and Louise flying glamorously over the cliff.

Those who fail to laugh along are, like the girl who doesn't fancy the bloke who fancies her, humourless, frigid, spoilsports, prudes. Nobody likes the Cassandra of Wine O'Clock. Nobody wants to be her. But all this jollity denies the unwelcome chemical truth that alcohol is a depressant. Used sparingly, it is an effective anti-anxiety drug (and yes it's wonderful to stop feeling anxious); used too much it both loses its effect and gets its claws into the genetically available. Booze is not actually fun, it just seems it, for a while – which for those of us lucky enough to stay in that 'while' is great. But on the strength of that seeming is built a massive industry and a wide and glorious culture with a hideous underbelly which we find easier to, yes, deny.

Half of the alcohol sold in the UK is not accounted for in the amount people report using. One and a half million UK adults[1] are alcoholic; many more drink every day. People who drink at risky or harmful levels (10.8 million in the UK)[2] account for 60 per cent of alcohol sales.[3] Alcohol costs UK society £21 billion per annum[4]; and in 2013–14 it cost the NHS £3.5 billion. Hospital admissions wholly or partly attributed to alcohol – including harmful use, alcohol addiction, acute intoxication, high blood pressure, cardiac arrhythmia, injuries, falls, self-harm and assaults – have gone up 115 per cent in ten years.[5] Then there is liver disease, diabetes, stroke and cancer. Alcohol is implicated in 10 per cent of the burden of disease and death in the UK. Alcohol-related deaths almost doubled between 1994 and 2013. Drinkers are paying their own way, though; indeed the government profits from drink sales: 67 per cent of the price of spirits is tax. In 2011 six UK alcohol and health organisations, led by the British Medical

---

1 Professor Sir Ian Gilmore, UK Alcohol Health Alliance.

2 Public Health England.

3 In England – *Guardian*, January 2016.

4 Insititute of Alcohol Studies.

5 *Guardian*, Jan 2016.

Association, very publicly walked out on a UK government policy initiative, the Responsibility Deal for Alcohol (RDA), saying it was a diversion from the evidence-based alcohol policies likely to achieve a real reduction in alcohol harm, such as policies on pricing and availability of alcohol. Even parts of the alcohol industry agreed that the deal would be almost wholly ineffective. There's a word for not listening to your doctor when it comes to your drinking. Yes, denial – but enough. This is a love story, not a treatise.

Here are a few things I wish someone had told me straight out about loving an alcoholic, right at the start.

You need to understand the difference between fault and responsibility. As in, if your dog craps on your neighbour's step, it is not your fault. However it is your responsibility, and you must clean it up.

Cleaning up after your alcoholic when s/he craps on your neighbour's doorstep infantilises them, denies them access to their own responsibility, makes them a naughty puppy. Which they are not: they are a human being. The correct response from you, oh competent perfecter, putter-of-things-to-rights, know-all, must be to step back and let them have their own relationship with their own crap, for however long it takes. It's their life.

Nobody imagines we can cure cancer, or Parkinson's, with love. Why should we imagine we can cure addiction with love? Because that *is* what we're thinking. We don't say, Oh, you wouldn't have muscular dystrophy if you really loved me. Oh, you have Crohn's disease; here, let me love you enough and you will be better, oh, my love is not curing it, I am a bad person, I must love you more.

But at least, with any disease other than addiction, you're allowed to look after them. With addiction, we are required to turn around the natural instinct which says to us: he's ill? Look after him. She crashed the car? Call the garage. He puked? Clear it up. She insulted someone? Apologise on her behalf. He's drunk all the time? Hide the booze, yell at him, weep, complain to others, blame yourself.

This instinct is wrong, all wrong. Turn it round. The trouble is theirs. Their responsibility. Theirs to clear up, theirs to apologise, theirs to call the garage, theirs to work it out. You are wasting time by confusing these issues. They alone can heal themselves.

But how? How can you do all that?

Like this: you say, 'I am here, I love you. The moment you want my help to get well I will give you all the help in the world.'

*

One evening Robert wanted to cook dinner for me. Art the jazz cat was coming over, and Robert said he'd cook for us all. Great, I said. Art came, it was 7 p.m., 8 p.m., 9 p.m. and then Robert rang from Bush Hall, saying, 'Come out! Come up here!'

I said, 'Art is here, you're meant to be cooking.'

He said, 'Get Art to babysit.'

So I cooked dinner.

When I said to Robert, the next night, 'No don't come over', he fell downstairs and broke his nose. So he did come over, covered in blood.

He'd insist on coming over when I didn't want him; he'd persuade me, then not turn up, nor ring till the next afternoon by which time I was cracked with worry. One time I turned him away and he got himself arrested.

I went into the Office after an evening out with a friend. I stumbled on the shiny floor and Robert made that 'Oh she's drunk' crack that made me so mad last time. I sat, and after a bit I said, 'You don't mind if I have this do you?' reaching for the complimentary Drambuie with cream on top (known as Nepalese Soldiers, for some reason), and he said, 'Yes I do actually', took it from my hand, and gave me a 'so what are you going to do about it?' sneery look. So I kissed him and said, 'Let's speak tomorrow', and went home, where I found five messages from him from earlier, while I was out. I left him one in return: 'Sorry to be so abrupt in my

departure, but I don't like to be with you when you're like that.'
And I went to bed.

At about 2 a.m. he rang, and got me out of bed to look up Cromwell and Fairfax for him, which I did because it was about work, and read me a Dylan Thomas short story that I didn't want to hear, and in the end I hung up. He rang back, full of strange sounds and sweet melodies, and I hung up again, and at seven he rang again, to tell me the fox cub was in his garden, and he's been on the phone for an hour to his ex-wife's new husband, wanting to see his son . . . Oh God, that'll help . . . And he kept me on the line till nine. He didn't know what time or day it was. The thing is, he was always extreme anyway. He never behaved to anybody's rules. He always wanted more of everything. But this wasn't sober behaviour.

When he behaved badly, I rang him, and he apologised. He was ashamed.

*

Lola hid his shoes. She said, 'I was practising to be a pixie in the school play.'

She woke in the middle of the night, I went in and talked to her, and when I said 'goodnight', she said well it hasn't been a good night. Why not? 'I can't sleep because of all that oohing and aahing and then all the whispering.'

'She's feeling left out,' said Robert. He guessed she'd nicked his shoes when he couldn't find them. He went home in mine. I told Lola. He's planning revenge: hanging all her shoes on strings, or something. I told her he had a plan. She looked gleeful: let battle commence!

But if you steal someone's shoes, you're preventing them from leaving, aren't you? How does that add up?

I'm overthinking.

When he was little, he'd felt unwanted by his step-parents. Now he was in a stepfather-like position, and Lola didn't like him. And who could blame her? And his own son was at home, with a stepfather.

*

Unmistakably very drunk, Robert rang from a restaurant. More precisely, he got the waiter to ring while he (Robert) carried on talking to him (the waiter) about whether he was from Eritrea or Ethiopia, ignoring the fact that I was there on the line saying 'Hello?' He often made waiters and cabbies and God knows who ring me, then pass the phone to him. I hated it. I don't much like talking on the phone, or to strangers, or being disturbed when I'm trying to work, yanked back into his chaos. He made friends everywhere, and forced inappropriate intimacies on strangers. (I didn't know yet that this is an addict trait, a corollary to avoiding appropriate intimacies – for example being truthful with those you love.) There was not a trace of snobbery or racism in him; everybody was treated the same. The good side of this was the Czech joiner delighted to discuss the niceties of Smetana and Janáček, knock out a few themes with him on the piano, and become a good friend. The bad side was the cabbies with very limited English bewildered and embarrassed by Robert's complex vocabulary and idiosyncratic choice of subject matter – Georgian polyphony, Picasso's sex life.

I said, 'I'm working, you're drunk.' I hung up, and left the phone off the hook.

It's a blip, I thought. Maybe he drank tonight, but he's not *drinking*. He's really trying. I mustn't undermine that.

An hour or so later he was at the door, saying, 'Don't let me in, don't get involved with me, it'll only hurt you.' His legs were corkscrewed, so skinny, so unbalanced. 'I can't come in, can I,' he said.

'No,' I said. 'I don't want Lola seeing you like this. I don't want me seeing you like this – actually, I don't want *you* seeing you like this. I don't want you *being* like this.'

He was leaning in the doorway, soaking wet, lurching and out of focus.

'And nor do you,' I said, so calm, competent and frightened that I disliked myself.

The rain was so heavy it passed in drifts behind him. *Les jardins sous la pluie,* he said. I invited him in. He wouldn't come. Then he did, and he fell into the piano stool, and he was crying, and I went to finish my article. Shut the door on him. He played the piano. Debussy, for the rain. Later he came up and sprawled sideways on my bed, talking about his admiration for Beethovenian structure but how only the French understand nature, and saying, 'Don't get into this, don't do it, Lou.' I said, 'I'm not going without you. You are not the problem. Your problem is the problem.' And he wanted to know why don't I have a piano in my bedroom so he could play me the Rachmaninoff Prelude in G, and it would sound with the rain in a . . . what's a good word for mixture – *mélange*, I gave him, he liked that – 'But why don't I just use the ordinary word?' he says. 'Why piscine aroma? Why not fishy smell?'

And he went downstairs and played the Rachmaninoff, and his Bill Evans-style extrapolations of 'Lullaby of Broadway', and 'Every Time We Say Goodbye', and 'Cry Me a River', with its magnificent lyrics: '. . . too plebeian / through with me an . . .' Great rhyme. Yes, cry me a fucking river . . .

I was thinking about rolls of loo paper and the turbulent pouring splashing incessant rain on the stones and leaves of the garden.

Just before he went to sleep he said, 'Do you love me then?'

'What?' I said.

'Nothing, nothing.'

'What did you say?'

'I said do you love me then, at all?'

'I love you completely,' I said. 'But don't be in that state.' He was sobering up now so it felt – what, all right? By some crazy logic, yes.

So, that night, when I let him in, was I padding out his rock bottom with pillows for him to fall on? Should I have thrown him out again, for another broken bone or arrest? Looking back, yes, I should have.

Chapter Eleven

London, 2003
I wrote him a letter, printed it out and put it in the pocket of his leather jacket.

Robert,

I've done a reality check for you. You may hate me for it. Please don't. It comes with unconditional affection and respect.

I may be wrong about all this in which case forgive me, but I think I'm not.

You're good
Kind
Generous
Funny
Loving
Talented
You work hard
You're honest
You're stubborn

You're tough

You want to do the right thing

You love your son, your father, your friends,

They love you too.

All these things are there in you. They haven't gone away. They're not going away.

You're killing yourself. Nothing new there, you've been doing it for years. You're taking the scenic route, yes. But every month that passes you're getting closer to the goal, and it's possible that you may achieve it without having thought lately about whether it's really what you want. (You may think about it every day, and be quite convinced. I don't think so though.)

You can't walk, because of the amount you've drunk, yet you're still drinking.

You're depressed, because alcohol is a depressant.

You drank through your anti-drink medication.

You say: don't worry, I'm fine, I'll be fine, I'm getting there.

It's as if some part of you doesn't believe it will affect you – it *is* affecting you. Either that or you want the effect – you don't. You don't like it. You've told me so.

You want: your son, your work, control over your body again, to love and be loved, to engage with your friends and the parts of life that do you good and give you pleasure. In the past weeks you've mentioned many things that could help you to be well and happy: sobriety, *mens sana in corpore sano*, therapists, exercise, Jim, routines, diet, sleep. You know exactly what you need to do. You know all about it.

Get a regular and permanent specialist doctor who can see you through the drink and its bastard cousin, depression.

It's still ringing in my ears, when you said 'I'm going to drink and smoke till the day I die'.

Please come out the other side and get on with your life, which is going to be lovely. That image I mentioned, me on the sofa reading and you playing the piano, and you said: 'It's do-able'. In it, you were well and sober.

When one thing is wrong it doesn't mean everything is.
It doesn't have to be perfect
This Too Will Pass
Be proud of what you've managed so far. Do more. Xx L

P.S. Here's a message I had from Boots, who's come out the other side of worse than you:

How do you deal with an alcoholic who you love? More to the point how do you successfully love an alcoholic?

Alcoholism is a twofold disease: a physical allergy and a spiritual malady. It's a disease that persists even without the booze and dope. Taking the substances out of the system just addresses the physical allergy. The so-called 'one was too many, and a million was never enough' syndrome. That's the physical aspect.

But beside that there is the aspect of spiritual bankruptcy. The feeling of total worthlessness. If anyone ever told me what I say to myself I would probably have to kill them. This is not a joke. Somehow I have been given the faith to break this vicious cycle. But if I am at the nadir my self-loathing, the grotesque self-image which I cultivate is my brutal reality. For instance: 'You betrayed your mother and let her die', etc. This is the self talking I now associate with the disease of alcoholism. It is very private. It was always either none of your business or something I wouldn't want to burden you with. It was unbearable, perennial, inescapable. I held it off for as long as I could. I chanted to keep it at bay. I worked like a demon to block it off. I drank and drugged to shut it up. And the gem: I hid out in the hood – none of my white friends would drop by down there and none of my black friends had a clue where I was coming from ('You from Paris, Boots?' 'No, London.' 'Same thing, right?'). I was in glorious self-dictated exile.

I spent ten years cutting myself off further and further from the succour of community because I was unwilling to have anyone close to me. When someone is close they see what and who I am. That external perception is not something that I wanted. It meant that I would have to acknowledge aspects of myself that I would rather disguise with bravado and enigma. My lying, cheating and manipulating others (particularly those I love, those who love me) come from the fear I suffer when they come too close: that I will be found out. And if I'm found out, then I'll find myself.

Isn't self-knowledge the goal of spiritual life? As an active alcoholic it was the thing I dreaded the most. Ergo, a spiritual malady – Don't try to reach out and help me. Don't try to understand. Those are threatening behaviours to me. I am feral.

None of your good deeds will go unpunished.

Just as there are tools and a program to deal with my addiction, there is Al-Anon to deal with the addiction to the addict. Lou, look them up, and go to five or six meetings. Keep an open mind. If what you hear there doesn't ring true then email me about what's going on. No. Email me anyway.

I love you long time B

It took me years to understand Boots's letter. That the greatest fear is of self-knowledge: the fear of what you will find there, when you strip everything away. Boots's mother died young too: depression, and suicide. I remember her in Maida Vale, 1976, making me my first ever American-style tuna mayo sandwich.

And my own letter? So sincere, so heartfelt, so humble, so damn carefully phrased, so generous in its effort to be constructive, not wanting to settle for a phrase that might harm his self-esteem if, by concentrating just a little longer, I could come up with one that was more helpful. All that energy wasted, all those words poured into the bucket with a hole in it, because the person I was writing to was too sick to listen, and had a much more balefully compelling thing to be getting on with than taking any notice of me.

*

Robert rings me at lunchtime. I'm in the tea room at the British Library.

'Are you masticating mackerel?' His words: aromae, sonorities, masticating, consummate ease, categorically.

'Did you read my letter?' I ask.

'I've read what was on the other side,' he says. 'The book about Byron. I'm scared to read what you wrote.'

I say, 'I'm so glad you rang because I just started getting scared too.'

'Thank you so much for your concern,' he said. This was where I snorted derisively.

He wants to know what I'm wearing, and says he'll read the letter when he's finished this track, which is going rather well. I don't know if he ever read the letter. Mine or Boots's.

Lola had been crying. She said, 'I wish I didn't exist.' She sent me away. She said she likes him but she hates me having a boyfriend. She said, Louisa Young would not do that. I didn't know if it was about sex, or about the whole wrongness of how Robert is. Louisa Young would not love something so wrong.

He said, 'You'll always love her because she's your kid, and she's not mine, and that's just true, so it'll always be, fuckin' 'orrible word, compromise.'

I said, 'No, not compromise – and anyway compromise is good, it's *real* . . . it's co-operation.'

He rang telling me to listen to some Rachmaninoff on the radio; I was already listening to it. I could tell which bits he'd grab my leg on with his incredibly strong piano-playing hands (many of his friends have dents in their knees still). He had recently nearly broken my ankle listening to Tchaikovsky. He had a game: he'd play a piece up someone's leg, and they would have to guess what it was. One Chopin nocturne had a series of leaps to a high D and then an A that would land practically in your knickers.

Another time we rang each other; our calls collided, we each left the other a message to turn on Radio 3 NOW, Etta James is singing 'I'd Rather Go Blind'. He rang again, and we sat together, each end of the line, in shared paroxysms at the absolute beauty. He hung up, came over, took me to bed. Back home, he says, settling in. He was his very best self in bed. Funny, open, appreciative, affectionate. When I took my shirt off he'd say, 'Oh my God there's two of them. Lucky I've got a decent span.' Or, 'A man needs eight hands, really, to do you justice.'

One night falling asleep I opened my eyes and smiled.

'What,' he said. Awake, of course.

'I love you,' I said. 'Oh gosh did I say that? Well I do.' And I fell asleep.

I'd said, earlier, 'So what do you think, how's it going?'

'Don't you start on that fucking analytical relationship crap,' he said. 'You've got my love and you've got my trust, all right?'

What a comfort.

His habit was to take the easy way out. To stay with women who would have him. He didn't leave; he drove women mad until they threw him out. Where did that leave me?

The year I had given myself was well over, but I was going nowhere. I was as tightly bound to him and his bandy legs and his bloody Chopin and his exquisite capacity to take the piss as I had ever been.

From me to him:

Reality checklist again, darling:

I did this before last night's fall from grace [I can't remember which fall from grace this referred to] but it's all the same stuff really. I've been meaning to give you the specifics of what I meant by 'straightening up' – here it is.

1) Looking after yourself: The booze you know I can only help you with by surrounding you with love … But there are the other

things, the smaller things. If you were to go swimming instead of lying abed in the mornings you would feel much better very soon. While wet, you could wash, shave, comb the lice out of your hair and deal with your toe-nails, blackheads, ringworm etc. I really don't want something as dull as personal hygiene to come between us, and I would really like to be able to approach your body without fear. It would be quite nice for you too.

2) If you stopped sleeping all morning and taking siestas, and instead took exercise, you would be far better prepared for a decent night's sleep, which would contribute to your happiness and sanity. Don't even think about sleeping pills until you have given this a go – by which I mean a couple of months, not a three-day effort and then 'Oh it doesn't work for me'.

3) Speaking as your girlfriend who does not accept the role of counsellor/therapist, it's time you got one: (here follows a small list of carefully researched possibilities; their phone numbers, the names of their secretaries). You are being unnecessarily cruel to yourself trying to keep straight alone. Talking of which, despite how Monday night turned out [I can't recall how Monday turned out either], I will come to meetings with you any time you want if you want.

4) Get a doctor who will look at all your stuff – sleeplessness, depression, booze, the legs, the sickness . . .

5) Go and see Jim

Now if you don't really want to be sober, clean, healthy and sane, that's a different question. As you know I don't want a drunk dirty sick mad boyfriend, and you're not one, but he's still too close for comfort. I made that clear at the beginning and it hasn't changed. I'm not with you to keep you just happy enough to carry on fucking up without quite killing yourself. I'm here for the love and the happiness. I'm not asking you for anything you don't have in you. I'm not asking you to be anything you can't be. You're right when you say I want a strong and decent man. You are the strong and decent man I want.

As I said before, you know what to do, do it. Be proud of what you've managed so far. Do more.

Love (really. Believe it.)

*

We went to Buckingham Palace. An ancestor of Robert's, William Ewart Lockhart, had painted an enormous picture of every potentate of the British Empire inside Westminster Abbey for the occasion of Queen Victoria's Diamond Jubilee – a massive item which nobody had seen as it hangs in the Queen's private area. Kath, Robert's stepmother, had been bombarding the Keepers of the Queen's Pictures for years, asking to be allowed to see it. Finally, Kath, her sister Chris, Robert and I were invited. He had washed his hair and put on a clean shirt and was being cantankerous enough for me to tell him if he didn't behave we were going home. Christ. A naughty boy in his forties and a nagging mother figure. Repellent.

We were taken upstairs and admired the painting, in a long corridor. Our guide turned out to be vulnerable to Robert's charm.

'Here,' he said, with a conspiratorial expression, and opened a door. We looked in: a large light-filled oriental saloon, full of mirrors and gilded *chinoiserie* like something out of Brighton Pavilion. Because it *was* out of Brighton Pavilion – extracted and recreated here.

'And look,' he said – and pointed towards French windows, the other side of the room. We went over – at this point we had no idea where we were: we had walked a long way through the palatial labyrinth. We looked out – across a balcony, and up the Mall, lined with trees and flags, wingéd Victory on her perch below. He opened the tall window so we could peek out – and Robert pulled me over and kissed me just where Prince Charles had kissed Princess Diana in those famous photos.

The thing is he would have done that anyway, drunk or sober. Taken it that bit too far. Kath and Chris were in hysterics, the official got us back in, it was funny, it was embarrassing, it was too much, it was great.

Kissed me on a balcony. Jesus, what's wrong with me?

And – was that how it happened? Could they really have opened that tall French window, just like that?

*

The twenty-eighth of January 2004 was a filthy night; snowy, wet, freezing on top of the slush. Unsurprisingly, I was at home. The phone rang.

An Australian voice said, er, did I know Robert Lockhart? And could I come? The voice had the edge on it which tells you you must go.

At the top of the road stood the bemused Australian. Robert lay at his feet, sacrificially recumbent in the filthy snow, propped against the side wall of the laundrette. Charles, our friend and neighbour, was kneeling by him, while his tough little dog licked at splashes of blood on the snow. It looked like some surreal Irvine Welsh nativity scene, a living Banksy, permeated by the hot, clean, incongruous smell of clothes dryers. And here came me; the third Wise Man, or Mary Magdalen, or something.

Robert's foot was hanging off, backwards, with a shaft of bone sticking out from blue-grey flesh. He didn't seem very concerned. He'd slipped, he said, down by Goldhawk Road. Or, he'd been in an altercation—

But he'd walked the half mile from his flat to my house, before collapsing.

On that? You walked on that?

He'd been thinking, he said, about my famous ancestor, about how impressed I would be at this heroic Scott-like trek across the icy wastes, defying the cold, ignoring the pain and the damage . . .

Ostensibly, at that time, he was sober: i.e., he said he was sober.

In my desire to make sense of it, I came up with:

It's a sort of hysteria, a euphoria, that thing that lets people bite off their own arms when they get them caught in combine harvesters. Or,

It's a hallucinatory response to the extreme cold. Or,

It's the pain.

To a clear-eyed person – to me, if it had been anyone but him – it would be patently obvious that he was off his head pissed. I didn't see it—

Why not?

Because when it is all around you, you lose your sensitivity. You actually *cannot* see what you desperately don't want to see. I finally had the man I loved loving me, being in my house and my life, stacking loo rolls in my garden to amuse me, writing music on my piano, coming to Christmas, playing duets with my dad, being my guy. I was still at this stage a naturally optimistic person. I was profoundly invested in his sobriety. I was in love with him. His wanting and working towards sobriety was the basis and *sine qua non* of the relationship. He'd promised me that getting sober was his prime aim and desire. I did not want to be the one to screw that up.

Because it was unbearable. Because it had been creeping around us like Birnam Wood and the Troops of Midian, slipping in and out of view, gradually normalising itself. Because I did not have the courage or clarity to say to my beloved – who declared, slurrily, that he was stone-cold sober and why did I have to fucking undermine him all the time – that he was drunk. Because I had not been long enough in this quagmire to learn that I had to make my own decisions based on the evidence of my own eyes, and ignore what my hyper-articulate, much-loved, lying-through-his-teeth boyfriend said.

Because if he was drinking I was obliged by good sense, sanity, self-preservation and my own promise to him as well as to myself, to leave him. Because in order not to suffer, we fool ourselves. Because, as Etta sang, I would rather go blind than see him walk away from me. So I went blind.

I hate the assumption that if you're with an alcoholic you are co-dependent. I was becoming familiar with the term: co-dependent, to me, involved colluding to protect the drinking, losing the boundaries between yourself and the alcoholic, blurring the responsibilities, being in love with their drunk self – whereas I fought and resisted the drinking every way I could for ten years. That's not to say I did it well or effectively, or that it necessarily did any good, or that I didn't lose boundaries and blur responsibilities – but fighting drinking, not protecting it, was my base. Some say that a co-dependent can become attached to the fight – that was not me. I had better things to do, and spent a lot of time doing them. Should I have had nothing to do with him? Arguably. But what undermined the fight at the time was that I genuinely couldn't tell if he was drinking or not. I couldn't believe myself – does that come under co-dependence, or denial? I found myself laughing: still living my life at the age of forty-eight to Rod Stewart lyrics: yes, he lied, more-or-less straight-faced while I cried, and yes I still looked to find a Reason to Believe. (I know Tim Hardin wrote it, but Rod sang it best. Or at least, sang it when I was fourteen, and most susceptible.)

And love anyway involves protection, losing boundaries, combining responsibilities. I was not experienced at actual love. Weakness at the knees, adventure, yes. But I had never lived with a man. I knew little about combining responsibility, or judging which boundary meant what and went where.

Robert both wanted to stop drinking, and didn't want to. It turned out this change of direction for him was not so much a 3-point as a 157-point turn. I'd said I'd give him a year; we had just doubled that.

So the ambulance came and took him and his foot away. I thought about my own foot, in the dream.

In A&E at Charing Cross Hospital, the doctor said, 'Do you smoke?'

'Like a fuckin' chimney,' Robert replied.

'Well you don't any more,' said the doctor – young, blond, and upright. 'Or you can't have the surgery. We need your blood flowing for it to work.'

Robert said he had a meeting at the BBC and wouldn't be able to make it to the operation. They looked entirely disbelieving. I said it was perfectly likely but I would sort it out. They gave me the 'Shine' look. It goes like this: part one – 'This pile of rags does not have a meeting with the BBC/a double first from Oxford/any reason to be lurching up to that piano'. Then part 2: 'Oh! Wow! Really?' (*Shine* being the film in which Geoffrey Rush plays a pianist who falls on hard times and looks like a tramp but remains brilliant throughout. See also, Susan Boyle, *The Lady in the Van*, etc, *ad infinitum*. The amazing miracle by which a non-fancy-looking person can turn out to have something after all! Who knew!)

Was it co-dependent of me to check if he had a meeting and if so cancel it for him? Because you'd do that for anybody, under the circumstances, wouldn't you? But he's not anybody. You're not anybody. The situation is caused by his drinking, therefore must be cleared up by him.

But then – how far do we take this? What if he was in a coma? Lying half dead in the street? Do I not call an ambulance? And – I didn't know he'd been drinking.

When he was sent off upstairs, they gave me his jacket to take home. It was a good leather jacket, initially. Agnes B. I think I gave it to him for Christmas, or I'd snuck it in as a ringer while trying to remove some foetid old favourite. Once he had something on he'd never take it off. His pockets became sinks of receipts, lighters, mints, dribbles of tobacco, actual fag-ends, a CD or two of preferred recordings of something abstruse, wads of cash. Today the pockets were heavy; I emptied them out. Among the detritus: little red lids from vodka miniatures; receipts for lunches with BAR in capitals at the beginning and end, 2x vodka tonic double, 3x brandy. Keys to his flat.

I felt bad at every step. A person is entitled to their privacy. I'm a writer; I know about space and creative solitude. That area of boundaries I am familiar with. I had four elder siblings and a strong history of 'Don't go in my bedroom' and parental 'Not now, I'm working'. I've never liked going where I'm not wanted.

Even the door was filthy. Inside, every surface bore vodka bottles full of piss. Fag-ends. Ancient newspapers. Cardboard boxes still not unpacked. An uncashed cheque for ten grand on the floor. The remains of my lipstick heart on the mirror. No sheets on the bed; no curtains. Just filth and manuscript paper.

Shame is a very particular kind of heavy, a clammy pain and disappointment. Surely the shame should be his though? Why was *I* ashamed? Because I felt I had been had, when all I was doing was keeping faith? Yes.

Of course I wanted to be the woman who meant so much to him that for me he would sober up. Then there is the version that says If He Loved Me then he wouldn't go prancing off with Lady Vodka, the Enemy. Neither of these are in any way real things in the face of actual alcoholism, but certainly it feels like a mighty slap in the face, it feels very personal, when you're on a lovely project together to sort his life out and it turns out that actually only *you* are on the lovely project, because he is locked away in a sordid room pissing in his empties. And even when you recognise that he's not doing it to *you*, he's just doing it – that's still an insult. A chopped-liver moment. Yes, you *are* chopped liver. And yes, he is ashamed. His shame puts your shame to shame. His shame about his drinking is so vast that the only way out of it, past it, round it, is to get drunk.

In hospital you can't get drunk. Instead, on morphine, he was shocked, sheepish, and charming.

'I do rather specialise in nadirs, don't I?' he said.

By the time I made my first visit, the mother of the Polish man in the next bed knew all about his passion for Chopin and had brought him in home-made pierogis. A week later the surgeons repositioned the bones of his right ankle, lining up his fibula (now in three pieces) and his tibia (in two); realigning his foot. When that was in order they sliced a deep circle of flesh from the front of his left thigh, and sewed it in, vein by vein, artery by artery, all the tiny blood vessels, over the fixed-up area. They drilled a hole across his knee and another through the repaired ankle and one through his foot, and put steel bolts through, held in place by butterfly nuts, and between those short bolts a long, elegant rod ran down the outside of his lower leg like a Meccano scaffolding. They encased all this in a voluminous bag, attached to some kind of pump, which breathed slowly like a hot-air balloon, protecting the whole caboodle, and delivered him back to the ward.

That night I went to my first Al-Anon meeting, in a hall on the King's Road. Everybody said, and when everybody says it is wise to listen, that *you have to look after yourself.*

But he is the one with the problem! I would reply.

They looked meaningful, and repeated, *You have to look after yourself.* I have said this myself, under similar or equivalent circumstances, to various people. Boots had said so, months before, as well. The analogy of the oxygen mask comes into play: on the aeroplane they tell you to put your own oxygen mask on before helping your child with theirs. Parental instinct says 'No! Help the child first!' Parental instinct in this case is a fool. No child wants their oxygen mask faffed around with by a parent who is gradually asphyxiating. So I must help myself; I must go to Al-Anon.

Al-Anon is a sister organisation to Alcoholics Anonymous, for the relatives, partners and friends of alcoholics who find their lives and emotions invaded by addiction. It works along the same lines as the Twelve Steps, and is a good thing. At this stage I didn't like it at all. The relation between alcoholic parents and their children, and that between a woman and her alcoholic lover, seemed to me to be quite different. They had been formed from childhood in the shade cast by their parent, someone they had not chosen; I had grown up with no such knowledge or damage, and was being poisoned now by the sickness of a man I was in love with, i.e. some part of me had chosen him. Totally different. I was chilly, miserable, I did not want to share or to be welcomed or given a cup of tea. I found their friendliness weird. I made one rude outburst; they all nodded sadly. There was a musician we knew on the other side of the room, in front of whom I had no desire to speak my secrets and betray Robert's. *Well, they told me to go and I went,* I said to myself. *Now I don't have to go again.* A very Lockhartian illogical reaction.

I rang the Japanese restaurant with an order for him that I was going to pick up: mackerel and ginger pickle make, mixed sashimi, agedashi tofu, miso soup, spring roll.

'But that's Mr Robert's order!' the lady said. 'Why isn't he coming in?' I told her he was in hospital. She was sorry to hear it and sent their best wishes. Was that co-dependent of me? Bringing him a takeaway? Surely you're allowed to look after someone with a massively broken leg? Plus he was sober. Admittedly, enforcedly.

I took him home. He was brave and funny about life in pylons, took care of his wounds, adjusted the little butterfly nuts as instructed. Our sex life became hilarious, manoeuvring the cage around the place – cripple-sex, he called it. I took him to AA meetings, helped him in and out of the bath, the encaged leg sticking out like an unwieldy joke. We were in it together, me and his sweet self.

Ten days after his surgery I was due to go on a book tour to Japan with Lola, then to Ireland, and after that there was a family trip to Ghana to see Grandma. I was glad about this, because it helped me to maintain balance and apply attention where it best serves. Judge a moth by its flame. Lola and my work and Robert were my flames. But his illness was not to be my flame. I loved *him*, was interested in *him*; not his illness. I was not in the least co-dependent. See? I was leaving him to get on with it. He was sober, and making plans to go into rehab. Breaking your foot off was a rock bottom, wasn't it?

Chapter Twelve

London, Oxford, 1978/2015/2004

Here is a small paper-bound booklet: Bartók Quartet no. 1 in A minor Sz. 40, BB 52 (Op. 7) (1908), a miniature score. The cover is grey, the font stylishly 1930s. There are very slight rust marks around the staples holding it together, and the binding looks like gaffer tape. It has the very slight smell of damp and neglect that books have when they've been unopened for too long, in the wrong place. It should smell of clean dry library, of rosin. It doesn't. Inside the front cover is a little beige card which tells me with a purple-inked date-stamp that the book was due back to the Oxford University Music Students' Library on 21 May 1978.

On the opening page someone with firm, rounded, neat hand-writing has written, in pencil: *Please do not draw on this score.* Underneath, in tiny spidery blue biro, Robert has written *Fuck Off,* and underlined it.

I looked at the Bartók score in May 2015, with a view to taking it back. But the Oxford University Music Students' Library no longer exists. I tried to pick out the opening on the piano.

*

He was out of hospital; I was back from Japan and Ghana. The honeymoon, such as it had been, was now over, again. He hadn't done anything about rehab; the footbreak-inspired sympathy was wearing off. I asked him to take me out somewhere, for it to be nice, just ordinary, and nice.

'I'll come to yours around eight,' he said.

He turns up at seven, on his crutches, unshaven, his grubby tracksuit trousers torn up the seam to the knee, and no shoe on that foot obviously, with its pins and screws jutting out. The unavoidable horribleness of his lower half he used as an excuse for crappy T-shirts; the difficulty of bathing as a justification for staying dirty. He says, 'There's Tchaikovsky at the Festival Hall.' He's got a cab, it's waiting, I'm to come now.

I am in a towel. I was about to get into the bath. I think: *You've been drinking*, but I dress quickly and look nice and get in the cab, because he's taking me out, and it is to be *nice*. I hope. I do, I hope. Though this is not really a date designed to please me – it is, as usual, him doing what he wants to do, and inviting me along, and pretending on some level that it is for me. On that level, he wants it to be for me, because he wants me to love what he loves, and I do love much of what he loves, including Tchaikovsky, but I need him to do something at the moment which is really about him thinking about me.

I remembered an elegant biker I had known long ago who, when he had a Meccano frame like this round a multiple fracture after a crash, had had it chromed, and etched with a foliate design to match the etched chrome on the oil tank of his Harley.

Robert is talking to the cabbie, too loudly, with words too long and too demanding for someone whose native tongue is Urdu. I choose to see this talking to the taxi driver, the movie star, the waiter, the priest, the child, all in the same way as a kind of integrity but it is also very annoying.

'You're drunk,' I say, pointlessly. He denies it. He can say he's not drunk till he's blue in the face; is he acting drunk is all I care about. I remind myself that I have promised never again to have a conversation which is a direct repetition of a conversation I have had before. We continue that conversation, a conversation we have had many many times before.

He is this alternate Robert, the one I have come to acknowledge as the Evil Twin. I'm so angry I shake.

The traffic is bad, it takes hours to get to the Festival Hall, and we're late. It's not Tchaikovsky anyway, it's Mozart and Bartók. I experiment by leaving him to do things without my help. Finally he finds the lift. He is standing in his socks, with his crutches.

'I actually can't do this any more,' I say. 'I am *that* far from saying "I'll see you when you come out of rehab". *That* far from saying "I'm leaving you".'

He's not listening.

He really wants to go in to the concert, and me to go in with him. Nothing is more important to him than this music, and avoiding what I am saying. We have time for all this because the first half is Mozart. He only wants me for the Bartók, because he needs someone's knee to grip. He goes up to the auditorium – he has both our tickets – and I stand by the lift and cry for fifteen minutes. Then I go and get myself another ticket.

In the interval he's at the bar, buying a vodka and tonic; 100-proof proof, if proof was what I wanted. Then he's outside on the concrete terrace, smoking and talking to strangers. I see him through the glass, with London spread out behind in summer evening light. I can see the oily vodka round the ice, the strangers' embarrassment as they think who is this person, crutches and socks, talking intellectual. The girl has very white bare legs. They are young.

Why am I still here?

I step outside and take the drink from him, saying, 'I assume this is for me.'

'No it's not!' he roars. The strangers are surprised but he looks like a madman anyway.

I walk off fast on my two good legs in their clickety high heels, breathless at my audacity, and put the drink down on a table. (Later I learned that coming between an addict and their substance is called 'Interfering in the Zone', and will always bring down punishment, a furious lashing out – as it did that time in Greece.)

I go back into the concert for the second half, and watch from two rows down and half a concert hall sideways as he listens to the Bartók. He doesn't see me. Throughout, his head is bowed, and occasionally it rears, in recognition, or admiration, or ecstasy. He is in conversation with the music; talking to a dead man.

Coming out with tears in his eyes, he goes for a fag on the balcony. I'm cold, no coat. He's crying for Bartók in New York in 1945 with leukaemia, only ten people at his funeral. I'm thinking, *Can't you cry because you're breaking me and I'm leaving and I've walked out on you twice tonight already?*

He wants to go for dinner.

'Not if you want to talk about Bartók,' I say. 'Only if you'll talk about reality and why I'm crying and you don't notice.'

We get a cab in the rain. He asks the cabbie if he can smoke, opens the window. I am shivering, wet and cold. I think, not for the first time, *It would be so good if you looked out for me. I don't mind if you don't look out for me. But do you have to actually sabotage me?*

He won't shut the window. I get out into the middle of the traffic at Victoria, and get the Tube.

I think he rang later, wanting to come round. I can't remember, it had happened so often.

*

I had friends, the closer of whom were fully aware of the novelist's capacity to paint herself in and out of every corner of the room, adjusting the narrative to fit, modifying storylines to suit her moods and needs. They thought it would be a better idea if I were to paint myself into a different corner, a different room even, hell, a different house, town, planet – better, they thought, if I were to write a version of my life in which I wasn't crying daily, in which my child wasn't living with an alcoholic. A version in which I stuck to my word, to myself and to Robert, and genuinely gave him back his responsibility for himself. i.e., kicked him out. They were right, they spoke from love, and sometimes some grew scared to speak because I bit their heads off. If they backed away from it, and from me too, it was not to a culpably unfriendly degree. I – we – must have been very difficult to be near.

We went round to a friend's house. Robert liked her and disliked her boyfriend, and the feelings were mutual. The boyfriend, already drunk, said Robert looked like something the cat brought in. Robert walked out, on his crutch. The friend and I made eyes at each other, women's eyes. *You-too-huh* eyes. I went after Robert. If it had been just her I might have stayed, but I wasn't staying there to give credence to *her* alcoholic over mine.

Another night, much later, they came over to my house. Robert played, I sang. I'm by no means a good classical singer – no timing – but I can hit the notes and have a decent accent, and he was patient with me, and it was something we both loved to do. Every couple needs a project, and his recovery couldn't be our only one. I think we did Duparc probably, or Fauré. Sad nineteenth-century French art songs about dreams and death. '*Après un Rêve*', which I hadn't been able to sing all those years ago. The boyfriend sat as if pinned to the back of the armchair, almost in shock. 'That's it,' he said. 'Oh God, now I get it. Oh God.' He was almost in tears.

I recall my friend Deborah, from Motherwell, a sharp and golden-hearted political journalist, saying, 'What has Robert Lockhart ever done for you?' For weeks I pondered this, worried at it, drawing up lists and justifications. The list included: Plays the piano. Sex. Piano lessons by phone. Offered to buy Ducati – meant it. Pays if we eat out. Gave up bed happily when Lola wanted it. Cooks – one time out of two so far. Offered to help clear up (didn't let him because he cooked). Makes the bed, badly, touchingly – 'You like that, don't you, because it implies respect.' Offered lunch on Sunday, inc Lola, didn't fuss when we didn't want to, and brought back baklava. Flowers on birthday. Remembers to smoke up chimney and in garden. Remembers to piss on compost heap not herbs. Makes Lola laugh (finsbury park backwards is krapy rubsnif). Talks, listens – sometimes. Not enough though. Pays compliments. Doesn't flush loo in case it wakes people. Working on: letting me go to bed, bathing.

I still find it both desperate and touching. The reality was simple though. What he did for me was what he had always done: sex, music and laughter. And a promise. We had promised each other.

I was so utterly relieved and glad that I had achieved a state of shared promise with a man, with this man, finally, that I doubt anything could have diverted me from it. I was one of a We now, and because of various issues with reality (see novelistic tendency to write my own story, passim) I had never really achieved We-ness before. My boyfriends had been in large part fantasy princes, as Swift called them: I gave them nicknames and attributes, simultaneously creating them in the image of what I desired and distancing them. They always included aspects of unattainability. The Deep Sea Diver, the Argentine in Rome, the Married Man, the Zydeco Fiddler, the Gorbals Intellectual twice my age, the far too old, the way too young, an array of musicians/charmers/foreigners/bikers/addicts in various stages of the condition reaching a peak in the Colombian coke-head war correspondent with an ex-wife on every continent, and the Born-Again-Christian Gang Biker in New Jersey, who I considered, momentarily, a contender. That my daughter's dear father, just as unlikely in his own sweet way, turned out to be so right for us is a small miracle.

Add to this pride, stubborn pig-headedness, a sense of loyalty which verges on the grandiose, and a total inability to lose face, and you will see something of why the little sister will never admit to being wrong. Anyway, I wasn't wrong (she says, even now). I just wasn't leaving without him.

We made lists of each other's irritating habits once, with a view to perhaps getting rid of some of them. I came up with two pages for him, from not brushing his teeth to not giving up smoking to setting fire to things to not doing his physio exercises. Things which were bad for him, basically. He came up with one: I would leave my bra hanging on the bathroom door handle.

Various images haunted me at that time:

He is a bucket with a hole in it. I pour in love; love pours out.

He is standing in the dark, torch in one hand, batteries in the other, complaining of how very dark it is.

He is in a deep dark hole. I stand at the edge above him holding my hand out, reaching, stretching, putting my back out, losing my balance. I will not get down in the hole with him, not even to try to push him out from behind. After a while I say, I have things to do, I cannot stay here forever holding my arm out. It's beginning to ache. I'm going to go and do stuff, I'll look in later. I'll bring a ladder. I can leave it in the corner for you. Would you consider using a ladder? It would be hard to get started maybe but you might like where it took you once you tried. I'll just leave it there for you—

Over and over, this phrase: I'm not leaving without you.

Before Robert's illness, I had never fought for anything in my life. For my first ten years I was the youngest of five, with three glamorous big sisters and a brother two years older. I soon learned that I didn't win anything by fighting for it. I didn't enter into quarrels; politicking and infighting still leave me cold. I had no interest in competition, retreated at the first sign of conflict, spent my finals year at university playing gin rummy. If someone else pursued a man I liked, my response was, 'Oh, after you.' It wasn't courtesy, or generosity. It was fear of rejection and of looking a tit. And it was that tiny voice sneering, 'You have so much, you're asking for more?' To be ambitious for myself in any way seemed greedy. It ran side by side with the tendency of female competence and motherly concern to shade into a gentle form of arrogance. Kindly generous women, often with an awareness of their own good fortune, feel that it is it right and possible to take on the misfortunes of others, and use their own happiness and luck to cancel them out. This is the Rescuer in the Drama Triangle beloved of therapists (the other two being the Perpetrator, and the Victim; family members caught in this triangle can swap roles according to circumstance, but generally hold one primary role). 'I have so much,' the Rescuer feels, 'that I can make things right for this poor other person.' Or, 'With all my advantages, how can I let this little thing derail me and my nice life?' She rarely phrases it: 'I am so fabulous I can take all this in my stride and solve all your problems too, just watch me, now shut up.'

I was fundamentally a person who liked safety over risk, and this was another reason for loving Robert. He was – or seemed – fearless. He pissed out of fourth-floor windows! He dropped his trousers to perform the opening bars of Beethoven's fifth in naked buttock-pulses! He had no respect for, or even recognition of, times of day! He wasn't scared to make a mess or to challenge a fool or to risk a friendship or upset a figure of authority. He delighted in it. Which of course made him a bloody liability.

A photograph comes to mind. He is standing in an arched golden-stone niche, halfway up a noble-looking wall – the kind of thing one might find in the garden of a stately home or an Oxford college, usually containing a statue of a nymph with a scrap of cloth draped over her. This one contains Robert, aged about twenty-five. He is wearing an unlikely dark blue wool cape, a jumper, jeans, and boots. He looks very pleased with himself. In one hand he has a cigarette, in the other you can just see his dick, which he has brought out – why? Because he was always getting it out. He'd say 'It's not the biggest but it's a nice shape, isn't it?' (He was dick-obsessed, actually. His own and other people's. He felt I must have had one in a previous life, and seemed almost sorry I didn't still.) Anyway, getting your dick out on a plinth is funny. And naughty, with a back story of 'Well, usually it's naked women in this position, and when they have naked men you see all of them except the dick, so I'm just redressing the fuckin' balance, this is actually an act of radical feminism, this—'

For the first twenty years I knew him, I didn't fight for him. Looking back, I see that I didn't start fighting for him until it was too late. I wish I had started fighting earlier; learned to respect my own strength in a balanced way, and know that it was not just my right but my duty to use it. I wish I'd known how very long it would take me to get my head around the situation. If I'd started fighting earlier I would have learned earlier that my fighting was not the point.

*

Which is not to say *we* didn't fight. One evening at the Office he tried to pretend the Nepalese Soldiers lined up in front of him were not his. I took his fag off him and put it out in one of them. He picked it up and drank it anyway, fag-end and all, sneering. I picked up the other three and knocked them back one after the other, and left. I could always leave because with his bad legs he could not come after me fast enough. I have no doubt he just ordered more, and that this made Ojay, the manager who had known him for years, very sad.

There were some horrible nights of yelling and crying (me) and sitting and sarking (him), followed by silences which got longer each time. I got hysterical. It turned out I had an Evil Twin too, who came out when invited – provoked? – by his. One thing he said – the one true thing, I felt – was that, at one stage, he hadn't had a drink for two and a half weeks. His hard little mouth as he said it. Two and a half weeks! The official version was it'd been four months! The lies, the lies, the things you find you've let yourself go along with . . . What had it all done to my child? To his?

But I saw people who got the cure . . . I saw it working.

*

He was having a coffee outside a cafe near his flat when a famous actor he used to work with and drink with at the National Theatre passed by, and stopped to chat.

'How are you?' said the actor.

'Not very well, as it happens,' said Robert.

'Is it booze?' said the actor. 'Let's have lunch.' They had lunch, then and there. Robert came home full of it, impressed. The actor, handsome, elegant, talented, successful, alcoholic, twelve and a half years sober in AA, had given him a fabulous two and a half hour bollocking of the highest order, his mobile number, and an invitation to a meeting next Monday. Me, I was starstruck and hope-struck equally.

Soon after, I saw the famous actor at a party. I whispered to him, 'You helped Robert, thank you,' and he dragged me into a corner, urgency, generosity and fellowship on his face, to enquire, to buck me up, to be kind. People were amazed. What could I have said, to cause the Love God who didn't know me from Adam to respond so intensely?

But did Robert go? Did he shite.

Faith, hope, love running on empty – that was how it drained away.

*

I always found Bartók difficult, from when I was given his simple pieces from *Mikrokosmos* to play as a child, to my first experience of hearing the Quartets. I found among Robert's music books a volume of Hungarian folk dances that Bartók had transcribed and arranged. There was one, very simple, called 'Brâul'. It was meant to be played very fast and cheerfully, with lots of staccato notes. I found that if I played it slowly (as befitted my skills, or lack thereof), it sounded eerie and beautiful. Its strange harmonies evoked distance and timelessness and the alien in a way which at that time felt right to me. He'd glance up and say, 'That's sounding great, love', and I could live on that for a while longer.

Chapter Thirteen

In a 1972 black Alfa Romeo Spider on the A29 outside Leatherhead,
25 May 2004
The Spider, a beautiful little car belonging to one of my sisters,
was in my care at that time. It's low slung and convertible and
left-hand drive, from the times when cars were made of metal and
canvas and leather, so worn now, aged, rusty and faded. The senses,
when you're in this car, are exposed.

After the Bartók Debacle on the South Bank Robert was hangdog.
So I said, 'Let's go now. You can have a look round and ask questions.'
Among the alcohol-related complaints with which he had been
diagnosed were liver inflammation, pancreatitis, with its pain and
nausea, and peripheral neuropathy which made his legs ache
and shake. As well there were the black eyes, the broken teeth, his
ribs that time, the foot, the months in Meccano and plaster, and
the insomnia, the pain . . . 'Please,' I said. 'Now.'

So on the Tuesday we went to Farm Place, rehab for the prosperous, the desperate, the metropolitan; pretty much the Rehab to
which two years later Amy Winehouse didn't want to go. Robert
didn't want to go either. He'd had a bad night, sleepless, retching

a lot. That was the pancreatitis. He thought that because he wasn't feeling well he didn't have to go. He didn't get that it was *because* he wasn't feeling well that he *did* have to go. I still hadn't properly understood that though you can lead a drunk to rehab you can't make him understand the first thing about what matters here.

It was a sunny morning, with big trees heavy in leaf, cow parsley and tall knotty grass and hedgerows full of May-blossom and a house full of people who looked as if they knew what was going on, and what to do about it . . .

Other people! Other people who knew that this horrorland exists, and who had a kind of bridge from it to reality! Functional people. Ordinary everyday life, with reason, and calmness, day and night, meals, manners . . . consensual reality. It was, then, a world from which I too had been torn. His condition was far too big for one person. Once it has its claws in, it eats up everyone in sight. It smells the love we have for them and hurtles down it like lightning down a conductor, and eats us too.

'He does look frail,' says one of the functional people, doubtfully. They are worried about his leg, how will he be, getting up and down the stairs with the plaster still on.

No music, it's banned. I think, *He won't like that*, but actually he thinks it's probably as well, as other people would want to play things he couldn't bear to hear. And rooms are shared. 'But I might want a wank,' he says. He's serious. Yup, he can't go to rehab to save his life because he might want a wank.

Everybody has to help clear up! This makes me laugh. (Our domestic arrangements are thus: he makes a lot of mess, is on sticks, will never tidy or clean anything in his life, and if he did he'd do it badly and break things. Even moving about, his natural progress is like one of those all-terrain vehicles on caterpillar tracks, which just goes wherever. He steps in things, and never looks before he sits down. He will sit in a plate of food and not notice. So, I could clean up after him (nope). We could fight about cleaning for the rest of our lives (nope), or he could pay for a cleaner. He pays for a cleaner. I have never had a cleaner before. I am happy. He's happy. He feels that he is contributing.)

There's a tennis court. He used to be rather good at tennis. *Yes yes yes*, I think, *take him, please, help him, please, help him save him help him save himself help him make him better.*

He talks to a woman called Carmel. I know he'll like her. Something in her face. Fifties, been through it. I have a small fantasy: he will sober up and get better and become a counsellor and help other addicts. He could go round schools and give talks to teenagers, saying yes, look – alcohol is not a joke. It's not a game.

A very pretty young girl is leaving, low-slung belt on her jeans, mother in a big car, a pot of dark mauve hydrangeas on its roof. The others are lining up outside the entrance, with their cigarettes, to send her off. Robert is interested in this.

On the way back to London I'm quiet because I don't want to say to him GO THERE GO THERE LET'S TURN ROUND!

Let *him* think, let *him* decide. That much I know.

Open car, English lanes, May morning, A29, A24, outside Leatherhead. Tooling along, back to town.

He's moving his feet. *Is there a spark from his cigarette, burning his ankle?* He's not smoking. *Has he dropped his cigarette?* He isn't smoking. No smell of smoking. He's waving his hands. *Is it a wasp, or a bee? At his feet? In his face?* He's calling out – roaring, arms flailing. No wasp or bee. He sounds angry. *Does he hate me? Because I took him there? Is he is he is he what is he?*

Robert!

He's jerking, head going back, froth at his mouth.

Bear left, mirror signal manoeuvre go left traffic coming up behind not too fast tension control nowhere to go ah grass verge wide under signpost for roundabout Dorking A2003. Pull up.

999.

Too long.

Not native English speaker.

North *on* A29, not north *of* A29.

Dual carriageway.

Near . . . ?

Before roundabout.

Heading north.

A24?

North of Bearsholm.

A fit.

In the car.

Yes.

No.

Please.

Handbrake? Have I turned the engine off?

Traffic. Blackbird singing.

Froth and blood. Kind of vomit. He hadn't eaten since yesterday lunch.

'Put your head forward darling. It's OK it'll be OK. Ambulance coming.'

Blood on his jacket.

He's calming down. Holding him in my right arm, phone in left.

Jerking. Have my calm. Give me your panic, have my calm.

What about my *panic, where is that going?*

999 again.

English speaker.

An ambulance drives past, was it our one?

Please. Please.

He's staring at me. Blue blue eyes white white face. Shocked.

Still now. Slumped.

Darling.

Holding him. Seatbelts.

Traffic.

Cow parsley.

147

Big sign, A2003. Last year.

Blank eyes.

'You'll be OK, the ambulance is coming.'

'Why?'

Oh.

'You had a fit.'

Blank face, questioning.

Oh.

Brain damage? Stroke?

For a moment I am thinking: *This is it. This is you, this is how it is now. And I must look after you.* So in that split second I made the decision: *OK. I will.* It wasn't really ever a question.

He's blank.

'Do you know who you are?' I ask.

Pause.

Oh shit.

'Robert,' he says.

Pause.

'Lockhart.'

Pause.

So I am pleased, and I breathe, for what seems to be the first time.

'Who am I?' I ask him, thinking *I am kind I am gentle I am not demanding I am me I am smiling I am not panicking.*

Pause. Quizzical look. *Is he teasing me?*

'Louisa.'

Pleased that he knows. Him and me both pleased that he knows me.

'Do I love you?' I asked.

What a strange question, I think. It's all in slow motion. Underwater. He needs to think.

'What a strange question,' he says. His mouth is frothy and unclear.

Yes, I am talking to his subconscious. Evidently I want to get the question in now, while he won't notice.

148

'Well?' I say.

Dunno gesture. 'Do you?'

'Yes,' I say, lovingly, cheerfully, as to a frightened baby. *I am calm I am strong don't be scared I'm looking after you.*

'What do you do?' I ask. I mean him to say, composer, or something, like holding up fingers, what day is it. He doesn't know what day it is.

'Pay the bill with a cheque,' he says. 'Very expensive.' *The fees at Farm Place perhaps?* I wonder.

He said 'play the bill'. His mouth is still bloody. He's bitten his tongue. It's swollen and white.

'Do you know where we've been today?'

He gives a shiver of a shake of the head – dunno.

And the ambulance comes, bearing a big man, with training. A competent man, who does the right things. A normal man. A layer of tension shivers off me – *I am no longer solely responsible for us.*

I answer the questions, and learn that it was an alcoholic epileptic fit, an electrical storm in the brain, and that he won't remember it.

Robert thinks we've been out to lunch. That's what he thinks he's paid for.

There's no alcohol in him now, blood sugar 6.9.

He is so pale.

No, I say, we won't go to hospital, if that's OK. Yes, his alcoholism is being seen to. Thank you. Rest, yes, of course. Repetition? Fine. Of course, yes, his own GP. Call-out report, thank you.

All the way home Robert and I repeat the questions, repeating the repetitions.

For the first time, it occurs to me, he could have killed me too.

Why did I not send him to hospital then? I didn't know this was the pattern of a disease. I didn't put things together, the trees to make up the wood, and the path ahead.

The doctor said, You get fits when you have been drinking heavily for a long time and then you suddenly stop. He hadn't had a chance to have a drink that morning – we had set off before he could make his customary trip up the road to get the paper and, as I now found out, the vodka miniatures he drank in the phone box. It was the lack of alcohol that caused the fit. That's what the doctors had meant, years before, about giving up being dangerous. His response, when the doctor explained, was still, 'So that means I should keep on drinking?'

And she said, You'll be dead in three years. She said, You need a brain scan and liver-function test and to see a pancreas specialist. He didn't go. I didn't make him. I couldn't make him. It's his responsibility, right? I ordered powdered enzymes for the pancreatitis though, because he didn't do the Internet (he never had an email address). He thought of it as mine. 'Have you got any Miles Davis on your Internet?' he'd ask. Yes. And I found him a clip of Rachmaninoff on a boat, smiling.

It was two and a half years since I'd said I'll be your girlfriend if you stop drinking and get a shrink. I was still asking the same questions: *Am I supporting? Or am I enabling? Do I stick around in hope? Or save myself now? Is this the time it's going to work? We've been in worse places before. Have we?*

If this had been someone else I'd have looked at them and said, What a fool, what a saga of wasted love.

The sadness. Self-pity whispered at me: Nobody has wanted your good love. You might as well waste it on him. What else has love got up its sleeve for you? All it has ever done is torment you and shame you.

Unspoken, I said, I hate him. Can I love him if I want to kill him? Just to see him I want to cry. To think of him I want to cry. When does a person decide what to do? How can a person decide when?

I didn't *want* to leave him. I wanted him to be well.

Chapter Fourteen

Either twin might turn up at the house, and you wouldn't know which was coming. I kicked the Evil Twin out of the house many many times, and refused him entry, but often it was Robert himself who reappeared, the Sweet Twin, apologetic, ashamed, beautiful, desirous of betterment, needing and asking for help.

The plaster stank when it was removed. They sawed down the side with a circular blade like a pizza slicer, and his leg was thick with dead skin. The bath afterwards was a corker. He showed his son the soft mound of flesh that had settled so neatly on to the inside of his bony ankle, and how the hair ran sideways, not downwards like the rest. Jim stroked it in appalled fascination, and Robert joshed him about turning the pad round like the dial on a washing machine, so the hair could be vertical like it should be on a leg. For Jim, Robert washed and shaved, girded his loins, pulled out his sense of humour. They played cripple football in the street on Robert's crutches, went out for lunch, never stopped talking. Jim's big eyes soaked him up.

He was writing the score for a Dutch film called *Lepel – Spoon*

– about a small boy who ran away from an evil button-thief to live in a department store with a wild girl and a lovesick store detective. It is an enchanting film, and his music was gorgeous, with the sweeps of full orchestral magnificence and lush, peculiar melodies that surprise people who didn't know Robert well, who hadn't clocked that his cynical presentation was closely intertangled with a ferocious, hungry romanticism. There is one yearning waltz tune I find myself whistling most days. This music made me love him so much. It was a sign. The foot breaking off *had* been a nadir. He *was* trying. He *wasn't* drinking. There *was* hope. There were plenty of days of *ah, yes, this is how it should be*, when good, relaxed, normal things happened: Robert working with Steve at the studio, picking him up there, running into old friends, Isobel the fixer, the musicians. The first screening. Meeting the director – Willem van de Sande Bakhuyzen. Robert loved to despise directors but he liked this one. *This is the kind of thing*, I thought. *We could live, like this.*

Lola and I were travelling a lot, doing book tours: Spain, Italy, Edinburgh. In September she started Big School, and we were on *Blue Peter*. In October the second of our *Lionboy* books came out. During half term she came with me for the first leg of the US book tour, then flew back alone from New York with her new skateboard to be with her dad while I went on to Connecticut, Milwaukee, Chicago, San Francisco, LA, back to London and straight on to the Frankfurt Book Fair.

The Evil Twin grew stronger when we were away. When we got home he sometimes scared me with his crashing about, late at night. I felt my vulnerability, so unprotected, feeling it in my breasts, aware that this was not how you should feel about your lover.

Sometimes he'd sit with Lola while she ate her supper. I'd tense as he'd chat, she would sense that and respond accordingly. Often she would just leave when he came in. He played for her approval; asking her questions, but about things which interested him, not what interested her. He didn't know what interested her. He might have guessed it wasn't how Scriabin had died of a pustule in his mouth – but the Evil Twin didn't think about other people. She was eleven. She'd given up piano lessons. I was sad about this but I knew why, and who could blame her? I would give music back to her later – I wouldn't let her lose the joy of it because of him. The irony of that would be too much. Or – in my dream – he would give it back to her. When he'd been sober for as long as he was drunk, the debt would be paid. They'll be back to square one, and she could start to like him, and eventually to accept his gifts. This was my idea.

'Sweetheart,' I say to him, in a cautiously admonitory tone. I can't bear the little drama unfolding around the kitchen table. And he can't bear the emotional tone of my voice, the patronising twist that I can't help, so he mocks my London pronunciation of the word: swee'heart. As well as the emotional offence he takes, he feels that for me, a posh girl, to drop an H or glottal-stop a T is pretentious. He is a great believer in the class system. Without it, and its being rigorously upheld, he would have so much less to resent. I feel that accents are as much geographical as class influenced, and that any Londoner might naturally acquire any London intonation. I don't like being called pretentious, because I'm not.

'You so enjoy resenting things, don't you?' I say meanly.

'No I don't!' he says. 'I sincerely wish there was less in the world demanding to be resented. Really I do.'

'If you just stopped resenting innocent things that you can't change, you would save so much energy.'

'Oh, fuck off and do some yoga,' he says.

'Yeah, I'll leave you to play with your imaginary enemies.'

'Yeah,' he says, mocking my way of saying it. 'Yeah.'

He protects himself with an armour of irrelevance, taking hold of the wrong end of the stick any time the right end doesn't suit him. How much easier to criticise the way someone pronounces a word than to deal with what they're saying. How telling that the pronunciation he most mocks is the way I say 'problem'. 'Prob*lim*,' he'll say, shaking his head. How incorrigible I am, honestly, listen to me. Prob*lim*.

Lola has left, slipping away to do her homework.

He has lost his house keys again. I've been wondering whether I should just not get any more cut for him. Leave him outside. Put a gate at the top of the garden path so that if he comes back at night without the keys he can just go away again, instead of waking us with his banging, making me lie there in misery praying that Lola upstairs can't hear him, until at last I can't bear it, and go and let him in, and put him in the sitting room, and build a barricade of fear and shame across the door so that he can't come out.

My girl, thank God, sleeps through most of this. I think. I can't ask her. Because if she *has* slept through, by mentioning it I would alert her to a danger of which she would otherwise be unaware.

In December Steve had a party at the studio, and Murray Gold was there, the young wunderkind who was doing the music for the new *Doctor Who*, and he said wow, Robert Lockhart, he's meant to be some kind of genius. I clung to this passing compliment like a woman with not very much to cling to.

And then a long-delayed appointment came up, and he just went. Finally.

Community drug and alcohol treatment and recovery services provide a range of specialist substance misuse interventions . . . Our outcome data shows people who use our services are more likely to overcome their dependence. We provide high quality, Care Quality Commission registered substance misuse services to help people overcome their dependence and achieve recovery . . . highly skilled, multi-disciplinary teams . . . personalised care . . . planned treatment and recovery packages . . . community detoxification and psychosocial support to either control drinking or maintain abstinence—

Gosh.

Three days later, he was in the Max Glatt Unit, part of a hospital in Ealing. I wished it was further away and for longer, but it was Rehab – Reprogramming Robert, he called it – and he was going. He cracked jokes all the way in the car. There was an undertaker's near the clinic with the same name as a rugby player. He looked at the pubs and said, 'It's strange to think I'm never going to have a drink again.' I held that phrase to me. I would have hung it round my neck on a chain if I could.

Check *us*! On the way to REHAB.

Also, he would be out of my hair and safe for the duration. This was a relief not to be underestimated.

The unit was a remarkably depressing place. A pool table, notice-boards, a junkie girl in a vest who locked him in the cracked-melamine kitchen and showed him her pierced nipples. All types. Asian boys, old Irish potato-noses. Hand in all your belongings. No bedside light, and when I took one in for him it had to be checked and it didn't come back till the day he was to leave. After three days he was allowed to go on the approved and accompanied team walk to the hospital shop. In the lead-up to Christmas, the addicts sat on their institutional couches, jaded and fish-eyed as the TV rolled out ad after ad for Tia Maria, for gin, for whisky, for Southern Comfort, for being young, sexy and drunk, because *that*, by God, is how to have a good time; or for being around a cosy laden table with your happy smiling children and loving spouse drinking Baileys and champagne and brandy and port because *that*, by God, is how to be a good and settled member of society.

He made friends, in his pubbish way. They nicknamed him Professor, of course, because he was educated. He was incessantly sorry for the other people there – for all the other things they had to deal with. Women with babies; people with no money, no family, no work, no alternative. He said someone brought in crack, and he didn't know what to do about it, not that he wanted to use it but because he was afraid if offered he might. But he didn't want to be the grass. It scared him and it offended him. He felt that being locked up with crackheads was not helping his recovery. I thought, *You feel that you have a recovery,* and I was glad. He said it hurt being made to look at things clearly. His past was a festering sore and hurt when he touched on it. I thought, if each time your glance falls on the past it hurts, then even as you do that, you're building what will in time become your past. And that will continue to hurt, when you touch on it in the further future.

He was out ten days later, in time for Jim's birthday, feeling it had done him a lot of good and proud to have made it. He was going to see his son, sober. I would go with him, and he would come back, sober. I felt – cautiously optimistic.

And then it was Christmas, and I wanted to go somewhere nice so it could be nice. God how I longed for straightforward ordinary niceness.

We thought – I thought? – New Year's in Norfolk was in order: some gorgeous little hotel on the coast, good food, we could tramp about in the mist and see some birds and sit by a fire, that might make him happy, and I would like it. I was Bridget Jones, searching for the right mini-break. Of course the nice hotels had been booked up months before by functional people. We spent New Year's Eve in King's Lynn, in a B&B which was not the nice old vicarage in the picture but a nasty modern annexe with plywood doors and overhead lighting, and the so-called double bed was two light singles (on wheels) pushed together with a double sheet across them, a potentially perilous hammock of cheap polycotton. It poured with rain and the cobbles were slippery. Everybody was drunk except for us. There was a good chippy though, on a beach. I was totally on for it to be all right, for us to make the best of it, because things were improving! But it wasn't all right.

There was someone on the radio, one of those glamorous 1960s actresses, talking about their marriage to one of the glamorous

1960s drunk actors – Richard Burton? Richard Harris? Peter O'Toole? She said, 'It was always just about to be marvellous.'

Anyway it was dismal. And a minefield. Simultaneously. Trying to get to sleep, I thought, *We're not even really in the same bed.*

Chapter Fifteen

On the train to Wigan, February 2005
We played a lot of backgammon. I always won, though we agreed that he was a much better player than me and my constant success was really quite extraordinary. He always wanted to gamble; I never did. He called it frontpork. It was for him the perfect combination of luck, skill and captive conversation; he loved to teach it to people, and spread it through his hospital wards and rehabs, challenging strangers, setting up tournaments. You know, when playing backgammon, that the person you are with isn't going to go away.

John's sister, Robert's Auntie Sybil, had died. We arrived on the train north to her funeral in a fluster and found seats at a table, next to a Russian in a flat black hat, clean-shaven, nice watch. His fingers were fat and he had a nineteenth-century air. Robert was in a mood of determined lunacy, making a fuss about not being able to smoke, getting up and down, saying it was too hot but not taking his coat off.

I said to the Russian, as we got out the clattery old inlaid-wood Greek backgammon board, 'I hope this won't disturb you too much.'

'On the contrary,' the Russian said. 'I am interested.'

I was winning. Robert appealed to our neighbour at the unfair luck I had, calling me '*Chair* of Backgammon at Trinity College Cambridge. She's so fuckin' lucky.'

'So have you been lucky,' the Russian says.

'Not like this jammy fucker,' says Robert.

'Perhaps she is more prepared for luck,' the Russian says.

These words dropped like jewels in slow motion through a storm, and I considered leaving Robert for this man, this character out of Flaubert.

'What does that mean?' asked Robert.

I was thinking: *It's self-fulfilling. Because you cannot understand the notion of being prepared for luck you never will have the benefit of what luck you get and you will always be unhappier than you need to be. And I who do understand all this will be equally sad as a result.* The Russian looked as if he understood all this. I was careful not to catch his eye.

At Sybil's funeral, the all-female brass band with which her daughters had played since childhood lined the path to the church, playing beautifully in the chill air. Robert had started to write a brass band elegy for her. We visited his mother's grave, and I left him in Wigan with John when I came back to London.

*

Things were meant to be better! As they weren't, the fact of them being meant to be only made them even worse. My step-grandmother had just died. She was ninety-five, and asked me, in her narrow hospital bed, did I think the doctors would mind? I said that she had lived a good life and she needed nobody's permission to die if she wanted to. She looked doubtful, so I said I didn't think the doctors would mind at all. I said, not entirely truthfully, I don't mind if you die, Pam. And a friend, a curly-haired big-hearted sparkly dancing man in his early forties, dropped dead, jogging to the gym. His funeral was one of those floods of love that leave you shipwrecked.

Robert was upset – if even people who jog to the gym fall dead in the street, what hope is there for anyone? This, like most things, was probably a reason to drink. He wasn't behaving right. He did stay sober after Max Glatt, but he was not using the support available to him, so became a bolshy dry drunk, sober on will-power, a toxic angry mode. His being crippled undermined my capacity to be disciplined about not doing things for him. He was in physical pain; I thought that was what made him bad-tempered. It was important to me not to be seen as pushy, bossy, enabling or a nag.

'Impairment of social and behavioural function' remained strong in my sweetheart. He had a bad habit of repeating to people mean things other people had said about them. Like 'What, Louisa? She looks like a man. And he'd be with anyone who'll wash his T-shirts.' I told him once that a particular person wasn't pretty, interesting or intelligent enough for him; he told me he'd told her what I said, and she didn't mind. I had no idea who was the lying lunatic in this situation. Consensual reality slips away in dribs and drabs; the first to go is often manners.

We went round to dinner with Deborah and her husband, Robert's kind-of friend Will (nickname Lurch, for his imposing demeanour, pale skin and deep-set eyes), a tall and famously articulate novelist. They knew a bit about recovery – including that you can't really call two addicts, as Robert and Will were, friends, at least not until they're *both* in recovery. They had invited some good rehab types, as encouragement to the 'newly sober' Robert. Robert arrived separately, late, edging to the piano to avoid the dinner table. They all knew that Robert was a faker. He knew they knew, and that's why he could hardly sit at table with them. All I knew was that nothing added up, all was disharmonious, I was comfortable nowhere.

Learning the ways of tough love, I put his clothes into bin bags. He was to take his stuff home because he did not live with me.

Included was a replica of the T-shirt Jack Nicholson wore in *Five Easy Pieces* (one of Robert's favourite films: 'I faked a little Chopin, you faked a big response'), the one with TRIUMPH written on the front, that Jack Nicholson wears in the sex scene where he's whirling Sally Struthers around and around and around. I gave it to Robert when he triumphed at the Max Glatt Unit. I never saw any of those clothes again.

Was this the occasion he described later in his rehab papers as me 'throwing my things down the stairs, saying fuck off (not like her)'? Maybe. I *was* angry. I sent his grandfather clock back to his flat; a family heirloom, Victorian with a bucolic scene of a lady with sheep painted on the clock-face. It was too big and though I liked it, it couldn't just loom in my hall being bumped into. At some stage around then I read somewhere, and wrote down: 'The life you are in danger of losing is GOOD and worth holding on to.' It seems extraordinary to me now that such a thing was worthy of note.

Late in April, I drove past the Anglesea, the local gastropub where we used to have long lunches when Lola was little and before his drinking became the enemy; happy stupid lovely lunches. He was sitting outside. There was a glass of something brown on the table.

I parked, and walked over. By the time I reached him the glass wasn't there, so I knew. It was under the table, on the pavement. Big round brandy glass. He said it wasn't his.

A kind of slow-motion disbelief descended, a suspension where everything around me – all these people sitting about, the geraniums, the remains of food on plates – shifted in relation to itself and to me, and my head floated.

I said, I don't think I want to see you for a while, and I left him to it.

And that became the summer of 2005. I'd see him outside some pub, and he would pretend he was drinking water, or I would give his drink back to the barman saying, 'He doesn't want it', and occasionally I'd pour it in the gutter, or knock it over and say, 'Oh.

Whoops' in the sarkiest tone of voice. And I would say 'Not dead yet then?' and 'Your next step is living rough, you know that, don't you?' and he'd say 'Yes'. Once a drunk person came out of the pub where I had left him, trying to persuade me to go back and be nice to him. Another time I overheard one drinker say to another, 'Oh Christ, it's him – hide or he'll come and talk to us.'

It's impossible, and wrong, not to love, when you love. Love will find a way to manifest itself, every time. Now, it made me Google rehab centres up and down the country, and talk to kind women who dealt with admissions. I slept a lot – undisturbed, my God, what a miracle – and forgot about him for entire hours at a time. This built up my strength.

One day I saw him in the street: a shambolic, lurching, unshaven damp creature, half dead, to be honest. Old man smell. Skin flaking off him, hair matted, teeth broken and scurfy and yellow. He tried to hide from me. 'Are you going to meetings?' I said, and he lied. I said, 'And are you going to go to the clinic?' And he said 'Yes, yes.'

In one of these encounters, we fixed on a rehab place called Clouds. I can't remember why. It was his choice. Random, probably, with me as a gun to his head. He said he'd sent for the admission papers. He hadn't. He said he'd talked to them on the phone. He hadn't. He said the application must have been lost in the post. He was a great master of masochistic procrastination.

I rang Clouds. I got the papers, filled them out, tracked him through the pubs of the neighbourhood and made him sign them, there in the street. I rang the clinic and put my phone in his hand, and made him tell them to let me deal with his things.

One by one the pubs banned him, and he was no longer visible on the streets outside. So I doorstepped him one morning. I took supplies and a newspaper, thinking I might be there a while, and I sat in the car outside his flat like a detective with a box of doughnuts. He shambled out quite soon. Saw my car. I had been prepared to bundle him in and drive him straight there, to wrestle him or hit him or anything. But he just came and sat in the car, quiet. I took him home, put him in the bath, peeled off his clothes and put the ones I didn't throw away in the laundry, washed his hair, shaved him. Behind his ears were strips of ancient soap scum, or dead skin, settled into the crevice: I peeled them off, fearing, because I didn't know if they were part of him. The skin beneath was raw pink and shiny.

While I was cutting his hair he began to shake, his whole body chattering like teeth. His hands started to go, and he straightened out, and his head shook. I stood back, and a sort of small trance descended on me. I was holding the scissors high like a totem, safe. Would he fall? Would I catch him? I put the scissors far away behind me; scanned the surroundings for things he would grab and pull down on himself, for corners he could smack his head into, for rugs he could clutch bringing lamps crashing around him, for furniture he might wrench his foot against, and rip apart his rebuilt ankle. And it passed. I laid him down and he was resting.

Later he had another. Big, frothing at the mouth on the sitting room carpet. He was on the floor on his back, rigid like a hawk's claw, gripped by it, still roaring, roaring at the outrage. Foam dribbled from his mouth. Every string of his body had been pulled tight and twisted; every speck of his own strength was doing it. Because I was trying to stop him hitting his head on furniture, I couldn't quite move. Lola, back from school, rang for an ambulance while I held his hand; calm as you like, twelve years old, yes we need an ambulance please, my mother's boyfriend is having an epileptic fit, yes he's had them before, and giving the address. 'It looks very scary but it's all right,' I said. No recovery position till he's stopped. Couldn't move him anyway; mustn't force him. Blood in the foam. Choke on your tongue? No. He didn't seem to be breathing. But then how could a lung swell or fall with breath in a body so utterly rigid?

I was very grateful for Lola's calmness and capability, and very sorry and ashamed that she should be having these experiences, so early in her life, and yes, of *course*, thinking how I could have protected her better.

'Does it hurt him?' she asked.

'He won't remember it,' I said.

Can I yet admit how naïve I used to be? Hope is a good breakfast but a bad supper. It won't keep you going all day, and it's folly to stick too long with it if it's all you have. I had a postcard of the painting by G. F. Watts on my desk in those days: blindfold *Hope* playing her broken lyre on a rock as the waters rise.

They came and took him to hospital, read him the riot act. I went to see him later. He was shocked, and tired. 'Is it over yet?' I said. Because this seemed like a different kind of rock bottom.

I went home and played backgammon against myself. It's one of the holding patterns I use in times of slow-motion crisis. To admit that you cannot help someone you love who is suffering is a very long, slow adjustment of the ego, and there is a limit to how long you can bear it. Particularly when their suffering manifests in their being a shit.

Part Three

2005–07

Chapter Sixteen

Years ago I wrote a piece for the *Guardian* about how men choose what to wear. Robert said, 'Whatever's nearest on the floor.' He was aware that other people washed their clothes and put them together in a particular way, but it meant nothing to him. Once he turned up in a pair of women's trousers – purple velvet, size 12 – and he honestly didn't know where he'd got them. Off the floor, no doubt. But he wasn't aware that they were a woman's, that there was a story in why he was picking a woman's trousers up off the floor – whose floor? – in the first place. They were excellent on him, with his *je dois me laver* look, so cool at twenty, so revolting after thirty-five.

As Will said, Robert took dishabille to the level of an art form, while displaying an anti-materialism that verged on contempt. Getting him into decent clothes was a problem. As it was not a need he recognised (except on the two occasions when he fixated rather demoniacally on having a white suit), he would not go to shops. So I would buy things for him, and after some days or weeks he might put one of them on, and then whether or not it fitted, or pleased him, he would not take it off, because the whole dressing/undressing thing was an expenditure of energy he resented. He would come to bed in his overcoat, and lie there declaiming about my southern bourgeois recalcitrance in wanting him to take it off.

I would say, Please don't muck up these new clothes you're not going to keep, I need to take them back. Meanwhile he would fall asleep in them, sit on the rainswept front doorstep in them, and burn a hole in them with his cigarette.

I lured him into Gap. With his sticks, he refused to come up to menswear on the first floor so I was running up and down holding things, waving them at him. I proffered a blue flowery cotton shirt which would suit his blue eyes and haggard demeanour. In 2005 there was an eruption of men's blue flowery shirts. It was the 'I'm still getting it' look for men of a certain age. I had bought a pair of black Levis, low loose 509s, size 34/32. Bought on 26 October at ten past six in High Street Kensington. Here's the receipt on my desk. They were new clothes for going to rehab.

He was going to rehab! Proper, long-term, residential, expensive. Clouds. The oddest people asked me if I was paying for it. No I bloody wasn't paying for it. He was paying for it.

The more physical damage his illness produced, the harder I found it to step away and let him get on with it, wherever it took him. How could I? He'd die. He'd get himself murdered, winding people up. He'd set fire to himself, the alcohol-related medical conditions he already had would take him over, he'd get knocked down by a car.

This is where I remained confused. When the alcoholics said, in Alcoholics Anonymous, 'I admit I am powerless against alcohol', I got it. An alcoholic is powerless in the face of alcohol, and needs constant supportive voices from his AA meetings and mentors to shout down the constant 'oh go on' voices from the demons, the booze, the shame, the self-loathing, the pain. That made sense to me. And I understood the higher power business: I'm not God, I'm not in charge, there are many other powerful influences on humanity: nature, science, brain chemistry, genetics, love, society, biology – I don't rule. I'm a termite in the mound – an aware termite, a termite with imagination – but a termite, and I acknowledge the mound. I acknowledge powers more powerful than me.

But when they say that the person who loves the alcoholic must also say, I am powerless in the face of alcohol – well, I thought, I'm not. I drink, but not vastly. I'd rather not drink than go up the road in the rain to buy drink. I'd rather not drink than have anyone say 'you're drunk' to me. I'd certainly rather not drink than upset my child, my true love, my friends, my workmates. Or did they mean us to declare that we were powerless in the face of the alcoholic? That we were addicted to that person? I thought this interpretation inhuman, bleak and unloving. In the end, I needed a leap of perspective. When the person who loves the alcoholic declares their powerlessness, it is not about their own relationship with alcohol, nor necessarily about their own relationship with the alcoholic: it is about the alcoholic's relationship with alcohol. What I was powerless in the face of was Robert's relationship with alcohol.

He didn't like the shirt, and told me so, in words of piss and vinegar. I left him there on his sticks, not knowing how he'd get home, sod it, he's an adult. Here, be responsible. Go on, on your sticks, rejecting the clean and the nice, the hopeful, the new – all in a shirt. You've said you'll go to fucking rehab. So buy a decent shirt.

He turned up on the doorstep later that day, clean, shaven, apologetic, and wearing the shirt. It looked good on him, and he looked good in it. He was sorry.

*

On 2 November I drove him down to the West Country. He wasn't kicking and screaming, but he wasn't happy. The house was solid and prosperous-looking among wet green English fields. Never mind him, I wanted to check in myself. It was a year almost to the day after Max Glatt; a very tender time. I dropped him off and my heart floated, because I felt again that he was somewhere safe. He was with people who knew about this; people to whom his tragedies were everyday occurrences, people who would help. We walked around the dripping garden; looked at cows, moss, black branches against the grey sky; rooks cawing away, wood pigeons crooning their five-note song of security and comfort. He couldn't get away. Six whole weeks. No visits to start with. I could relax. At least, apropos him.

The day after dropping him off, I flew to Ghana with Lola and Louis. Osei, Louis's big, handsome, teasing brother, had been killed. The aeroplane he was in had exploded, mid-air, in the hot blue sky over Nigeria. Louis had been at Abuja, waiting for the flight that never arrived. So now there was the memorial, in Accra. His beautiful children and his kind wife, his mother and father, his brothers and his sister, their children, Lola, me, all standing for hours in a line for people to shake our hands and say, 'I'm sorry, he is with God now'. When you are obsessed with a long, slow danger to one person, you do not imagine some other swift and deadly danger will suddenly swipe somebody else entirely from the very sky, and never even give back his body.

*

Each day, as part of the therapy, Robert and his compadres filled in a Significant Events Sheet. I didn't see these at the time, of course. I found them under the piano, in a mass of rehab papers. God, the power of reading, years later, personal papers that were not meant for your eyes! Fat files of his writing, in which truth and time do their dance. Things that happened long ago; the understanding of them that emerged only years later, and here I was reading them and trying to understand them years after that. This is the fabric of a lifetime. And drunkenness at Robert's level is its own dimension of blindness. 'Blind drunk' is not a nonsense phrase, nor one necessarily describing a temporary state. Robert's sober accounts of what he did in the drunk past were quite different to how he had represented himself at the time. Reading them, I understood him better and better. They were relentless though. Recovery is relentless. (I don't want to misrepresent that. I haven't included all their relentlessness here: I quote from them, and I include some fuller accounts, in Robert's own words, in the appendix on p. 383.)

On his first sheet, Robert announced that there were 'no "significant events" as such'. Dear God, I thought, what on earth counts as significant if this doesn't? But then he allowed 'except for the fact that I eventually got here'. A tiny acknowledgement.

The first weeks were bad sleep, not liking to wake early, eating lots, wanting to be given drugs for anxiety and getting instead an interesting lecture and the doctor's insistence that anxiety comes from the brain to the body so therefore no calming drugs, 'which would make things easier. However one would have to get off them at some time'. His counsellor is perceptive and sympathetic. The meetings are exhilarating; sometimes too much so – 'combustive'; 'stomach-turning aggression'; 'but I suppose that is the nature of the process'. The Life Stories recounted by his companions touch him deeply; he begins work on his own, and on the First Step of recovery, admitting that he was powerless over his addiction, that his life had become unmanageable. Like 99 per cent of newcomers, he doesn't take to the God/higher power/spiritual concept. He gets bored with all the drug talk and repetitiveness. He'd like more one-to-one counselling. He is knackered.

He finds people to play backgammon with. He goes walking, and sees a greater spotted woodpecker, a badger, goldcrests. He likes 'the crows, wood pigeons, jays, cows and lovely deer. Fields, trees, sky, rain – simple but powerful stuff – ideal for contemplation'. He's amused by someone's snoring during the relaxation class. He starts writing a song with one of the others: 'I'll buy Clouds a better keyboard (if my music royalties pour in).'

His fellow recoverers report that he 'beats around the bush', is not 'pacific', 'reads the paper too much', and 'plays too much backgammon' but also that he was 'integrating really well after just five days'. There is a 'hilarious' acting workshop: 'Acting (except in life – not any more!) is not one of my talents.' A TV celebrity with a famous haircut was exposed, and Robert was 'not sure if he'd be elated or distressed if his picture appeared on the front page of the *News of the World*. He is becoming involved: 'Backgammon tournament off with a bang . . . Funny mixed day – busy enough to occasionally forget anxiety – walking, eating, listening, talking, reading, not drinking – it's a cinch (not).' Someone suggests that the 'God as you understand him' could be the sense of community felt in AA meetings: a Group Of Drunks.

They all have to write their life story: 'The Life and Times of Robert Lockhart', he calls it (see p. 383). And his sweetness suddenly shines through: 'Have a nice weekend to whoever has the dubious privilege of reading this.'

I learned a lot from 'The Life and Times' about those parts and periods of his life when I hadn't been around. 'I have caused trouble courtesy of the booze,' he wrote, with maddening simplicity. 'I would go to the shops for supposedly fags and newspaper but in a phone-box would pour a 1/4 of vodka into a half-full bottle of 7-Up, fully equipped with the tools of the trade: extra-strong mints, chewing gum, toothbrush, toothpaste. It must have been a strange sight seeing someone clean their teeth whilst pretending to listen to someone on the phone. The booze antics I got away with for a while but when I broke my ankle in 3 places Louisa got keys to my flat which she had never visited. This was no bachelor pad. It was a disgusting shit-hole . . .'

It was impossible to read it, years later, without a cloud of old regrets and resentments swarming up, as useless and painful as a cloud of midges. There I was, looking for nice things he'd written about me. I wanted to see 'I love Louisa she saved my life' in his handwriting so I could get it tattooed across my heart. I found: 'My old friend Louisa'. And, 'Biggest mistake of my life', he says, of breaking up with someone else. I decided to suppose he was not writing for my eyes, saving time, trying to keep things simple, and to bear that in mind as I read through. Or – here's a later interpretation. Virtually from the moment Robert began having sex, he was already simultaneously being unfaithful and feeling nostalgic for the beautiful relationship that might have saved him if cruel circumstance hadn't robbed him of it. 'Alcohol destroyed us,' he wrote of one. 'She would criticise my drinking while drunk which is no way to conduct a relationship.' Each woman, once lost, became the lovely thing without which he was bereft – while he continued to behave in ways which made it impossible for any woman to stay with him. Only I, the 'old friend', failed to earn that romantic halo. Because I didn't leave.

'The booze antics' – what a phrase! 'Louisa said if I started again that was it.' 'I don't think that was quite it . . .' He refers to my child as 'an equally big problem'.

'Not so, not so,' I murmured as I read. And 'Really? Oh!' But addicts, while active, can't hear you.

I was touched that Robert, sensitive to the snobbery at Oxford, used the basic inverted-snobbery technique of referring to university – and that particular university – as 'college'. And I was amazed to learn that his parents had both remarried on the same day. How – careless?

He read his Life Story aloud, 'nervous, sweating and shaking (never thought I'd get that again!). Everyone said "You must feel better, feel relieved". I didn't feel that. Just emotionally totally drained.'

'Nervous about seeing Louisa tomorrow,' he wrote. 'After all I've only known her for 29 years.'

*

On the eleventh day, I cruised down the A303 in white frosty mist, listening to the Sunday morning love-song show on Radio Two, iced-up cow parsley skeletons all along the hedgerow, Stonehenge, so tiny in its field. After that I went every Sunday, the light and mist and rain and frost different each week. There was a hill where the reception always failed in the middle of Snow Patrol singing

'If I just lay here, would you lie with me and just forget the world?', or Coldplay 'Fix You'; or 'The Drugs Don't Work'; the Athlete song 'Wires'; and 'How to Save a Life' – 2005 was full of dirgey songs to make an addict's girlfriend weep. Turning to Radio 4, the civilised world was still a circle of hell and confusion. Out there, everything still existed: politics and poverty and art and war and love and space and terrorism and fashion and babies and knowledge and murder and Ken Livingstone and TV and climate change and dying animals and the sales were all going on. The whole human race, addicted to its comforts, poisoning itself, rank with fear and violence, self-destructing. It didn't need my attention, to continue to exist. *My boyfriend is a microcosm,* I thought, and laughed and immediately cried, which was how it was in those days.

That first time, we sat delicately in the big reception room with its sofas, fruit cake and cups of tea, alongside other people's tragic parents, fearful mothers and angry girlfriends, wide-eyed children, boys with eyebrow-rings and tight T-shirts, smeary babes of a certain age. The fireplaces were blocked up, the coffee tables bore the Sunday papers and the dried rings of mugs of instant coffee and depression. Robert was sharing a room with a convicted murderer, and feeding bananas to the badgers who came up on the lawn late at night. He told me who had dropped out or run away since the week before, who was coming in. The tabloids had now stopped hiding in the woods; the TV presenter was upset because he'd only made page five. Wednesday night was music night, because let's face it half of them were musicians of one sort or another. Robert played the piano and made friends with a heavy-metal bassist. They called him Professor again.

So much sadness. Semi-literate people writing their life stories on lined paper in biro; washing-up rotas, desperation.

'Two out of three of the people who come in are dead within three years,' he said.

'Well you've only got a year left on the last three years they gave you, so that's an improvement,' I said.

'I'm not fucking dying,' he said. 'I'm not. Don't you worry.'

I was very proud of him.

We walked around the grounds. We had a session with his counsellor where I said the same things I had always said, and it seemed possible that he was hearing them, possibly for the first time. Later he was rude about her; he said she looked like a horse, and neighed when her name was mentioned. Afterwards I sat in the car park and cried because I was so happy; though whether that was because I could go home to bed whenever I wanted and sleep undisturbed, or because he was safe in professional hands, I didn't consider. I ate chocolate while I drove and felt safe because I felt *he* was safe.

*

I had entered worlds which I never intended to enter. Self-help world, which previously I had scorned, as a righteous virgin and an intellectual. Addiction world, which I found alien, controlling, pathetic, tragic. Drug world, which I had first noticed at thirteen, when some people started to think it was a good idea to take pills that strangers gave them, and put powders up their noses, and stick needles in their veins, and the lives of my generation began to divide inexorably into those who found that exciting, and those who thought it insane. Once or twice, I had tried to follow the drug-takers as they went round the back of the pub, to the *other* pub, to dark and dirty places where I didn't want to be. They came back weird and moody, scrawny and spotty, violent and mad, half asleep with their pinpoint eyes rolling in their heads. Or talking nineteen to the dozen, dripping dirty glamour. I minded enormously my friends falling away. I didn't want to play this game, but that put me among the dull ones, and I didn't want to be one of the dull ones. I was always aware of the injustice of this. It was the same everywhere. Drink was healthy and clear-eyed and normal and a bit unimaginative: drugs were wild and free and romantic and creative. And now here they all are in the clinic together, and it turns out that it wasn't drink v drugs, it was whether or not you had the killer streak of self-hatred. And it was sad, and boring, and it killed you.

Is it genetic? I asked the counsellor.

That is certainly a factor.

What causes it?

We don't know.

What can be done about it?

They have to stop using.

Using! Using alcohol. Abusing alcohol. No longer an amusing turn of phrase (picture a guy yelling 'fathead!' at a pint of beer).

How long does it take?

Long as a piece of string.

How can I help?

You can't.

Can you give me answers?

No.

Why not?

There are no answers. You have to work it out for yourself. He has to work it out for himself.

Work what out?

You'll see when you do.

Have you seen a million people go through this?

Yup.

Does it get better?

Sometimes.

Are children damaged by it?

Sometimes.

Do couples survive?

Sometimes.

By the time I was sixteen I knew four dead people: one who drowned, opiated, in a bath in Chelsea; one who couldn't tell cocaine from Ajax, two in drug-influenced car crashes. Alcohol had been my drug of choice. Cheap, legal and so many flavours, plus you know what you're getting. Nobody thought of alcohol as a drug. Nobody seemed to have noticed that Britain has basically been drunk for a thousand years. Or longer – who knows? It's so normal no one would record it.

*

It is a big pile of papers here: Self-Esteem, Unmanageability, What Does Sanity Mean to You? Through his notes, I can check what happened on any particular day, revisit any poignant moment, eavesdrop on him and the past. The evening after my first visit he wrote: 'Very sad when Louisa left. Emma, if you read this I need to go into detail (big detail) with you face to face. The issues feelings etc would be many sides of A4.' And the next day: 'Still frail after yesterday. Bollocked aggressively for using my hand to sprinkle cheese on my ragu. Totally habit. Subconscious. Apologised profusely and got the chef who very kindly brought more out. Tiny thing – but for that to make me hot and trembly proves what a delicate condition I am in. I am facing up to a lot of things. I found hurtful that "arrogance" was a term applied to me. I am more than willing to accept this when given more detailed explanations (there wasn't enough time).'

Another day he wrote to his counsellor: 'Thanks for the family meeting. Revelatory. I've heard all that Louisa has said before, but in this context, in this atmosphere, in your presence, it made me think and react in a very different fashion. Very valuable—'

I remember that day clearly. This time, I saw it in his face, in the eye contact, that he heard me. It made me glad – and sad, too, that alcoholics need so much help before they can hear the people who love them. What space is there for an actual, progressing relationship of equals, when someone is this compromised? Where can the love be?

'Talk about things you did, drunk, that you shouldn't have done,' the counsellor had said.

'How long have you got?'

'All the time you need,' she said.

'In chronological order, or in order of importance?'

He no longer said she looked like a horse, or neighed.

These were the lines that made me cry in the British Library where I was typing them out: 'Looking forward to church, chair-moving, guest-tea preparations, Louisa, Patrick, mini-group. Hope you've had a good weekend.'

*

One winter Sunday, I went down with Will who, having cordially disliked Robert for years, indeed thought him 'a sleaze-bag', was now offering to be his sponsor in AA. We sat outside on the damp, slimy wooden bench, the soles of our boots wet from walking, wet brown leaves on wet grey paving stones, dark by 4 p.m.

Robert was wearing the flowery shirt. His *Best of Tommy Cooper* DVD had been missing for four days, and I was hit by a surge of poignant protectiveness. Had someone nicked it? To stop him putting it on? 'I'm sure it'll turn up,' he said.

He used the weekly visits to show his improvement and his determination, and used our acknowledgement of it as fuel for the following week. Other friends had visited: 'Oh God it's like getting him back again. Oh God it's fantastic.'

The turnover was constant. A girl of nineteen whose father had agreed to pay for her to have the breast enlargement she wanted if she agreed to go to rehab. (Later I saw her in a tabloid, on the arm of her footballer.) The guitarist from a Goth band: the week he came there were photographers in the shrubbery again. A very nicely spoken boy with a sweet and fragrant mother; we were in family sessions together, she was worried because it was Christmas, the neighbours would be coming, should she not have any drinks in for them after all? I loved her. I loved everybody. I longed to spend my time in sessions. For the first time, as well, I realised that my knowledge and experience of Robert's alcoholism could – maybe – be useful, to someone to whom it was all new. This idea amazed me.

We did a questionnaire together: 'What Is Co-Dependency?' Now there's togetherness. How domestic, how romantic. We gave the same response to almost all the questions:

'My mental attention is focused on pleasing you' (NO);

'My self-esteem is bolstered by relieving your pain and solving your problems' (NO);

'I am not aware of how you feel I am aware of how I feel' (NO);

'My dreams for the future are linked to you' (YES – and also, hurray).

We differed on: 'With my help you could reach your true potential' (Robert: YES; Louisa: You'll do it if you do it);

'Your behaviour, clothing and personal appearance are dictated by my desires, as I feel you are a reflection of me' (Robert: NO; Louisa: Fat chance.)

Some of the questions suggested to me the titles of psychologically aware country-and-western songs, and I came away humming 'When something is wrong with my baby, something is wrong with me'. Looking back, I see that I gave the answers that I wanted to be the case, not, as it seems to me now, true answers. My mental attention was very much focused on his well-being, whether it pleased him or not. Of course I felt good about myself when things went well with him and he did the things which I felt would help him.

My own everyday feelings had rather dried up by then in the glare of his pain and sickness; or perhaps I had shut them down in a subconscious act of self-protection. In the chapel, which became a quiet place to sit on our own during a visit, Robert asked me if he had hurt me much. Of course every hurtful thing he had said to me hurt me, but what hurt most was how much he hurt himself. If anybody else had done to Robert the things he did to himself they would be in prison for attempted murder. Such are the dichotomies. You can't punish or reject the Evil Twin – and believe me I would have killed him – because he lives in the same brain and the same body. But now, each visit, we snuck into the chapel and kissed like teenagers, like we were

crazily in love, because he felt physically alive as he had not
for years.

*

Here in his papers I could see the precise moments he was introduced to vital factors which he later taught me. The difference
between a trigger and a reason, for example: 'Robert was *triggered*
to drink by an emotional response to realising what he had lost.
The group considers that anything can be a trigger, but the *reason*
we relapse is because we're alcoholics. If we blame relapse on
circumstances it leaves things wide open for future relapses.' And
that if an alcoholic drinks again after a long break, they are immediately back to where they were when they stopped.

And I saw him recover his capacity to take the piss out of himself
constructively: 'I raised my issue with defensiveness – at one point
I interrupted (to justify myself, obviously). This caused great
laughter from some peers and my counsellor, who later tapped me
on the shoulder and said, 'You just don't get it, do you, Robert?'
One learns humility in these situations. Very useful.'

*

Lola expressed an interest in visiting him. She and I talked about
it. It felt right. She's intelligent, balanced and wise. But we were
nervous, as we sat side by side in what had been a country gentleman's grand study, now institutionalised with whiteboards and
plastic chairs, listening to a lecture on the shame cycle.

Robert explained it too: 'You get drunk. You do stupid terrible
things and hurt people. You wake up, and remember. You can't
bear it. You are completely ashamed. The only way to get away
from the shame is to get drunk. You get drunk. You do stupid
terrible things and hurt people. And so on.'

I know perfectly well the friendly penumbra, the little trippy mist, that after a drink or two starts to obscure and blur your private list of discomforts and horrors, and how after the third you can't really make the list out any more, and what a relief that can be.

'It's so simple,' I said.

'Simple, yes, but not easy.'

'Is that a slogan?'

'Yes. And you end up believing that you don't deserve to be sober because you're such a cunt, so you drink to punish yourself. You're not a fucking idiot.'

'And how do you get out of that cycle?'

'You find the moment to jump off the carousel. You do something else about the shame, instead of drinking on it. '

There was a diagram on a whiteboard during the lecture – a circle, with the entry and exit points marked on it. Lola took it all in, and I told myself that understanding is the crux of everything. On the way back in the car, we talked about one of the slogans we'd heard: 'If someone calls you a horse, you can call them a fool. If ten people call you a horse, think about getting a saddle.'

*

Another exercise was a No-send Letter to his father. 'A funny concept,' Robert observed. 'Half thinking you're going to send it but knowing you won't – hence more *real* big honesty (don't over analyse, Robert).'

3rd December

Dear John,

This is an extremely difficult letter to write. Don't think for a moment that I want to appear critical or downright nasty but I have to get things off my chest. First of all I'd like to apologise for my lack of contact. The three reasons are my horrific descent into a pit of alcohol, my resentment towards your travel problems plus your affairs when I was young, and finally my dislike for Kath (your wife).

As you know I have been alcoholic for many years now. Because you don't understand the condition and because we don't see each other very often it has been impossible to gauge whether you would have given me more support . . . I believe that you would have. Having said that, your post-Victorian Northern working-class ethics would probably have been 'just fuckin sort it out'. All well and good, and I am, by being three weeks dry before coming into this rehab clinic a month and a bit ago. This is only the start of a very long process but at least I've started and have finally realised the enormity of the problem and have a lot of belief and self-confidence. I can hardly believe now that after the fourth doctor told me I had a maximum of three years to live, I went to the pub and got slaughtered. There are a myriad reasons for my alcoholism, all of which I am trying to explore, some of which I think may be connected to you. However please bear in mind that my lack of communication with you also applies to everyone else: Louisa who as you know I love to death, ditto your grandson, almost all my friends, and also those I don't like: Customs + Excise, Inland Revenue, Council Tax, BT etc. Bailiffs have become regular visitors to my flat. I built a big round wall round me and became an ostrich in the sand. The only people I did see were local drunks hanging round me mainly because I would buy them drinks and meals. I see them now and with one exception they are repetitive bores, which doesn't say much for me.

When I went to university at 17, your travel phobia didn't really concern me because I was engrossed in my new life. But gradually it began to affect me, usually triggered by me doing concerts. My graduation was particularly painful. All the proud parents and families and me on my own. I can't remember whether I asked my mother or not.

Having moved to London I started doing concerts at the Wigmore Hall, on the South Bank, and live on Radio Three. At least you could listen to that one . . . Never did you make any attempt to get help, to get medication, nothing. Only when I came home did you meet some of my friends and people I was amorously involved with. When I turned to writing music for TV and film it was easier for you I suppose because you could at least see my name on the credits. You never really opened up about it. Pivotal moments – my wedding, the birth of my son, his christening – where the fuck were you?

Finally Kath – it must have been very difficult for her to deal with an arrogant, grandiose, self-centred and precocious sixteen-year-old. I think she tried hard, but to no avail. I'm delighted that your marriage works but at the moment because my resentment of her has grown stronger due to my new-found mental clarity, I don't really want anything to do with you both. I really hope this will change. I want to forgive and be humble. I know that I've often been an awkward, difficult little shit. Give me time. After all that I love you a lot and always will.

Your son Robert

'Then the most extraordinary thing,' he wrote. 'I wrote a postcard to my father and stepmother some while ago, merely saying where I was. I got a letter today and would you believe he echoed certain sentiments of my no-send letter to him. He's never written to me before.'

Letter from John to Robert, blue biro, wobbly capitals.

"The Poplars"

24.1.06

Dear Robert

After your stinging reminder about only ever writing to you once I thought I would shock you and make it twice. I've been thinking about our recent telephone conversations and it seems you apparently have the need to have confirmed the love your father has for you. This is not in doubt and never has been and I don't think will ever be. There are many other people who also have love for you here in the north. Kath and Christine Diane and Denise for example and others who seem to always be asking "how is Robert". However there is a difference and it is called blood relationship. I have to love you because (as you often tell me) you are my son! At times in your life of major success and of troubled times your father has not been there, and that I know you must've felt pretty sad about, but life is far from perfect and I also have felt very sad about not being with you at these times. However it is totally unconnected, relevant to whether I love you or not. That is just not in question. It is just that your father is one of many thousands of people who have a totally irrational fear of something. Unfortunately mine is of travel. Your great-grandmother was frogs. Two people at Greenhalghs [the bakery at which John worked] I knew were afflicted one with spiders and one who was terrified of birds. To cope with these problems is not easy because other insensitive people cannot understand. It certainly inhibited my progress in the commercial world to an extent but the main drawback has been the inability to see you at important times in your life. However it hasn't been life-threatening and has given me a greater understanding of other people's problems and inner thoughts and feelings. I think it gave me a degree of humility and a much lower sense of self-importance. So I have no regrets.

Enough of me. What about you! It has become apparent that you seem to possess a formidable memory and can recount little insignificant events of the past which many times surprise me. What bothers me a little is that they are of the past. The modern mode of speech for progress is that you have to <u>move on</u>. Many people use it today, "you have got to move on". I don't like it because Mr Blair has moved on and in the process has destroyed most of what England was about. Having said that I feel sometimes that shortly you should be thinking of <u>moving on</u>. Instead of a tendency to talk of the past I would like some conversations about what you are planning for the future. I am convinced there is lots of wonderful music to come from you yet and it's getting time we heard some. I know it is not easy with the problems you've had but they can be overcome. It needs a degree of humility, a certain lowering of self-importance and an understanding that many thousands of people have far greater problems than you and me (I) have so far had to face. Even though one seldom feels like it, work is a great antidote to many ills, and if I may be allowed to talk of the past for a moment, you showed quite often the extraordinary ability to work hard.

   love Dad

*

As the time came for Robert to come out, we both got nervous. 'It got quite distressing in the family meeting with Louisa,' he wrote, 'who revealed one or two things that were obviously upsetting her. Productive for both of us, but painful nevertheless.' I had been grabbing at what might have been my last opportunity to speak in front of a sober third-party representative of consensual reality, in that magic place where Robert heard me. I was a bit panicky. I hadn't yet realised how it upset him to hear, without the anaesthetic of alcohol, how much he had upset me. I didn't want to let him down.

'Art class produced my usual genius in pastels,' he wrote. 'My leg is killing me.'

*

On four sheets of lined A4, I see the walls around him come tumbling down. So much joy for me, from lines of blue biro, a series of answers to a set of questions which is lost.

*

Shame, a difficult assignment.

I often compensate for feelings of shame – or not feeling good enough – by interrupting people when they may be just giving good advice (or not) and trying to justify myself. A subconscious fear of people finding me out.

Isolating myself became virtually constant. Wallowing in drunken self-disgust. Alarmingly, there was a masochistic pleasure to this. A tooth fell out. Barred from four locals and a local tandoori (I've only been going there for fifteen years!) Saw nobody. People crossing the road to avoid me.

Even when accusations are truthful – they mainly if not always are – I have used blame to deflect from myself in order not to be found out to be the evil disgusting person that I believe myself to be.

I have almost always been unfaithful – the exceptions being my marriage (until it broke down) and with Louisa. Sometimes I felt guilty, sometimes I didn't. I have felt incredible shame re my behaviour over the years. I think in some cases I may well have caused serious emotional damage.

Because for many years I had the facades of being drunk and trying to be entertaining, I rarely allowed people to know who I really was. I'm not afraid about revealing my inner self. Quite the opposite. I look forward to it.

I definitely used to avoid responsibility.

I rarely felt special, except when I was very drunk and would think that boring sober people were on a lower emotional plane – especially when it came to listening to classical music and appreciating nature. That state of mind was totally self-delusory.

I feel that a great weight has been lifted. Shame suppresses optimism.

*

All the way down in the car to fetch him home I was humming 'Re-Hab', by Stew and The Negro Problem, which was my earworm of that period. I loved this song for its gentleness, and its combination of tender affection and bitter realism as Stew sings of how very embarrassed and optimistic his friend is at getting out of rehab for the twenty-second time. And I hated it for the same reasons.

Robert was wearing the blue flowery shirt. 'It's your favourite,' he said. We kept smiling at each other, putting things in the car, saying goodbye. In his pocket he had a sheet of paper, which he gave me to read:

CONTINUING CARE PLAN: Robert Lockhart

Recommendations of the counselling team
  *Abstain totally from all mood-altering chemicals one day at a time
  *Attend AA at least five times a week – find a sponsor immediately
  *Explore further counselling options as discussed with your counsellor
  *Attend Clouds reunions
  Robert, you came to Clouds ravaged by your addiction. Others had expressed grave concern as to the severity of its consequences to all aspects of your life. You had been told by doctors that if you continued to drink your life was in danger.
  Despite this, you continued to question or minimise the severity of these consequences. You were open and honest about your underlying desire for the 'pleasures' you associated with drinking. You came to realise the reality of your alcoholism: that its impact had been devastating to you and to others important to you. Relationships in your life had been affected, as had your previously flourishing career and your sense of self-worth. You also discovered that this denial and minimisation of consequences was the very nature of the illness by which you were afflicted.

During your time in treatment you have learned to listen to others. You have learnt to value and make sense of their feedback, challenges and suggestions. You have taken action to identify and change your behaviours that are 'blocks' to your recovery. You have started to become realistic about the true effects of your drinking and to identify what you really care about. You have started to acknowledge and express your feelings and have taken risks to share these feelings. You have received identification, support and a sense of release. You are discovering a new sense of interest in yourself and in others. In letting go of justification, defensiveness and intellectualising your problems away, you are accessing a new sense of inner wisdom and serenity. You are using this to develop your understanding of recovery, yourself and others . . . We wish you ongoing success and happiness in your journey.

Matters Requiring Further Attention:

Taking responsibility/Asking for help/Connecting to the fellowship

Robert, you cannot recover alone. When you take responsibility for yourself and access the help and support you need and deserve, you find a way out of the blame and negativity which is so familiar to addiction.

Expressing your thoughts and feelings appropriately

You have discovered how you easily avoid difficult feelings, especially sadness, pain and anger. Keep finding healthy ways to express yourself honestly.

Family relationships

You have accessed the support of family sessions to address the consequences of your addiction. You have highlighted important concerns and identified a need for you both to seek ongoing support.

I have read and agree with the above recommendations

Patient RJ Lockhart 14/12/05

*

AA and the Twelve Steps come in for mockery. People say it's religious, fatuous, new-agey, profiteering, culty, only for fools who can't run their own lives; they hoot with laughter at the idea of a Higher Power. Some who do this are the very ones who might benefit – as an addict, or as someone close to an addict – from what it has to offer. Mocking denial is, I would say, behavioural Trait Number Two of the intelligent addict (Trait Number One being ringing up at all hours to talk without listening about how everything is somebody else's fault, and Number Three being hiding empty bottles in places where they are bound to be found, and saying somebody else left them there). After all the discussions and the articles and the books about AA and NA, only one thing matters: if you can do it, it works.

Everything was inconceivably tender. Everything was – or might be – possible. Robert planned, as well as his own four or five meetings, to go to two meetings a week with Will ('being an ex-junkie coke addict and alcoholic he knows a bit about it. Extremely helpful. He's been clean six years now'). I let myself dream about him getting back to work, living well, writing glorious music, playing the piano again and being happy and useful. I fantasised again a future where he would go round schools to explain the dangers of drink, and this time it seemed plausible. There would probably be a honeymoon period, they said. I was prepared for that. I was prepared to be very happy.

Chapter Seventeen

Home, 2006

My father was ill: Alzheimer's was moving in on him. He remained himself, a very nice man, intelligent, judicious. And a charmer. He had a melancholy streak which came out at dusk each day, and he loved music, talk, social justice, his children and our mother. All of this is what came out. It wasn't easy, but it wasn't as hard as it is for many. In February he was in hospital with the usual problem: is it his heart? It often had been. He'd had his first surgery when he was fifty-six, and plenty more since. Now, because of his dementia, one of his numerous offspring would always spend the night on the borrowed mattress on the floor behind his bed. That night it was me. We were all used to early hospital mornings, the clattering of cleaners and the vicious fluttering of overhead lights, but neither Dad nor I expected to be woken by our core family – seven or eight of them, led by our ghost-pale mother – gliding and crowding into the small room on a cloud of trepidation.

'Good morning,' said Dad, cheerfully. I rose squinting from behind the bed. It was about 6 a.m.

A night nurse had rung Liz in the small hours and told her Wayland was dead. She had turned two pages in the nurses' book, and rung the wrong number. 'Hello, this is the hospital, is that Mrs xxxx?' sounds much the same whatever the surname, at four in the morning when your eighty-three-year-old husband is in hospital. But Wayland was not dead. The man in the next room was dead, God rest his soul.

How happy we all were! 'Lazarus!' we cried, and sent the youngsters for coffee and were glad to be all together and wondered if there was a word for the opposite of disappointment, because that was the elation we were feeling. Later it occurred to me that for everybody apart from me this had been a practice run at losing him. In the next room the other man's deathbed had been made up again.

And Robert was recovering. The slow, hidden self-slaughter was over. Clouds was a success, an effective, strong re-introduction to a new life of sobriety, possibility, health and hope. Robert was to demonstrate to me his sober life; making the territory safe, bit by bit, so that I might, at some stage, not become hysterical at the idea of thinking about starting to trust him. Aspects of daily life were to improve, and the improvements were to become manifest. I had told him often enough that nothing he said meant anything to me now. By his deeds I would know him and witness the change. He would go to ninety meetings in ninety days. He would carry on with the Twelve Steps, study them and apply them. He could have secondary rehab if he wanted. He would bathe and shave. Will would be his sponsor and he would get a shrink of some sort. We would go to a counsellor together. When he felt ready, he would get work. He would go to bed at night and get up in the morning, and try to eat regularly whether or not he felt like it. He would have physiotherapy for his leg, and training to make him stronger all round. He would make his flat nice. I would be invited round. We'd see friends. Easy nice things could happen now. And did! We were at a neighbour's house eating fish pie. Robert, fearing there would be no gherkins, brought his own, loose in his coat pocket, and had the children fish them out, squeaky green and wet. He'd been thinking about a haircut: he invited the children to do it. Three deliriously happy six-year-olds, almost sick with excitement, clambered over him with scissors, snipping wildly and quickly in case someone made them stop. Robert sat statesmanly, quelling his own laughter, looking like Sid Vicious with extra bald patches and mock dignity. Easy to love.

I found myself writing songs. This was new. Robert was the music in our house, and at such a level that any musicality in me had only ever been in relation to him. With him, I *could* now sing those intoxicating French songs '*Après un Rêve*', and '*Clair de Lune*', and 'Lydia', with their air of absinthe and green velvet and drippingly emotional Parisian nights. And homegrown songs: 'Down by the Salley Gardens' (the Britten and the Ireland – yes, he found the names very funny), and 'O Waly Waly', where pale youth believes in love, and is belied, in crunching chords of heart-piercing stringency. And American songs: he snorted at the piano arrangements of the Cole Porter songs in the book, and improvised new ones as we went along, in whatever key worked for me, cool, spare jazz versions which felt mine, ours.

This was an area in which he and I were right: the home life where he played and I sang. He taught me, so kindly and with astonishing patience given the standard of musician he was used to working with. He gently guided my utter lack of rhythm. We did Fauré and Duparc, Cole Porter and Billie Holiday, and then he would indulge me with sweeping arias from *La Bohème* and *La Traviata* where I would just start crying in the middle. And not forget to go TING for the most sublime use of the triangle in western civilisation. At the piano, he was superb, I was pretty terrible, and together we weren't bad. He liked the humility it brought out in me who was usually such a know-all, and I loved to see him doing what he was so good at. At the piano he was himself, his best self. I would weep at the lyrics, and he at the chords, and we would laugh at each other and at ourselves, because that was always the same: words and music. When we watched TV or a film together, I would make my comments when there was no dialogue, and he would shut me up because he'd be listening to the score. And then when the characters started talking again, I'd have to shut *him* up. When he was sent a tape (in the old days) or CD or link to watch something for which he was going to write the music, I'd often sit with him, because though his talent for mood and character was spot on, he was terrible with plots and never knew what was happening. 'Are they lesbians?' he'd ask, or 'What are those cows for?' I (not surprisingly given my line of work) knew not only what was happening in the plot but often enough what was going to happen. He thought this miraculously clever of me.

So when I found myself writing songs, bluesy, countryish, guitar-type songs in three or four chords, it was a bit surprising. They were – still are, though they're more sophisticated now – all about him. In this period, they veered to the happy: songs of world-weary survival.

But. Slowly and against every desire of my heart—

Things did not improve.

Those things which were meant to come to pass still did not come to pass.

By March, though I didn't know it, couldn't see it, didn't want to see it, didn't dare see it, Robert was drinking again. As a result, I drove myself actually mad, trying to reconcile opposites. To match up what he said with what I saw, I entertained total contradictions as if they made sense. He looked drunk, talked drunk, behaved drunk, but my judgement was so bamboozled by now, reeling in the renewed onslaught, that I did not have the confidence to respect it and to say: You are drunk, and it is my judgement which stands on this, not what you say. After climbing that long, hard ladder, with such a shining prize at the top, you have fallen down this fucking snake.

Here is something I wish someone had said to me at the time: This is part of it. It is a three-point turn with many many points. Falling down the snake is not the end of the world. You just have to start again.

Actually, they may well have said it. Anybody could have said anything to me at that time. I was not hearing because my ears were stuffed with contradictions masquerading as alliable truths, with Dirty saying, 'Hey, I'm Clean', with Putrid going 'I can't smell anything', and Drunk drawling, 'Of course I'm Sober, Jesus, and it's a fucking miracle I am the way you go on.'

There was an argument where I sort of came to, in a moment of clarity. Robert was living in his flat nearby. I didn't go to his flat – he didn't want me to; I didn't madly want to anyway; periodically I'd try and he'd make excuses and I would think 'hmm' but not want a fight about it. My home is nice and has my kid in it. He stayed every night with me, and went off when he woke (which could be any time) saying he was going to do his VAT. VAT! Well. He was not an organised man. I had moved my – our – bed from the big bedroom at the front into the little bedroom at the back beyond the bathroom, to be further from Lola's bedroom in the middle. Why? So that she wouldn't be disturbed, because he was up and down all night, unable to sleep, searching for painkillers, grimacing with tinnitus, feeling sick, in pain, stomping about, refusing help, going out to smoke, getting up to pee, retching, keeping me awake, coming in at all hours, going out at all hours. One evening he was on the floor on the landing, for ages, saying he couldn't stand, and I was so distressed – and then he stood up, and said he'd been pretending. It was not the rehabilitatory behaviour they had told us needed to be achieved. I was concerned for him and I was pissed off too, because I was a writer and a mother trying to finish books and make a living and look after my youngster. Could he not perhaps, I suggested, do the things? Go to the counsellor, to AA meetings? Get up in the morning? Sleep at night? Brush his teeth?

Eat? Perhaps even at mealtimes? With me, even? And he would call me a nag, and I'd say 'Show me a nagging woman and I'll show you a man not doing what he should', and during an argument in that back bedroom I found I was banging my head on the bedroom wall.

Just as well I had swapped bedrooms.

But Jesus – you step back and you see yourself. Swapping bedrooms so your daughter should not hear you arguing with your boyfriend. Banging your head on a brick wall. Literally. Bang bang bang.

*

I thought people were thinking, If only he'd pull his socks up and sort himself out. I thought they thought me a fool. I used to fight them in my mind, the way you fight the voices which torment you when you're fourteen, telling you you're fat and will never be loved. 'It's an illness,' I'd say to them, in my head. 'People die of it. It takes time. He's doing his best.'

I didn't have these fights out loud because actually no one was saying anything to me that would warrant that reply. So who was I fighting with? Myself, of course. And trying to live by my own rule: help him if he asks; other than that, do nothing for him or about him. And longing for him to ask.

*

I was writing two novels at the time. One was a children's novel, *Lee Raven, Boy Thief*, about a dyslexic boy who ran around the sewers of a futuristic dystopian London with a stolen magic book which gave a different story to whoever opened it – the story they needed. I reread it recently and yes, the hero stuck in darkness and shit, and the obsession with the desired story, do throw some light on my preoccupations at that time.

The other was a novel for adults about an alcoholic concert pianist in the 1960s, his wife, his girlfriend and his dysfunctional family, entitled *How Do You Like Living Here?*. The dedication was '*For RJL. You probably think this book is about you*', and the epigram from Liszt's mistress, the author Marie d'Agoult: '*Rarely do those we love deceive us; we deceive ourselves in them.*' I adapted liberally from our own home life. It never worked and was never finished, but it contained lots of our conversation, more or less verbatim.

'Beethoven piano sonatas?' he says. 'Fucking Germanic four-square plinky-plonk crap. And I hate that fucking self-congratulatory pompous laughter you get when a middle-class audience just has to demonstrate that it gets some stupid little Schubertian joke . . .'

I take his talk personally. I don't feel equipped to judge Beethoven, or Schubert's facetiousness. I flinch when he talks like that. He doesn't notice. Why not?

'Because I am so hypersensitive I have to block out what other people are feeling,' he says. 'If I have to deal with that on top of what I am feeling myself it's just too much. I can't handle it.'

'Oh,' I say. There's a word: mimophant, meaning sensitive as mimosa regarding one's own feelings, and as an elephant regarding those of other people.

'I think that's why I'm a drunk, as well,' he says. 'I drink to desensitise myself because it's all too much.'

A week ago he said he drank because he couldn't bear reality in all its inordinate ordinariness; to maintain the intensity of the day's musical experience. Or intense anything. To maintain intensity.

I try to think of a way for both to be true. I am still trying to square his circles. But he's talking about it. That's good, isn't it?

*

We were sitting miraculously by the fire in the sitting room, London dim beyond the windows, him sober-seeming, me relaxed, patience and affection sitting with us. He was looking at the paper and I was looking at him. How handsome he was, how weary he looked.

'This is nice,' he said softly, not looking up.

I tucked my feet up under me, and he reached out for one and squeezed it. My feet are always cold. His hands are always warm.

'It is,' I said.

Comfortable silence.

'I'll run you a bath, shall I?' I said.

'I don't want one,' he said.

'It would be nice,' I said, kindly, thinking it safe. 'To bathe.'

'I do bathe,' he said, sports pages aweigh.

'More often,' I said, hideously embarrassed even to be having this conversation, again, with a grown man.

'Why?' he said. 'I don't smell.'

'Well, you do, actually.'

'*Act*u-welly,' he said, mocking my accent now for being well-bred.

'Well, you do. You smoke, and . . . well, you do. People do.'

'Ah. People.'

'Yes, people.'

'Mmmm,' he said, in a camp, eyebrow raising, slightly mad, slightly bored way.

It really irritated me when he said 'mmm' like that.

'Darling, please,' I said.

'Don't call me darling,' he said.

'You're behaving like a stubborn schoolboy,' I said. 'Don't make me mother you just so you can be clean.'

'My mother's dead,' he snapped.

'I know. Funnily enough, over all these years, I'd noticed, actually . . .'

'*Act*u-welly,' he murmured.

I breathed out through my nose, gently.

A moment ago he was a charming bon viveur, a drinker, for sure, but a professional, a man, a life being lived – How come now he smells peculiar? When did his glamorously tousled look become stale and ugly? When did his loucheness begin to turn? When did that elegant cigarette, held as if slightly too heavy for his wrist, change his skin to grey?

'Please don't mock how I speak,' I said automatically. How many times have I said this to him?

Perhaps this endless repetition is just how things are between couples.

A different thought assails me. Everything is terrible, and I won't see it. I am force-feeding us. I am dragging us around dressed up in a party frock. I am parading us like a fucking corpse in lipstick.

'You chose the wrong man,' he said. And this too is something he has said before, many times, something to which I refuse, in turn, to listen. 'That's all. Don't do it. Don't try and help me. It's all a waste. You need some strong man in a clean shirt, with a big dick and biceps. You deserve that.'

'I want you,' I said, as if from far away. 'I want you strong, in a clean shirt. Your dick is fine, I don't care about biceps. I love your arms. I love you.'

'Well don't,' he said.

'All right,' I said. 'It's dead. It's over. You can take your things. Go on then. Goodbye.'

'No!' he said. 'No. I don't want it to be over. I don't want it to be dead. I want it to be alive and all right. I want to eat naturally and sleep at night and go to parties looking healthy and happy. I don't want it over. I want—'

'What?'

'I want you to—'

'You want *me* to?'

What he wanted, was me to forgive him.

'That doesn't matter,' I said. 'I forgave you long ago; I was born forgiving you—'

'It does matter!' he cried. 'Every horrible thing I have done to you matters because while you sit there saying they don't matter we never get beyond them – you're denying their existence, not forgiving them. Not the same thing.'

'Well I can't go through them one by one,' I said. 'Did you keep a list? – and we're all right now, aren't we? I'm all right, you're in recovery—'

'Do you know Schubert's Sonata in A?' he said.

'Um – what – A major?'

'Of course A major. A is major, unless you say it's minor. Do you know it?'

'I don't know – you know I don't recognise music by name – which one is it?'

'God, you can't be wrong, can you – you can't admit not knowing.'

'Well I might know it, if I heard it—'

'So, what, could you play it?'

'Not know it in that sense, of course not—'

'So you don't know it.'

I gave up.

'If you listen to it,' he said, 'it's all in there. It's just a fucking catastrophe, but it doesn't stop. It goes completely mad, but the theme keeps coming, but you know it's all over, this fucking funeral march . . . the scherzo tries to cheer you up but you know it's all bollocks, and the finale, Jesus, there's these little scraps of Schubertian birdsong in a fucking catastrophic vortex, and the guy was dying, he was dead a month later, thirty-one years old, but this fucking skylark won't stop, it won't die . . . Syphilitic cunt . . .'

I closed my eyes.

'Darling,' I said.

'Don't call me darling,' he said. 'You call everybody darling.'

'There's lots of people I love.'

'Subtext, you don't love me any more than you love all of them, whoever they might be. Subtext, you don't love me that much. Which I quite understand, though you might be woman enough to admit it. You don't love me, and I can't blame you. '

'You know I love you.'

He started laughing. 'Without the piano, my modicum of talent as a decomposer, I don't think so.'

'Without those things you wouldn't be you! You can't just abolish part of you for some academic experiment in hating yourself . . .'

He stared on out of the window. His head swung infinitesimally.

After that he mostly talked about Bartók, Red Garland, Art Tatum, diminished sevenths, the circle of fifths, syphilis and the *Tierce de Picardie*. I went to bed. Later, he went out. Soon enough I was lying half asleep, grateful that we hadn't shouted at each other, that he hadn't stormed off at least, and wondering whether forgiveness was in fact something one couldn't do by choice after all, and dismissing the grey nebulous thought that recovery was surely not meant to be like this. And he, presumably, was staring at the streaking lights of the traffic through the grime of the telephone box window, or sitting bony-arsed in a doorway, his fag-end burning his fingertips.

*

He said, again: 'I am the wrong man.'

'That's for me to decide,' I said. 'And you're not. You're the right man. You're funny, and handsome, and kind, and intelligent, and talented beyond belief, and you kiss like a dream, and you have that look in your eye . . .'

'What look? A bit vulnerable?'

'Yes, that too.'

'Apparently girls like that. So I'm told.'

'And I can talk to you, and when we have a conversation you pick it up again the next time we meet, as if you've been thinking about it, at least you used to—'

'Well of course I've been thinking—'

'Not everybody does that,' I said, and he was bemused.

*

Rereading this, I think: 'I may have written this before.' I'm not sure. Alcoholism is repetitive. I wonder how many of *my* brain cells his alcoholism destroyed. And I see that alcoholism is profoundly selfish, and feeds off kindness.

*

'For example,' said my agent, after reading a draft of *How Do You Like Living Here?*, 'When he gets drunk before the concert, the big charity gala – we're given no reason why he did that . . .'

If there was a reason, I'd have given it. There being no reason is the point. Reason, as I had learned to my cost, has no sway, and serves only to torment those who cling to it in these irrational areas. Or – OK. He got drunk because he was an alcoholic.

'. . . and we would have an opportunity to sympathise with him, because as things stand he's not very sympathetic . . .'

No, he's not, is he?

'And it seems to me the two women are basically the same woman . . .'

Yes. Alcoholics turn every woman into that same woman – the Heartbroken Nag.

'. . . and it's just the story of a man's decline, really . . . it's pretty harrowing.'

Yes, it's pretty harrowing.

'But you have that lush setting, Italy in the sixties, all that Venice and sunsets and cocktails, that's all great . . .'

That was the one bit of the novel that was made up.

'The problem,' said my agent. 'is that you set up this question, here on page two, where the daughter is on the terrace, wondering whose fault it is – a lovely opening, by the way, and a very good question – but it's clear, all the way through, that it's *his* fault. There is no question, at any stage, that it's anyone's other than his fault.'

And there it was again. Fault.

That addiction is the addict's responsibility, but it's not their fault, is a significant part of the Twelve-Step approach, a way in which the addict can acknowledge that he is not in charge of everything. Step One: I admitted I am powerless. How can something be someone's own fault, if they are powerless?

Perhaps both that novel and this memoir represent me clinging desperately to something that protects me from my greatest fear – to whit, that if I allow myself to perceive what many others believe, that an alcoholic's behaviour *is* entirely his/her own fault, and that when Robert repeatedly told me that I'd chosen the wrong man he was for once telling the truth, I will be swamped by an impossible toxic flood of emotion because he was in fact a bastard and I am, still, a fool.

*

That March I was to do an event at the Oxford ('fucking Poxford', he called it) Literary Festival. It was our birthday weekend, and I, still living in La La Land, thought we might make a nice weekend of it.

Robert suggested a charming seventeenth-century place at the top of St Giles. He was hot and ill and wanted to lie down, but he came to my reading and was adorably proud, and when a youngster asked were any of the characters based on real people I was able to point Robert out as the original of Sergei the manky one-eared Rachmaninoff-obsessed cat with the heart of gold, and he miaowed at them. The next day was *his* birthday, and Mother's Day as well. He slept late, then we ordered brunch in the restaurant among the daffodils and the good mothers of Oxford being taken out by their children. I was thinking *Isn't this lovely!* in a terrible artificial voice, even in my head, and just as the classy cheeseburgers arrived he collapsed dramatically, on the floor: the sudden sharp roar that kicks it off, stiff, frothing, shaking, eyes rolling back. Now, though, I know what to do.

An ambulance came, and while they were putting him on the

stretcher a waiter gave me the bill, even though we hadn't touched the food and Robert was being taken off in an ambulance. I paid it, and followed on to the John Radcliffe, and there I was in a corridor, waiting.

The next day I read the bill and saw it had a Bloody Mary on it. Robert said the waiter made a mistake, he ordered a Virgin Mary, why, what was I trying to say? And I was thinking about fits coming when you don't drink after a long period of heavy drinking, and about the benefit of the doubt, and to whose benefit was it.

Two days later Robert got himself arrested. 'A fight with someone dropping litter,' he said. Ojay rang from the Office saying Robert was at the bus stop, covered in blood. Two friends were visiting: Osei's widow, and a friend whose husband was having an affair. We had been talking about how in any group of women at any time there will be at least one whose marriage/relationship was a shambles because of what men do – die, have affairs, drink – and I was so embarrassed, sad, eroded, because they had been thinking I was the happy one.

I dragged Robert home, physically, as his legs were giving way. The presence of my friends, their clear, calm eyes, their natural shock at this situation which to me seemed almost normal because of the long, slow decline that had led to it, made me get him an appointment with a neurologist. If he wasn't drinking, as I still desperately wanted to believe, then he was clearly ill in some other way.

At the beginning of April I went away to Italy and planted fruit trees. I could, looking back, feel bad about leaving him alone and going about my own life and business with Lola. I can think myself inside out with how things could, should, would or might have been – but I was beginning to take on board that while it is foolish to provoke a crisis it is equally foolish to try to prevent a crisis which is determined to happen. This was very much against my nature. I always wanted to put things right.

I said, as I went, don't use the house while I'm away. I came back to find he'd stayed there all through my absence. There were empty vodka halves in peculiar places, left there, he said, after he'd invited Mark the neighbour in, and Mark had brought some friends. I neither liked nor trusted Mark the neighbour, a semi-violent and incomprehensible junkie whose only merit was that if your kid's bike was nicked Mark could probably get it back for you. The idea that having Mark and his mates round to my house was the excuse that would get Robert off the hook was laughable. Mark coming round was neither true, nor any defence. The truth was, Robert was drinking and I was paralysed.

I didn't like thinking of my house as my house. My house, my bed, my life. I wanted it all to be ours. Me, Lola, him, harmonious.

That gave impetus to a string of appointments, made, missed, and finally, kept: 31 May, brain scan.

*

I had my own appointments. I was seeing a counsellor regularly by this time, an icy-haired six foot four Viking of immense tenderness and wisdom, who I got free on the NHS because my boyfriend was an alcoholic. I made him cry once. He said, 'Louisa, why is it so hard for you?' in such a sweet way, with tears in his eyes – though it occurs to me now the question should have been 'Louisa, why is it taking you so bloody long?' I told Robert, and he said, 'He's in love with you.' But he was just sympathetic. He sent me to a family support group, to which I only went once, because this was not about family. Family was my daughter and her father, which remained a healthy, affectionate set-up. This was about a lover, and that seemed to me very different. I felt that with Robert not being Lola's father, and not actually living with us, and her father being very present and a good and lovely dad, the trouble was between me and Robert, and therefore still not really anything to do with these people with alcoholic relatives. Also, on that one visit, I received a gift of such magnitude that I had to take it away and think about it. A father and son started talking about how much they had both wanted to murder their wife/mother, and how they had first discussed how they would do it. They laughed about this. Others in the circle laughed too.

'Weedkiller in the tea!' the man said. 'Not very imaginative.'

'I was going to push her downstairs,' the son said.

I had been going to push Robert down the stairs. No one would have ever known. With his bad ankle and his unsteadiness it could easily have been an accident. I had mulled over the possible permutations with an Agatha-Christie-like eye for detail.

Is fantasising about killing the person we love so much an aspect of the family illness?

It is powerlessness. I was desperate for something to go on: proof, reassurance, comfort, reconciliation, reparation. He could not give me anything. Certainly not any of those. The situation could not function, because it was based on a big fat lie. The constant and ferocious grinding of reality against pretence makes progress, stasis, decline, breath, everything, impossible. It is untenable. So all kinds of absurdities, wickednesses and lunacies offer themselves. Many years later, Robert wrote, of this period: 'Louisa put up with it'. No, my love, that was not what I was doing.

The imbalance in our living arrangements had come to represent other imbalances which to a reasonable person were unreasonable and to an addict were vital. I said, flush with reasonableness: 'Well, if I can't come to your flat, after all these years, you can't come to my house. How about that? You have keys to mine. Give me keys to yours.' And he gave me back his keys to mine.

*

205

On the kitchen table I found one of his questionnaires:

Questions to Help You Find Alternatives to Anxious Predictions

What am I predicting will happen?

What is the evidence to support what I am predicting?

What is the evidence against what I am predicting?

What might be an alternative view on the situation?

What evidence do I have from the past that would be helpful now?

What is the worst that can happen?

What is the best that can happen?

Realistically, what is most likely to happen?

If the worst does happen, what could be done about it?

If someone I cared about had the same worry, what advice would I give them?

What are the costs and benefits of worrying about this? Divide 100 points between the costs and benefits (i.e. 40–60, 30–70, etc.)

I applied it to me, and I applied it to him, and then I took the line Churchill took with Hitler over the invasion of Poland in 1939: if he didn't do what was necessary (withdraw from Poland/demonstrate sobriety), within a set timescale, then we would be over. If he couldn't demonstrate sobriety to me within six months, I would no longer be his girlfriend.

But Robert was not Hitler. I was not Churchill. I was in love with him – not just with what he used to be or could be or what I wanted him to be, but with the actual him, battered and snarling inside the sticky web of his addiction.

His response was to lock himself away. He said I'd banned him, and refused to see me. He rang me most days, sometimes chatty and amiable as if nothing was wrong; sometimes a vitriolic slug in a puddle, miserable, vicious, drunk and hurt, rank and hissing, immobilised, interminable. I would put the phone down, and go and do something else; he'd still be there half an hour later, talking to the ether.

Three weeks in, he told me he was in a deep, deep depression. I wasn't allowed in; he wouldn't come out. How many reasons are there why an alcoholic locks himself away, all alone?

In his Recovery papers, he describes this as 'Louisa threw me out'.

That summer, both my parents were in hospital.

*

Robert had not read the novel. He was willing to read it, he said. He professed to want to read it, but so far he had not, and as long as he remained locked up in his flat, chances are he wouldn't. Feeling bad about having shown it to my agent when Robert had not seen it, I offered to post it. Robert said no, it might get lost.

'Doesn't matter,' I said, down the phone, old-fashioned receiver tucked between ear and shoulder, half an hour into a long conversation. 'I can always print out another one.'

'You know I don't open my post,' he said.

This was going nowhere.

'You can't write it till I die,' Robert said, with some bolshy pride. 'You don't know how it's going to end so you can't construct it.'

'I don't want you to die,' I said.

'I'm not going to,' he said.

'Yes you are,' I said. 'We all do.'

'Not yet,' he said.

When is 'yet', anyway?

I opened a new document and called it Structure. I stared at it, then saved it and went to make a cup of tea. It is still empty. Even now, every now and again, I open it, to laugh.

*

He saw nobody. He had no friends – he'd gone silent, or scared them off. Everybody still loved him as far as they knew, but he was one great big Piss Off personified. The aggression had long ago overtaken the wit, the obsessions and intrusions became unbearable. Nobody was around to see the naughty golden boy, our little genius, our sharp-tongued, foul-mouthed Orpheus, slide away, over the limits, from designated *wunderkind* to world-class fuck-up.

I only saw him twice in those six months. In August, he and I went together to the funeral of a sweet neighbour, a hardcore drinker and smoker, lung cancer. The second time, in the street, I was driving, near his flat. Looking out for him? Perhaps. He tried to run away from me when he saw the car. I parked and followed him. 'I haven't seen you for so long,' I said, and he said, 'I'm not fit to be seen.' He tried to get away, and when he couldn't he turned his face into a privet hedge, as an ostrich turns to sand. I hugged him and told him I wanted him well, I loved him. I persuaded him to come home, made him bathe, tried to make him eat, took his dirty clothes and gave him clean ones. But then he left the house, saying: 'I'm going back to my private world now'. It was twenty years since he'd told me, in the street, that he was dead.

*

My piano, sitting in my house, seemed utterly pointless.

'I can't bear it,' I told him, 'taking up the whole bloody room, just lying there like . . . like . . .'

'Like my coffin?' he said, and yes, that was what I hadn't said.

'Don't get rid of it,' he said. 'I'm not going to die.'

He said, 'I've done nothing, have I?'

I said, 'You've sat and watched as I drift off into the distance.'

'Are you in the distance?' he said.

'Further every day,' I said.

'Don't go,' he said.

'I'm doing nothing,' I said. 'For years I've been chucking balls into your court, every ball in the world is in your court, I have invented balls, pulled them out of thin air, in order to have something to throw into your court and give you another chance to do something . . .'

'I've done nothing,' he said.

'Oh you've done so much.'

'I can't walk,' he said.

'I'm sorry,' I said.

'I haven't eaten for a week,' he said.

'I'm sorry,' I said.

'If I can prove to you – if I can get better – can I get you back?' he said.

Was I leaving him to make him try harder? Was I leaving him because it was killing me? Because it was killing him? Because I had become part of the problem?

'I'm not leaving you,' I said. 'I've just stopped trying to keep you.'

I felt as if I had been pressing my hands to the edge of a doorway for years, and now I had stepped out of the doorway, and my hands flew up of their own accord, free.

*

I gave Robert a print-out tied with a piece of string, with a card (Van Gogh's 'Almond Blossom', 1890) saying that it wasn't finished, but I wanted him to see it, to understand my side, to see how I saw his side, to recognise that there simply shouldn't be sides. I didn't expect him to read it.

It wasn't really a novel. I don't know what happened to that print-out, or to the card, which I'd bought on a trip to Amsterdam with Lola to meet the Dutch publishers of *Lionboy*. I used the painting again in my later novel *My Dear I Wanted to Tell You*, where Nadine the unwilling nurse is sheltering in a trench outside Étaples, where she has scarpered because she believes Riley Purefoy's lie that he no longer loves her, whereas in fact he has had half his face blown off and rebuilt, and he does not want her pity, and she sees almond blossom against the dawn sky, and recalls a pre-war dream of going with him to Amsterdam to look at art.

*

After weeks of silence, he rang me on 13 November. Six months to the day since my Churchillian ultimatum. He got the bloody day right.

'So we're broken up now,' I said.

'Not yet,' he said. 'Not till the evening.'

'Are you going to do anything about it?' I said.

'Yeah,' he said, 'I'm going to do everything about it.'

Parrot. He did nothing.

I thought, by doing nothing, he is telling me, quite clearly, that there is no hope for him, and I should step away, just like he said at the beginning, like a melodramatic teenager, only it's true. A phrase recurred in my head: 'Please, tell the lady that I have the honour to be a thorough reprobate and not a woman alive can save me now . . .' Where's that from? (Dostoyevsky, as it turns out. *The Brothers Karamazov*.)

It was not for me to save him. I had faith in his ability to do it himself. I looked for our happy ending. I believed in happy endings.

So, November to March. Four winter months. I know which shops he hobbled to, while he could still hobble. I know which shopkeepers sold him drink. I know which cab firms he rang to bring him vodka and fags, every day.

Should I have moved him to the middle of nowhere in the countryside? Should I have bribed the cab firms and the off licences not to serve him? Should I have tied him up in the cellar?

I knew nothing but sadness. Did I feel anything? Yes – cut off and blank. Brutalised. Nasty word. It all seemed such a waste. My hopes had been so high, and now that I had no hope, I couldn't even remember what hope was. I felt foolish, to remember how I had felt. What kind of fool hopes? A foolish fool. And that cynicism made me sadder.

I could not write because my feelings were cauterised. How could I entrance a reader when I was so bogged down, so untouching, so nothing?

The only feeling that rose, from time to time, like a dragon rearing out of mud, flaming on its long neck, was fury. It aimed for Robert, and bit and stung him, which was not fair because despite his stupid choices and his many abused opportunities he did not deserve to suffer more.

I didn't like anything. There's a word for it: anhedonia. Same root as hedonist. I wanted desperately to write this story of Robert and me, and the enemy. I knew it was a story worth telling but I'd start thinking about it and I'd start crying – because of all that had happened, and because I couldn't write it. And apathy was killing me. Depression, procrastination, going back to bed. I was afraid. I didn't know where to take my poor mind now. It felt so tender; so small and scared. I was all frozen up, the frozen sea within to which Kafka was so keen to take an axe.

I remember sitting in Swift's car outside her house in floods of tears, and her saying, 'But would you and Robert get back together?' and me almost throwing up, retching and shaking and saying 'NO. NO. Never.'

Chapter Eighteen

An Italian Restaurant, 2007

I went on a date with another man. I felt I owed it to my friends who would like to see me happy. I met him at a wedding; let's call him Jack. He took my number and invited me to dinner. He was shaggy, intelligent and quite attractive. A journalist.

He was there at the restaurant when I arrived. He was drunk. The service was attentive, so we ordered quickly. The third thing he said, as the starters arrived, was, 'All Muslims are bastards and should be nuked.' I thought of my friend Amira and her sons Younus and Ali, of nice Mrs Bhutt next door. I would have left but because of the starters I followed the rules of propriety and not being mean to restaurant staff. I disputed his point and we ate.

He wanted to arm wrestle. I felt not.

The main course arrived. We talked about travel, his work, my other life in Italy.

He started to cry. I was sorry for him but not very.

I declined pudding, and he invited me to go to Italy with him. He felt I would love Italy, had I ever been?

I was out of there by 9.15, hiding in my car as he walked past, me on the phone to Swift, in desperate need of someone human to wash my brain with sane talk.

The next day he rang to apologise.

'Which bit are you apologising for?'

'The crying.'

The crying had been the one bit I hadn't minded.

It seemed clear to me that I preferred my own alcoholic.

Chapter Nineteen

Australia, March–April 2007

On his forty-eighth birthday – 26 March 2007 – a year to the day after the fit in Oxford – Robert was in hospital, and, after some thought, I visited him. He was thin beyond belief. Five foot eleven, seven and a half stone. His hair was long down his back; his beard was scraggy, his cheeks sunken, his skin waxen and yellow, like, though I didn't recognise it then, a dead person's. His pale eyes were enflamed. He looked like Franz Liszt painted by El Greco, or a very old candle, or someone dug out of a peat bog where everything had kept on growing after death. I hadn't seen him since that time on the street when he had told me he wasn't fit to be seen by me. He'd been in a coma, and had not been expected to come round, but he did. He'd been expected to die, but didn't. This I heard secondhand.

He heard me coming and recognised my footsteps.

'Oh my word,' he said, in genuine pleased amazement.

He thought it very kind of me to have come all the way to Australia to see him. We weren't in Australia. We were in Hammersmith. He was concerned about my luggage. Was it still at the opera house? Sydney, I assumed. He meant Covent Garden. Apparently I had left it there after a row we had in the bar. We'd never been there together.

He offered to send a taxi for it. I said it wouldn't be necessary. Had I come straight from the airport, he wondered. Where was I staying?

'At home,' I said. 'This is Charing Cross Hospital.'

Amazement again. Why was he in hospital? He thought it was a hotel. George Best had been coming in every day for a few rounds of backgammon. Debussy had been by as well. There was a tournament. Spike Milligan had accused Robert of cheating in the final.

Nobody would tell me what was going on, because I was not Robert's next of kin. They would only tell him. But he was in Australia playing backgammon with George Best, so what good was telling him?

I had carefully not made myself next of kin. I knew all about co-dependence now. I knew now that alcoholism is a weird, sneaky trickster, where rule number one of being anywhere near the afflicted is to act against your natural instincts. He's ill? Don't look after him. Don't even feed him or put his T-shirt in with the rest of the washing. You love him? Don't carry out any of the normal acts of love. Respect him by leaving him the space to see clearly what he has become, and only then can he learn, and know, and seek help. So I was not next of kin. I was just the ex-ish girlfriend who they'd rung because he gave them my number.

I made a list:

- Alcoholic neuropathy: nerve damage to the extremities, when your feet cling to the ground and your knees circle like the little jointed wooden mannequin on elastic strings; push a thumb up under the wooden base and you topple, but your feet don't want to move. That was him at the bus stop, him on the landing saying his legs didn't work.

- The fall on the icy night in January 2004. Was there a fight, as he said at first? I still don't know. The triple fracture, the Captain Scott heroics in the snow.

- Pancreatitis: the retching and vomiting all night because you can't produce enzymes properly, so you don't digest food and don't get your vitamins and minerals, you are malnourished, you are sick.

- Hepatitis: your liver swells and hurts and can't process the toxins with which you are flooding it. You turn yellow. Next stop cancer or cirrhosis.

- Insomnia. Not surprising, but don't underestimate it.

- Ditto tinnitus

- Depression. Strange how we forget that alcohol is a depressant. Because it is so very cheerful in the beginning, and we can take it at face value for years and years. Strange how we forget how hideous depression actually is, and how we can fail over and over again to put two and two together.

- Epilepsy.

Today there was something new: Wernicke-Korsakoff Syndrome. Imagine being blind drunk, legless, slurring, you can't remember a thing the next day. Imagine that the wind changes, and you're stuck like that. If you don't eat, but drink vodka instead, for months on end, you starve. Vodka is not a balanced diet. The lack of vitamins, particularly vitamin B, damages your brain and nervous system. Your walking, movement, eyesight, speech and memory begin to fail. If you do it long enough you go mad. You don't know where you are or what you're doing. You are at the mercy of fate, defenceless, hopeless, starving, raving, on the streets of the city. Your legs fold beneath you, words fail in your mouth, thought flails in your mind. You froth and fall. Anything could happen to you.

You could die. You would die. Thousands of people die every year of drink and its sicknesses.

His good neighbours had found him naked, shit-stained, bony, comatose and foetal on the stairs, and had called an ambulance. They did this twice a day for a week, because the hospital wouldn't or couldn't hold him, and he would hobble home. In the end, because you can't be sectioned on private property, the doctor upstairs (I don't know her name, but if she's reading this: thank you, and I hope you got the letter he left for you) escorted him out into the road so the police could section him and take him back yet again to A&E, which forced the hospital to keep him in for long enough to notice that he wasn't just drunk, he had this condition, where the wind had changed.

Under the new wind, his mind struggled like the God of the Old Testament to separate the light from the darkness, to bring order to chaos. The tough, rational brain, longing for order, tried desperately to do its job: to make sense. The brain deprived of normal memory finds snatches of memory within itself, and patches them together into something that looks vaguely like a possible truth – and then believes it. It invents what it longs for, out of whatever is to hand. It's called confabulation: putting the stories together.

*

I visit again. He calls to greet me before I am visible. His father is a Parisian taxi driver. He had dropped Debussy off!

'Paris? We're still in Hammersmith, darling.'

'What?' he cries, astounded. He's forgotten that he can't remember. 'What do you mean?'

'You're not in Paris. Any more than you were in Australia last week.'

'I was in Australia? Oh, no. Wasn't I?'

'No.'

He laughs, remembering, and says, 'Well, at least I'm getting closer to home . . .'

My own knees give way a little with tenderness at this. I remember how much I adore him. Remember – the opposite of dismember. To put back together the parts and recreate the whole.

We talk about his condition, and about what's happened. I steer his stories towards consensual reality. He warms up, as it were; reconnects, slowly. Then after about an hour of pretty normal conversation, he says, 'Anyway, how's your son? Still playing the saxophone?'

*

The hospital staff have had trouble telling what is confabulation and what are more glamorous aspects of his former reality. Debussy, no. But Dustin Hoffman on Broadway, and the double first from Oxford? Actually, yes. But why should they be able to identify the scraps of truth? It's all peculiar enough at the best of times. Sitting in a hospital corridor I thought: we all confabulate. The difference is that most of us will put together more or less the same observations in more or less the same order and call it facts. But I know that I too have invented what I long for, or even what I can bear, out of whatever I had to hand.

I sit with him. We talk. I watch him sleep. He squints at me when he wakes. Late in the evening a doctor comes round, a young and pretty woman. She says, almost in passing, that he will be like this forever now, and probably never walk again.

Oh.

I cry, which means I don't watch his reaction. Then I look up, ashamed of the immediacy of my selfishness, and take his hand. What does this mean to him? I don't know if it has been said before. Is this how they tell you something like this? It doesn't seem proper. Don't you get a special appointment in a little room; someone saying, 'Sit down, we have bad news'?

And yet a doctor has just said it.

Does Robert know?

218

It seems at the same time desperately serious and utterly unreal.

'Why are you crying?' he asks, sympathetically. He has already forgotten what the doctor just said.

I cry more.

If the lorry driver I yelled at on the way home is reading this, I'm sorry, it wasn't your fault.

I just started immediately on the important job of confabulating a reality in which the fact of his psychosis and disability could co-exist with some sense – any sense! – of things being somehow bearable.

Of course that's what I did. It's what people do.

I was getting there, too.

*

I read up. The overall message was vast, complex, and either contradictory or so dependent on variables that it had to be presented that way. Whatever. It scared the daylights out of me.

Wernicke-Korsakoff's Syndrome consists of two stages: Wernicke's Encephalopathy – disorientation, confusion, mild memory loss; the person being very underweight, involuntary jerky eye movements or paralysis of the muscles that move the eye; poor balance; followed by Korsakoff Syndrome – severe loss of memory. Loss of initiative. Confabulation: experienced by a small number of Korsakoff sufferers. Difficulty in acquiring new information or skills . . . personality changes . . . apathy, lack of emotional reaction. Not knowing they have the condition. Believing that their memory is functioning normally. Problems with concentration, planning, making decisions and solving problems.

What's happening is that the front of the brain is shrinking. Thiamine is used in the formation of blood vessels; without it they begin to leak. High doses of injected thiamine can reverse the encephalopathy in a few days, otherwise permanent brain damage can result, and can be fatal. Where it's untreated, or treated late,

219

Korsakoff syndrome usually develops. Blood leaks from capillaries in the parts of the brain that form new memories and control muscle co-ordination. If the leaking continues the patient becomes unconscious. The leaked blood then clots and, as it solidifies, damages the brain tissue around it.

I had written in my *Book of the Heart* about the physical sensation of the heart sinking; of people claiming to have felt it. I had not felt it before, myself.

Initially I took away three simple messages. His memory is physically filled with clotting blood. Those failed hospital visits where thiamine was not given were several of his nine lives. And the phrase 'what level of recovery (if any)'.

And then others leapt out, alarming, sometimes contradictory, specific to him and to how I was going to respond.

'They may need weeks of practice to learn simple information. For example, if they move to new accommodation, the route from their bedroom to the kitchen.'

'Sufferers may have difficulty in telling whether two songs are the same or different.'

'If left to themselves, they rapidly sink into silence.'

'Testing carried out immediately after detoxification can give misleadingly pessimistic results.'

'Long-term residential care.'

'Traditional therapeutic alcohol treatment regimes involve . . . exactly the skills in which the brain-damaged person may be deficient.'

'For some people [alcoholism] ceases to be an issue as they forget their need to drink.'

I think about how funny he would find that. I wonder if he will ever find things funny again.

But he joked about being closer to home now he thought he was in Paris. I read somewhere that being able to take the piss out of yourself is a sign of certain sanity.

The disease had come roaring out of the emotional, the moral, the behavioural, and lurched into view as the unmistakably physical. Everything that had been creeping around was now out in the open; all those symptoms added up. Now he's not just unsteady, he's ataxic. He's not just shaky, he has peripheral neuropathy. He's not just thin, he has malnutrition. He's not just drunk and a pain in the arse, the capillaries of his brain are leaking blood which is clotting in his memory. Wernicke-Korsakoff Syndrome. He was in a coma. He's in a hospital gown. It's real.

And again, thank God, at last, I was not alone with it.

*

Lola and her friends were watching *The Notebook*, a film in which the heroine has amnesia. By the end of each day, for about five minutes, she remembers her true love, and everything he has done for her. They are together and joyous. Then the next morning she's forgotten him again. The girls all came out of Lola's room weeping.

I thought, *In the past six weeks I have had to tell Robert three times that he left me, because he didn't remember. Is that not tragic?* I can't say this to the young girls: 'Hey, looky here, it's real.' I don't want them to know it's real.

Each time I told him he left me he was outraged. 'No!' he cried. 'Why would I do that? I didn't do that! I love you!'

*

The two most stupid things Robert ever said to me were: 'You were never in love with me, were you?' and 'Did I hurt you much?' Oh yes and – 'I know exactly what's going on, I know what to do.'

I thought he was dying, all the time. Why? Because I always thought my father was dying, with his heart problems. I longed for Robert's death, and I dreaded it. I planned for his funeral as a girl plans for her wedding – 'Pale Blue Eyes', I thought, Velvet Underground. Joni Mitchell's 'Trouble Child'. And '*Der Leiermann*'

221

from Schubert's *Winterreise.* And him playing of course: the Chopin. At last everyone would remember how they loved him. I saw them flee from him that sometime did him seek. I heard them, reluctance in their voices as they sensed the vampire in him, and retreated . . . And they would see how I suffered. Ah, the self-pity! There was a lot of that too.

*

I never saw that young doctor again – and just as well. In the course of conversations with other doctors, it became apparent that her view was not necessarily correct. The consensus was that there could be no definite prognosis, yet. Whatever was going to happen would take a while. Robert wasn't going anywhere immediately, and when he did it would be to a long-term NHS residential rehab centre, probably for six months.

Oh, OK. That's good, isn't it? I mean, better?

I picked up my confusions, my fear and guilt and helplessness, and went to my other life, in Italy. I felt there was nothing I could do for him. What good had I actually done him so far? Judging by results?

I can't pretend it was a rational decision. Some kind of extraordinary curtain was drifting across my mind, hiding him from me, due to my fundamental inability to take on board what was happening. Fear. His face like a blank ecstatic monk, gentle and completely ignorant of consensual reality. Self-starvation. Crooked, unworking legs. The state of his flat, after he was taken away to hospital. Bottles and shit again; maggots and fag ends. Blood dried up in the basin. Puddles of what turned out to be, probably, ancient vomit. Food that I had given him months before rotting in the fridge.

Walk away from who you love. Leave them, literally, in their own mess. A man who cannot deal with his own mess is going to remain forever in his own mess.

Really?

But he'd said, 'At least I'm getting closer to home.'

But.

All right: other things and other people exist, apart from Robert. Two days after I visited him on his birthday, my daughter was in A&E at the same hospital. She went on her own, without ringing me, having what she thought was one of her bad asthma attacks. But it wasn't asthma – her peak flow and oxygen levels were fine. It was a panic attack. She'd never had one before. I did not want her having panic attacks. I did not want her taking herself alone to A&E. She was fourteen.

And, three sets of friends and their children were due to visit in Italy and had bought their flights, including Israeli friends on the only visas they would get that year. It was ten days. It was all arranged. Easter. Daughter. Family.

So Lola and I went to Italy, and in the meantime friends came and, God bless their sweet hearts, helped Robert. I don't know who emptied the months-old piss from the vodka bottles, threw out the rank piles of newspaper, cleaned off the layers of filth. No cleaning company would touch it. But someone brought some tea-lights and lined them up on the mantelpiece, thinking I suppose that he might go back there, and wanting it to be nice. Hopeless kind gestures fluttering in the face of this catastrophe. And then someone took away his furniture – a table, his desk, a trunk full of letters and old programmes, the sofa on which Truncheon and I had slept – in a van and put it into storage. His piano had moved in to Bush Hall. The grandfather clock had disappeared, nobody knew how or when. He has friends apart from me.

Leave him to it, the small voice said.

So I went about my business. In a daze. Thinking, *Where is his sweet mind? What the hell is going to happen? What am I going to do about it?*

One thing at a time. That's what you do.

I rang John and Kath in Wigan from a sunny Italian courtyard.

I hadn't told them earlier because nothing seemed definite enough to tell, and it seemed too horrible to inflict on them when there was nothing they could/would have done about it anyway, other than suffer from the knowledge, and because I was struggling with my responsibility here. I was staring at a dense rosemary bush when I told Kath what was happening with Robert, harshly, thinking it would be better than faffing about. Looking back, I frightened them, and I am sorry. I should have gone up there and told them in person. I had a tendency to think people are stronger than me, and know what I know, and more besides. And of course that's not always the case. So there was John, in Wigan, hearing this news third-hand, at a distance, about his only son, his genius boy. Would John have gone to Robert if he could? Would it have helped? Who knows. One of the first things I learnt reading Narnia under my father's piano was Aslan's great piece of wisdom: you don't get to know what would've happened. John couldn't travel and that was that. And there was Kath, who loved Robert (though he couldn't see it, thus denying himself a measure of parental solace he could've benefited from), having to find a way to support John. And me, in Italy, trying to be straightforward, and so concerned with myself and Robert that I forgot to be kind to these old people. John's health was not great – he was a huge smoker, and a depressed man – and this was I'm pretty sure the biggest shock of his life. Though his initial response was, apparently, 'Trust Robert to get something Russian.'

This gift of time allowed me to think, but I knew already that, whatever happened, I was going to look after Robert. It would be a challenge to my creative skills to romanticise being a carer; and to my personal abilities to make the adjustment from caring about somebody emotionally to caring for them physically. But actually, it's the same damn thing. And anyway I'd made that decision years before, in the little black car on the A29.

Part Four

2007–09

Chapter Twenty

Camden Town, April–November 2007

By the time I got back from Italy, Robert had returned to consensual reality. After all that, it took only six weeks or so. We spoke on the phone. He was in Camden, and I was to visit.

I felt relieved, disbelieving, buffeted and weirdly disappointed. If I'd known he would be back so soon I would have spent more time with him in Australia and Paris, in that semi-real land where shafts of clarity pierce the murk and join up to make unexpected patterns. I'd have asked impertinent questions, taken notes, and made friends with the madman he was then, in that place. But I had been accustoming myself to the terrifying possibility – probability? – that he was staying there. Now, in my relief, it didn't occur to me that he might have left some of himself behind. I hadn't thought how changeable things still might be. I was in yet another new land I knew nothing about.

This rehab was in a Victorian house with disability-friendly annexes and a paved yard out the back, but it was again the world of duty managers and overhead lighting and encouraging slogans, with cleaning rotas in Comic Sans stuck up on corkboard in the kitchen and separate cupboards protecting people's instant coffee and Cup-a-Soups. I walked through. The paved garden was full of thin people, smoking under a tree in blossom. I knew their expressions, if not their faces, from Clouds and Max Glatt. They eyed me and directed me through to the lounge, from sunny day into dimness. There he was, opposite the door, sitting on a low institutional couch, a walking frame at his side.

He stood up, and I started crying. I hadn't known he'd be able to stand up. He talked. He was sane and sober. He hugged me. My head in his neck. He was sane. He was sober. I made a promise then, in my heart: I love you and I will stay with you forever.

I could fill the next ten pages with those words. SANE and SOBER. SANE and SOBER. SANE and SOBER and HERE and ALIVE. I want to do that joy justice – to give it as much space and attention as I've given to all the pain.

In another blue file under the piano, I find another batch of Significant Event Sheets. Among them I find that on 24/04/07 his 'significant event or general mood of the day (Please be specific)' was 'The visit of my "girlfriend" – she is ex, or semi, non. I'm not quite sure. We had a very lachrymose session. Extremely upsetting for both of us. I insisted on her telling me about the last few months – many things have been forgotten due to chronic inebriation. Very painful but potentially creative. Crying. Lots of deep breaths. The panicky feelings remain. I have to come to terms with the damage that alcohol has caused both to me and to her. Being so drunk I distanced myself from my eight-year-old son. I just hope to God that I can fix the damage caused and for him not to feel alienated from his father.'

'Could you just write down what happened when?' he asked me. 'Because I can't really remember.'

I leapt at the opportunity, and produced an efficient timeline of his life since divorce. Writing his own life story at Clouds, he'd got factual details wrong – the year of his divorce, the number of breaks he had in his leg. He had become his own unreliable narrator, which was unsurprising but also oh fuck. How do you tell someone that, when you're trying not to be controlling and also trying to work out whether you're going to have to compensate for brain damage? I was trying to find the truth in memories of things Robert had hardly registered as they happened. Later, I would be in charge of all his old love letters, his father's LP collection and his rehab papers, but already I was becoming arbiter of his truth; editor of his version. Questions re-emerged which have been on my mind since I first wrote my grandmother's biography; about truth, fiction and memory and the relations between them; about the writer's responsibility.

What I really needed was to settle myself, to take nothing for granted, to protect myself and Lola, and take care of him too. But we were all over the place. I was overwhelmed by this unforeseen possibility of survival, another chance at life – hasn't he used up his nine yet? I felt unbalanced. I came home wanting to splash about in SANE and SOBER and HERE and ALIVE. Instead, while he returned to the life of Group and Assignments and Significant Events, I wrote and wrote and wrote: for self-definition, I think, in the face of his chaos. 'I became overgrown with self-pity,' I wrote, 'looking in the wrong direction, caught in the thicket like any rescuing prince, snagged with the thorns, confused, fighting the wrong battle, no direction home. Every patch I clear in my mind grows back more tangled; a hydra thicket, out to get me. It never loses. It never goes away. The one I am trying to rescue never escapes. But is that him, or is it me?'

*

Robert was to be in Camden for six months, till November 2007, alongside these people with whom he had everything and nothing in common. The Prof, yet again. They liked him. He liked them. I liked them. I offered him country-and-western lyrics; Townes Van

Zandt's lines about drowning tomorrow when you cry too many tears for yesterday. Someone printed it out and stuck it up in the kitchen. As Robert wrote in his notebook: 'Nothing that comes from the outside can cure us, because the problem is inside us. Only the things we do will bring recovery.'

Among his papers I found a battered envelope from that time in Camden, with this written on it:

Robert's Wishlist

To never again pick up a drink

To regain mental + physical health

To rid myself of envy, bitterness, jealousy and resentment

To have a mutually fulfilling rewarding relationship with my son and for him to be a happy, fulfilled and eventually rounded man

Ditto with ~~Louisa Young~~ my father

Ditto with Louisa Young

Ditto with all the people I love and am fond of and even one or two who I don't actually like, for the benefit of others with whom we are mutually connected.

To write beautiful music, perhaps eventually for the concert hall but to become more successful than before in the media milieu

For our planet to become a more peaceful and beautiful place

For Wigan Rugby League Club to regain their former status as the world's premier club side.

This makes me laugh – not Wigan to win the rugby, though that was a sign of life – but my being crossed out and then added in again, after John. I think Robert was less worried about losing me than about losing his dad. I hope it meant that he believed in us. Though later, reading through the new file of rehab papers, I saw it was more complex than that.

I found these papers almost unbearable when I first looked at them. I stopped and cried. I scurried from page to page, looking for themes, for chronology. I cross-referred to my own diary. Sheets flew across the desk; forms filled in in his spidery handwriting, crossings out, parentheses; folded pages with his nickname for the counsellor written on the back: 'The Marchioness of Istanbul'. I typed it all up – I couldn't tell how to use his words until I saw them out of his potent handwriting and into print. This turned out to involve a curious and painful physical/emotional overlap, as his words from long ago went through my eyes into my brain and came back out through my fingers, my physical means of production – which recalled the means of *his* production, his fingers on his piano keyboard, and his 'first language', how he expressed himself. I type up so much sweetness, so much pain and physical frailty, so much concern for his fellow recoverers and gratitude to his friends. And I type up myself: almost continuously coming through as a negative.

Here is a simple line diagram of a head with a sausagey brain coiled up inside. Robert has added a moustache, a blacked-out tooth, stubble, and an earring, for some reason. (He didn't wear an earring – earrings on men were another fucking poncey southern bourgeois affectation.) It's a self-portrait. On the right, he has written a list of positives; on the left, negatives. I am not on the right among 'passing moments of happiness like watching the sun come out, the clouds, wildlife', 'a stimulating conversation' and 'friends'. I am on the left, between 'increasing angst about practical issues' and 'fear of not being able to work again'.

I type out: 'The relationship with my girlfriend is in tatters. Not sure that either of us has the strength to resurrect it (and sometimes not even the desire). It has either come to an end, or is going through a non-existent patch. I decided not to have any contact with her except by post until the completion of my first three months at Herbert House. We love each other, always will, I think, in a way, always did, in a way, since we met when we were nineteen. But the effects of my drinking have had a wearing effect on her and I think it's best, as does she, to call it a day. Don't get me wrong she can be a real pain in the arse even when not provoked. I started going out with her when I was drunk. However I still have some good friends who can be supportive.'

Of whom I was apparently not one.

Reading these papers from 2007 for the first time, my own 2007 emotions leapt to life again, as if he was still up there smoking in that Camden yard. I wanted to head straight up there and have it out with him. 'A wearing effect'? It makes our romance sound like a trying attempt to get through to the tax office; an uncomfortable pair of shoes during a longer-than-expected social occasion. 'Best call it a day' is not how my love for him would end. And did his vodka-drenched blood-clotted thiamine-deprived brain cells miss the fact that his intention and desire to get sober was the mainstay of my being with him at all? And while I don't deny my capacity to be a pain in the arse, at what stage, ever, in any addict's life, were they not being provoking?

Then, as usual, I rationalised. He was a brain-damaged man in the early stages of understanding the effects of addict behaviour. He wrote of still being 'pretty wrecked, very nervous, unstable, very stressed, full of regrets, remorse, embarrassment, fear, pessimism, neuroses, obsessions, thoughts of suicide, thoughts of leaving here and drinking which may well lead to death. There is no anaesthetic, little protection.' And also of how 'there is now much more than a glimmer of optimism, of hope. I'm slowly gaining strength – inner strength, not relying on people so much – as I did on Louisa last time round.' He couldn't yet bear to listen to music. When bad things happened, bad thoughts, it tore him apart. But, he wrote too of his genuine belief that 'when, rather than if, I get that poison out of my mind I will be able to enjoy my own well-being, to enjoy all the wonderful things that are out there. I want to be a good father, I want a fulfilling relationship and friendships. I want to have the hunger to learn, to enjoy life instead of being trapped in that dark ominous frightening tunnel.'

I had to be – I was! – grateful that he was able to do any of this.

His significant event of 5 May, he writes, was seeing me. I remember that night. We tiptoed round each other with great kindness. His fears about his physical well-being and mental health were well-founded. On top of the usual symptoms, his speech was slurred, and he had developed accommodation lag which, along with dizzy spells and his weak legs and limp, meant that he had fallen over several times. I didn't understand why he couldn't see that now he was sober, for the first time in years there was a possibility of these other problems being overcome. 'The atmosphere is difficult when we only have three hours,' he wrote, 'both of us self-conscious – knowing that if we embark upon analysis we don't have the time or emotional energy to sort anything out. We love each other a lot but there are big issues, big problems (not just my alcoholism but of course that has played a major destructive role). Lonely, remorseful now. Lonely with other (nice) people around is not nice. Sad that Louisa had to leave so soon. Sad that it has been and will be a long, drawn-out process. Angry at myself for abusing her love. Ashamed even.'

He was frightened too about his father's health, and the alienation that had grown up between the two of them, knowing that 'my recent demise has unquestionably had an effect on his clinical depression'. Homesickness was strong in him at this time. One evening returning to Camden Town, he took a cab. 'The driver had a very familiar, very strong accent – totally shocked, confused: WIGAN! Too many feelings to go into.' He rang home, and Kath answered. 'I tried to be polite and nice. Mentioned that I may come up at some stage. She said, "I don't want you staying up all night with your friends" etc. Cold inconsiderate shitty non-comprehending. I talked to him. He sounds weak – trembly voice, confused, old.'

And there was a terrible echo of his separation from his father in the situation with his son, with whom he had not been able to be in touch. 'I've checked that he's OK but I am increasingly petrified by the idea that I'll lose him. He loves me, I love him more than anyone on earth but I've not been mentally or physically fit enough to see him. I feel so guilty and sad and remorseful that as we speak I am due to my alcoholic state incapable of having any positive influence on him. I hope to God (despite being an atheist), that I can resurrect our good relationship. This situation, excuse the pun, is crucifying me.' Kath sent Robert some photos. As a little child, Jim had been blond: now he was dark-haired. Robert was shocked. 'I feel as if I've lost him. I'm daunted by trying to rebuild.'

I felt that Robert should *always* see his son, whatever his own health; that Jim would want to see him, and needed to see him and know him, and that was what mattered. Jim's mother and her family had been saintly in keeping the channels open and making contact possible. What I didn't get at the time was how deeply Robert felt the pain of having to part from Jim, and his terror that he would drink after having left him – and sobriety *has* to be the alcoholic's first goal, because without it there is nothing. In fact, loving Jim and wanting to do right by him kept Robert alive and sober more than anything else.

And he was worried about money. He had royalties coming in, and savings, but chaos ruled: a savings account had gone missing, tax was unpaid, his rent was still going out and things were a mess. More to the point, he had a proud loathing of not earning, and of not working. Work was where he had always proved himself, and coming back to reality he feared that he wouldn't be able to work, creatively, and that even if he could he wouldn't be able to handle the stress of the world of work, and that even if he did nobody would want him; nobody would forgive him. (See p. 389 for more of Robert's own words from this period.)

What I hadn't noticed, because I was so deep in the woods, was that because I had been aware of Robert's problems for years, I was almost inured to them, whereas Robert, coming out of his drunken blindness, was seeing clearly for the first time what he had been like, and what he had done. 'Is part of my insanity the belief that my addiction is my only problem?' asked his workbook. 'Addiction was in many ways avoidance of other problems,' he answered. 'Inferiority, insecurity, confusion as to who I was or why I was here. Indefinable fear.' No wonder he was terrified now, looking on his works and despairing.

*

On 20 May, something magical happened. We went out for the day, to Rousham, a quiet country estate that he used to visit from Oxford, a bucolic heaven. We sat on the stile at the end of the lane, his sticks leaning against the wooden fence, looking over the fields and the parkland with its great cedars and brown cows, the shafts of sunlight lying across the landscape like blessings. And we sat on the bench in the corner of the old wall, by the river, where the branches hung low, their leaves dappling in the light. And in the folly, like a tiny temple. We learned together how to walk together, him needing help but not wanting to lean; me wanting to help but not wanting to carry him or look – for his dignity and for mine – as if I were carrying him, arm in arm on the paths of the formal garden, trying ways of taking the weight between us. I remember the utter beauty of the English summer's day, the weight of the leaves on the trees, the grey walls and green lawns. The sense of the wreck of a man returning from somewhere terrible; a quiet, chastened, wounded tough man beginning to conceive of the existence of healing and forgiveness. It felt like the bloody First World War, like 1919. In my mind, in my heart, it was at that moment, at that stile, that we got back together. Of course it was. We kissed. If you kiss, you're together, right?

'Louisa and I didn't really discuss the state of our relationship,' he wrote, 'just enjoyed the day. Exquisite sun. Happy – being in a beautiful place having a great time with my (?) girlfriend. Sad – very sad – to leave her tonight but will see her next week. Enjoying having felt happy – yes happy!'

Renewal approached me. Images I had found when I was writing *The Book of the Heart* crept into my mind: washing the heart, baptising it in a clear flowing river. Upspringing. Meadows. Sweet waters. Moss. I listened to Al Green singing 'Take Me to the River', washing me down. Renewing and refreshing. I dreamt about a green heart with little new green leaves, and heard the line from *The Wasteland* about coming back from the hyacinth garden, your hair wet and your arms full. Perhaps in the midst of winter I *would* find there was within me an invincible summer; perhaps we *could* do to each other what spring does to the cherry trees. That was the day when it began to roll off me, and I began to think all things were possible. Perhaps I would be able to trust my own judgement again one day. My own judgement which said: He is really doing this.

First I wanted to see less of him: 'She wants more defined temporal limits – because I'm more together, looking (a bit) healthier – it confused her (her remark!),' he wrote. Then he wanted to see less of me: 'We went up to Parliament Hill and sat over the view, seeing the windsheer under the clouds, and talked. I mentioned that it was going to be easier not to see her until at least the end of the first three-month phase here – no phone calls etc. She agreed, we went out for a meal and just as she dropped me off she said "I still fancy you, you know". Thanks a fucking bunch. Turmoil, anger, great sadness, despair but strange form of relief.'

We were trying, we really were.

He couldn't go places on his own. But the relief – my God, the relief – that he was not after all a textbook WKS case. It is hard, even now, to estimate what damage was left by the WKS. He was not as articulate – at least on the page – but then his peripheral neuropathy made it physically difficult and shaky for him to write, and he was constantly tired. His dates are all over the place. This seems to me some kind of metaphor for his state of mind – confabulating, though on so much lighter a level. Looking for order because he knows it is necessary. Even when it is not entirely accurate.

But he couldn't play the piano. 'The brain is telling the fingers what to do,' he wrote, 'but they won't do it.' He tried to play piano duets with a friend, a fairly capable amateur, and just couldn't play any more. 'It was one of the most important things in my life.' The neurologist said there was nothing she could do about his deteriorating condition. 'As you can see,' he wrote, 'I can't even write properly now. Never mind speak or walk or see properly. The condition is incurable. Will never get better . . .'

Where the SES asked how he dealt with his feelings, he wrote: 'I can't.'

*

In August, his Target was to 'ascertain exactly what nature of relationship will exist with Louisa, now that the amorous aspect has, we assume, cessated.'

Specific needs/concerns #4 Relationships/social: On-off girlfriend – friends since 17, want to retain friendship

Action strategies/resources: Talk about feelings and issues, and explore legacy for future relationships.

Desired outcome: To have a good relationship with myself. To have a close loving and supportive relationship with my son and others I love. To make amends where appropriate, and where not, let go of regrets. To be aware of beliefs and behaviours that do not help me.

Legacy! 'Future relationships'? With WKS, remember – though I didn't remember – 'the person may show . . . lack of emotional reaction'.

I was often confused, reading these papers. His moods flung around the place like a pinball, pinging off all and sundry. One day he's writing 'Happy? I can hardly spell it'. And then soon after: 'Up at 7.30 – saw a robin feeding her young!' or 'Determined. No reason I can think of – oh yes! I want to live, and live well' or 'My significant event 2 blackbirds (adult male and female) in the kitchen on the floor during group', or 'I've laughed, I've cried, I've smiled, I've frowned, I've skipped + jumped, I've fallen over flat.' What I didn't understand was the phenomenal sensitivity of someone who is peering and blinking at reality for the first time after years in the dark, anaesthetised cellar of drunkenness. I gave him Oliver Sacks' books *The Man Who Mistook His Wife for a Hat*, and *Musicophilia*. I wanted, really to give *him* to Oliver Sacks. I thought they might be right up each other's streets.

I was in Italy. I had no idea the amorous aspect had 'cessated'. I was, I thought, being delicate. I thought we were good.

*

In September we went to see Bill Bailey at the Riverside studio. 'The good bits were mesmeric,' he wrote, and gave him 'hunger for creativity. Went with my ex-girlfriend and her daughter to whom I said "SORRY". "What for?" she said. "For not being as good a person as I am slowly becoming." . . . ?!'

I desperately needed him to be sorry. What I didn't see was that in wanting things from him I was, from his point of view, finding him wanting. The obsessive perfectionism which so illuminated his music could in other areas define anything less than perfect as worthless, humiliating even, and therefore jettisonable. By wanting things from him I was finding fault with him, which by the flawed logic he still lived in made *him* jettisonable. My desire was to support him while maintaining my integrity and independence. When I wrote letters about how much I loved him, my intention was happiness, possibility, togetherness. Now I see that any complaint, weakness, grief or anger on my part was unbearable to him. I was looking forward to the step where he could make amends. Christ, I dreamt of amends. But meanwhile, yes, I was still chopped liver.

But – he was not drunk. He *was* tough, determined and amazing. I hadn't failed him. He *was* coming back to life. Hope and relief were dancing about casting spangly fairy-dust all over everything. The grievances were details, because there was so much now to live for.

For six months he talked about his condition, in groups, in pairs, one-to-one with his counsellors. There was an acupuncturist for whom he started writing a piece of music, a fifteen-minute meditation piece, and he wanted his keyboard, could I bring it up (YES!!!!) and he wanted his assistant and he wanted a shedload of sushi and could I not bring him posh Duchy organic elderflower, it was a bit embarrassing, could I just bring Lucozade? Yes I could, and I could get over the fact that Lucozade bottles made me shake because they were what he used to hide his vodka in. He was really *really* doing it, a thousand per cent more than he had done at Clouds. He was talking, telling the truth, being straight, admitting failings, investigating complexities, making jokes, making friends. He sobered up, straightened up, stood up and strode about. His brain regained quite enough of its original intelligence and natural glory. He was gallant. And he *was* unbelievably fucking sorry.

Now, though, I can see how the things that were wrong with him gave him more pain as they became clearer, and as new ones rolled up. Not being able to play the piano, dear God. Because I was trying to stand back, I didn't see how much these things were hurting him. 'What has made it difficult to achieve your target?' reads one of his work-sheets. His answer? 'Fear and dread of the pain of complete self-honesty.'

'A terrible day,' he wrote, towards the end of his stay. 'One of the worst. I am so grateful to all here for turning my life around. There is respect, admiration and great fondness for the staff and some of the peers, past and present. Even at this increasingly delicate, frightening time I have to balance "here, now" with "what, when?". I have neglected one of the most important things: finding a safe, secure, conducive home. I am now almost in a state of panic. Seeing my flat – the bad state could be reversed, but not my feelings towards it. I'm going backwards tonight. But tomorrow I'll go forward again.'

I didn't know he was concerned about housing. He could stay with me – I thought he knew that. I thought he understood the basic premise which for me had always been the same, and which God knows I had told him often enough: sober, I love you; drunk, you're out. Sweet Twin; you're the love of my life; Evil Twin, piss the fuck off. (That's one of his. He could always be relied on for lucid profanity.) At the time I thought he wasn't asking to come home with me because he didn't want to, because he needed to stand on his own two ataxic feet. Now I see that he didn't know that I wanted him home. I didn't get it through to him. And was that because of alcohol/WKS-related memory and understanding issues? Or my failure to be clear? Was it residual muddiness from years of him not saying what he meant, and me trying to make sense of that while also being a dingbat romantic? Or his exceptionally friable and delicate state as he began to approach reality for the first time in years?

The fact was, apart from Robert's illness, I had a secure life, full of things he did not have: a home, a close strong relationship with my child, good health, capable legs, an iron digestion, a good professional reputation, command of my faculties, own teeth and eyesight, a regular sleep pattern, earning power, friends, two parents, nice siblings. I was OK. He was not. I should not have waded in so early with my desire for him to make things right *re* me. I was not the most important thing – either for me or for him. Me needing him to appreciate all I had done and be really sorry his illness had hurt me so much was all well and good, but it was not the first step.

(Actually, it is Step Nine.)

Chapter Twenty-One

In meetings, Autumn 2007

He was coming out for the third time. It didn't look like a pattern. It didn't look like a minefield. We really were very very very very very very very very very very very optimistic.

He went for a few weeks to a dingy third-stage support place in a street called Lymesdale something (which he immediately christened Limescale Gardens), hated it, and came home, back to mine. On his first return, he sat down by the piano, ran his creaky neuropathic Wernicke-Korsakoffs (Wear Knickers Corsets Off, it had become by now) fingers over the keys, and said, with a rueful little snort, 'Well, just have to start again then.' That, for me, sealed the silent promise I'd made when he had stood up in front of the couch in Chalk Farm. That gallantry. That humility. That determination. You don't desert that.

*

I have been reading about the seven basic plots of western culture on which all stories are based, and came upon this one. It is a variation on tragedy, and it is called Rebirth.

A hero, as a young man, falls under the shadow of a dark power;

As the poison gets to work, it seems at first amusing and empowering; it takes some time to get the upper hand and to show its full destructive effect;

Eventually the darkness emerges in full force, plunging the hero into a state of total isolation;

This culminates in a nightmare crisis which is the prelude to the final reversal;

The hero 'wakes from his sleep', and is liberated by the power of knowledge and love.

In Tragedy, the hero, caught irrevocably in the dark side of himself, plunges on to final destruction. In Rebirth, light steals in on his darkness, and he can escape his frozen, lonely state and return to the world a transformed man.

Just thought you'd like to know Xx L

*

Both of us had to relearn help altogether – because it was all right to help him now he was a cripple, 'a fuckin' *RARS*berry', he said (cockney rhyming slang: raspberry ripple). He needed helping. Now, he was coming to terms with the paradoxes of early recovery, and with his disability. He had graduated from the walking frame to his two NHS sticks, metal and adjustable with grippable handles like shiny worn black vertebrae, on which he would ease himself about, crabwise. The piano was worse. He would sit, play a few bars, stop, crack or stretch his fingers, try again. He might look up and make a tragicomic face for my benefit, then glance down again, cough, and continue, more seriously, attentive, listening to himself and feeling his way. 'I must learn that,' he'd mutter, and sigh and push himself up, and go outside for a fag.

He accepted that he had lost his mind, and been psychotic; that he had been in a coma, that he nearly died – that his mind and body had done all this to itself. All his previous nadirs faded in the darkness of this one, and the miracle of surviving it. Gratitude rose off him like a summer mist, constantly: for not being dead, for being forgiven, for being loved still by people he'd assumed had forgotten about him, and by new people; for the burgeoning understanding he was getting about what had happened to him, and what his future could be.

We talked about loving yourself. Before, he'd sneered and made faces: 'Oh yeah, he *loves* himself, he thinks he's just *great*', as if he were still in a primary school playground. Now he could see that everyone can love themselves like they love other people, as an active thing. Be kind to yourself. Help yourself out. Or even just don't consistently undermine yourself and tell yourself you're shit and deserve everything you get; don't abuse and attack yourself. Don't fill yourself with poison and lock yourself in a dark room and starve yourself. Understand yourself. Listen to your fears. Make yourself a cup of tea.

He could not believe his luck.

Sometimes he invited me along to an open AA meeting. I loved going, because the meetings were full of people who were getting better, clear-eyed cynics, former miserable wrecks, who had decided to save their own lives and were making a bloody good go of it.

Here is something I learnt at a meeting. Twenty years earlier the speaker, a healthy, cheerful woman, had been jobless, thrown out by her husband, banned from seeing her children, depressed, insomniac, skint, hopeless, sick, shameful, in constant pain. Suicidal. She thought it through and made her decision. She spent her last money on two bottles of gin. Back at the flat she was about to be kicked out of, she drank one bottle, and put the plastic bag it had come in over her head, and tied it, and prepared to die. But through the clear plastic she could see the other bottle, sitting on the side. The alcoholic in her couldn't just leave it there. She had to drink it. She tore the plastic bag off her head, drank the remaining gin till she passed out, was found by her flatmate and rescued. So, her compulsion to drink had saved her life.

This story confirmed to me, very clearly, that it is addiction itself before which we are powerless. If a person can't even kill themself because their addiction wants them alive to drink more, then what could I ever hope to achieve by trying to punch Robert's alcoholism on the nose?

Chapter Twenty-Two

London, Wigan, 2008–9

Sobriety clears the air – and then there are all the other things, plain as day, needing to be dealt with. Quietly and carefully, he did so. Officially, he lived in Wigan; half the time he was with me. There, he rented a room from his good friend Patrick the prison tutor, in a trad red-brick terraced house with the backyard and the alley behind. There Robert relaxed into the loving, piss-taking affection of the old friends he had neglected for years: his cousins, old school-friends, Gary the headmaster and his wife Julie, GFW, the cleverest man he ever knew, who delivers vegetables. He'd head off down the platform at Euston or Wigan North Western on his two sticks with his carry-all slung round him Sam Browne style, slowly and with a polite 'No thanks, I'm all right.' He had regular AA meetings in both locations. I wasn't looking them up for him, or encouraging him to go. He went on his own. I was saying 'I'll give you a lift!' and he had already booked a cab.

He was amazed that his friends still wanted to be his friends. He thought we wouldn't like him when he was sober. He thought he would be boring. We mentioned how boring his being drunk had been. I remembered Lisette saying years before: 'He's really boring when you're not in love with him.' He wasn't boring now.

He sat on the doorstep at home, or among the pretty flowerpots in the backyard at Patrick's, smoking in the sun, listening to birds singing, smiling. I'd go and stay, and he'd take me round the scenes of his childhood, pointing things out. We visited John and Kath, went to Southport; to Haigh Hall where we saw grebes dancing on the lake; up to White Coppice where you could get very easily on to a bit of moorland. He learned to text and started sending me sweet messages. Snatches of music started to reappear in the margins of the *Telegraph* sports pages. Guests took to visiting, at both houses. Songs reappeared on the piano. I'd been trying to write a funny feminist young adult book about a band called the Rodeo Dodos: it hadn't gone down well. I came back to an elegant melody on the piano stand, and these lyrics: 'On the day that your book was rejected, try not to be so dejected, don't retire to a farm, [Note Cole Porter reference, from 'Get Out of Town'] just remain really calm, for a publisher can't be too far awaaayy . . .' I'd written a song called 'Goldhawk Road'; he wrote out a piano arrangement for me, and did it in two keys, because he wasn't sure how I would want to sing it, or which guitar chords I could play. I didn't find it until later.

And best of all, he was now able to reconnect with his son, and the sweet loving friendliness between them rekindled.

His higher power, as required by AA, changed frequently. Group Of Drunks, his dad, music, nature, Black-tailed Godwit. He was a life force of the first order. People came to warm their hands on him, because he was a survivor.

He left Lola and me a note:

Dearest Audrey and Dearest Adders,

I would like to thank you both for making me feel so welcome here, so I will. Thank you. Don't forget to invoice (with VAT) the Kennet

Trust for your services. [There was a long-running joke that my dad paid Robert to keep me happy. And possibly vice versa as well.] Additional rewards will include an autobiographical first edition of Enid Blyton's 'Two Don't Do the Washing Up and One Sleeps in his Clothes', and a hydraulic smoke remover.

I realise that the next three weeks will be very tough for you without Count Coccium bestowing his love, warmth, wit and tautologous humour upon you, but the Northern Star will be watching over you both as you sleep with your aristocratic hot water bottles.

Love from Robert XX

N.B. No drawings
   (said John Thomas to Willy and Dick)

The tail of the S on drawings does stray perilously close to a phallic/bollock twirl.

Will, who had offered at Clouds two years before, now became Robert's sponsor. He lent him his 'Narcotics Anonymous Step Working Guide', a green plastic-bound A4 book, and together they went to meetings. Under Will's aegis, Robert set out on the task of Doing the Steps (the steps/questions of Narcotics Anonymous are effectively the same as those of Alcoholics Anonymous). This is a complex process of self-investigation, an incipient lifetime's habit, manifested in Robert's case by answering, at length in a ring-bound orange notebook, the series of intimate and demanding questions that each Step brings (see p.393 for more).

I didn't know he was doing it. I never even saw the notebook, and when I found it after his death, I read it with a potent combination of greed, fear and shame. I try to be a respecter of privacy, but by nature I always want to know. And when your beloved dies, you just want more of them – and here it was: a big, fat, engrossing, detailed, file of him. The steps are repetitive, banging home the messages of recovery in order to counteract the equally repetitive voices of addiction saying, 'Go on, have a drink.' (The same repetitiveness is why meetings work. You need to hear, think about, and do recovery, every day. Otherwise you will be back to drinking, every day. It's like the repetitiveness of taking prescribed medicine, eating meals, breathing. It's what you need.)

Above all, for me, the file was a tremendous gift: a tall clean window into the depths of what he had been trying to do, both without me and for me, in excruciating honesty. It was a conversation we started in his sobriety but had not got round to having in detail. We were going carefully there, because we had all the time in the world.

The first of the Twelve Steps is: 'We admitted that we were powerless over our addiction, that our lives had become unmanageable'. It's a considerable concept, and many addicts either never get past it, or return to it over and over. The first question, 'What does the disease of addiction mean to me?', brings up another of the great points of dispute: the word 'disease'.

Whether or not you think of addiction itself as an illness, it is always a secondary condition, arising from self-medicating for some previous damage or mental-health issue. Robert doubted it himself. He felt that addicts are greedy, self-obsessed people, always wanting more of a good thing, always wanting the good thing to be better, always trying to mollify or nullify the bad things; always trying to change the overwhelming cocktail of fear and self-disgust, to become more ambitious and hence successful, to improve relationships. The opposite happened.

'Many believe we are born addicts. This may be true,' he wrote. But he acknowledged that he repeatedly heightened the moment and blocked out emotional issues for years, 'until alcohol became the most important thing in my life. The love for my son, my girlfriend, friends was there but I could not demonstrate that love. Oblivion seemed to be the most conducive option. I went into an oblivion from which I very nearly did not emerge. I am an extremely fortunate, grateful person.'

'The healthier I become,' he wrote, 'the more I physically desire a drink. I have the desire now as I write; 9.30 pm, Monday 20th July. For me, there is little point reading or, ironically, writing about this. I need to hear it, see it, smell the suffering. [I have been] severely upset and shocked by what drink has done to those who have gone back out [resumed drinking], and it gives me a great sense of guilt to realise that I am getting better by seeing this suffering. However one of the most crucial aspects of AA is that aspect of fellowship – most members are happy that divulgence of their pain can help others.'

He had to look at how the self-centred aspect affected him, learning to differentiate between self-centredness and self-protectiveness. In a way, putting not drinking first is self-centred, but it is absolutely essential. He had learned that without sobriety he would be incapable of helping others, loving others, loving anything. 'As an active alcoholic,' he wrote, 'I loved too much, hated too much, and finally became almost totally numb. Now I have the ability to love a lot and the ability to tolerate. Of course there are many nasty sadistic selfish people around. Unlike Jesus, I do not forgive them for they know not what they do, but I try at least to understand what has led them to behave in such a fashion. Fear, I believe, answers many questions. It's always fear or desire. Or both.'

And soon the equally contentious 'spirituality' aspect comes up: 'How has my disease affected me spiritually?' Robert was the kind to snort at spirituality, but, made to think about it, he decided that music counted, 'which though written by man sometimes acquires a significance that transcends the human condition, with a directness and an almost mystical impenetrability'. Nature, too: 'the extraordinary powers of certain birds. No one can as yet understand why or how the arctic tern migrates from pole to pole or why a strand of the black-tailed godwit flies from Ottawa to Auckland'. Simon's farm in Somerset: 'Fields, trees, and of course birds. A beautiful place which provokes a sense of nostalgia for an emotion

I've never felt before, a sense of balance, of rhythm, the place where I get a sense almost of a God as I do not understand him.' And he did carry with him a prayer Granny Annie had written out: 'Courage for the great sorrows of life, patience for the small ones; and when you have laboriously accomplished your daily task, go to sleep in peace. God is awake.' (I borrowed this prayer, and gave it to my character Jack Ainsworth.)

The Step questions touch on aspects which had been part of his – and perhaps every addict's? – character forever. Obsession, for example. 'Have I recently been obsessed with a person place or thing?' the Step asks. 'Being obsessive,' Robert wrote, 'I'm obsessed by the fear of becoming obsessive. I know we should apply ourselves as rigorously to recovery as we did to drink. But I need to control my almost addictive attitudes – perfectionism for example. A piece of my music, a plate of my food, my relationships will never be perfect. When they disappoint, either myself or others, my senses of futility, underachievement + failure are so intense that I think I might as well have a drink.'

This too it would have been useful for me to know earlier. I find the idea of perfection nauseating, insane and somehow hilarious. But this does explain how I ended up being a negative, why he couldn't handle my needing reassurance.

And he wrote about being obsessed with two 'ridiculous quasi-adolescent "crushes" in AA'. He was 'shocked and confused, humiliated and amused by how I could have succumbed to this. The sick nervous tingle, the heavy breathing anticipating her arrival, the despair if she didn't appear. It seems risible now but at the time it was quite alarming, like being in my early teens again. I love and fancy my girlfriend, so why did this happen? Perhaps my sponsor had the answer – I'm "alive" again.'

That was a kick in the guts when I first read it. Much as he loved me, some lingering insecure bit of me never felt he was 'in love' with me. We had a fight about that once. Again, I was asking for reassurance, and he responded with anger at me for finding him wanting. Neither of us recognised the pattern, and I had to comfort him. Here, the sad romantic in me was jealous for the sick nervous tingle. Like being in *my* early teens again. However, Will was right. Sign of life. Suck it up, chopped liver.

But here he was, on paper learning and acknowledging that it was absurd to think he was better than 'an old former friend who would need to go to the off licence before going to the pub, to the pub before a restaurant, a pub after the restaurant, and an off-licence after the pub before home', or another who 'smoked weed, sometimes in the morning. I would comment on this, often with a drink in my hand. It didn't occur to me that my habit was just as bad if not worse.' It wasn't, in hindsight, 'fussy and obsessive' of me to mind his 'lack of cleanliness, lack of clean clothes'; and his ex-wife was not to blame for divorcing him. 'What I didn't realise,' he wrote, 'was that the behaviour, moodswings and illness caused by alcoholism are basically unhandleable.'

*

In spring, Robert went to stay with friends in France. It was so normal and yet at the same time so ambitious. I thought I would be in a state of constant alert and terror. But I wasn't. It was just . . . normal. A kind of normality that made me want to sing and dance and buy normality a crown of flowers. He took a nightie of mine to wear – an Egyptian galabeya – because he had no pyjamas. One evening I had come home to find that galabeya and my own nightie lying on the bed with their sleeves wrapped round each other in an embrace, and I had to sit on the bed, my heart full. Sweet Twin.

And I was working. My *Book of the Heart* had inspired a curious music performance piece involving early music, Hank Williams, Frida Kahlo, dance, surgery and high religious symbolism in the National Gallery in Dublin, so I was spending time over there. I was writer-in-residence running creative writing courses at two local secondary schools, through the charity First Story. And bits of journalism; an experimental radio drama for the BBC co-written with students; and my new novel: *My Dear I Wanted to Tell You*, set during the First World War, about love and truth and pioneering maxillo-facial reconstructive surgery.

*

And Robert's work on himself continued. 'Over what exactly am I powerless?' the book asked. 'I *was* totally powerless over alcohol,' he wrote. 'I could not talk to people, work, eat, without having a drink first. I thought I became alive, receptive, appreciative. In these early stages, alcohol is very effective, a good social creative drug. I envy people who can keep it like that. I couldn't. It gave me a purpose in life. That purpose, I see now, was to drink more.'

'I've done things while acting out on my addiction that I would never do when focusing on recovery,' the book says, unforgivingly. 'What were they?'

'Insulting people,' Robert wrote. 'Principally to show my verbal superiority, my sharp cutting sarcastic wit and my boldness. Pathetic. Succumbing to masochistic obsessions: drinking straight out of a vodka bottle knowing that more would merely rot my guts. Sticking fingers down my throat to wretch [sic] even more, knowing that I had wretched more than enough.

'I felt I must go through with it, because the initial feeling, I believed, was not only intuitive but honest, and had to be honoured, and anyway, being a masochist I would enjoy the guilt and relish the sordid memories. This is what I deserve. I am worthless. Or so I tell myself.'

'Do I become arrogant?' asks the relentless book.

'Yes,' he wrote. 'I thought that I was a better film, theatre + T.V. composer than most . . . I convinced myself and tried to convince others that something was their fault when it was often obviously mine. I assumed I was clever and sexy when I most probably came over as a drunk arrogant wanker.'

'Do I manipulate people to maintain my addiction? How?'

'Yes – convincing my girlfriend that I was sober. It has, in recovery, transpired that she knew I was still drinking—'

Not as such, darling.

'—but didn't want to admit it to herself never mind anyone else.' Really, that wasn't it. Was it?

'A classic case of co-dependency I assume . . .'

Or denial? God I could scream. Reading this, I wondered which of us had more to learn on those topics, co-dependency and denial.

'How has my addiction caused me to hurt myself or others?'

'I think I may have hurt quite a few women – I'll never know about many of them due to loss of contact. I presume I hurt my ex-wife but it's hard to tell. I was often drunk enough not to notice or care. I really don't know about my son. Perhaps I'll never know. Perhaps he'll never know or never want to know. My ex-girlfriend Anna. Daughter of an alcoholic who died of the illness and a heavy drinker herself. We were fine for a while. She loved me. But one day – sudden coldness. I hope I didn't hurt her but I think I must have done. Perhaps I might, however, in the long run, have done her some good. Louisa. I loved her but I loved alcohol more. I love her a lot more now. She put up with it for a long time—'

Put up with it . . .

'—but eventually to protect herself and her daughter I was thrown out. She loves me enormously but then perhaps loved what she wanted me to be, or rather what she remembered me as being. I hurt her a lot. However I now feel that I should be wary of succumbing to the notion of "compensatory love". Not to love in an apologetic way.'

I would have quite liked some compensatory love, actually.

On Boxing Day that year, he wrote me a letter. I found it nine years later, unfinished and unsent, in a box under the piano.

Coccium, Lancs
26/12/07
7.10am

Dear Hon. Audrey L. Young <u>M</u>A. Cantab, F.C.B [This M is underlined ten times, and surrounded with a charming circle of asterisks.
I think this may be a reference to the Oxbridge habit of giving you
an MA free (well, for a small fee) with your BA.]

Thank you so much for your <u>incisive</u> article in the National
Geographic magazine 'The Girth of the Kennet'. I could not but
help associating the fertile flow of the aforementioned river with
the resulting ornithological progeny (Thoby the Twite and Easter
the Egret to name but two) [This string of jokes is about the names
of members of my family, starting with my father, Wayland Kennet,
and following up with some siblings.] from these fecund loins.
(Excuse the protracted tautology – I must correct, find fault with,
improve and ameliorate my literary style with more semantic élan.)

To change the subject, I love you. You've seen nothing yet. Many
tenets are beginning to surface. I am not a 'new' person. Not 'born
again'. But . . .

Whilst listening to King's College Cantab Choir on R3 alone on
Christmas night, preparing a frozen Tesco Weightwatchers fish pie
with frozen soya beans and accompanied by a cold refreshing glass
of 2007 Tesco Sparkling water, I experienced an extraordinary
epiphany: admittedly for less than ten seconds, I liked myself,
approved of myself. I have always abhorred the notion, thinking it
narcissistic, self-absorbed etc. Transference, avoidance, esp. exaggeration of 'outward' emotions. Projected out and if in, contorted,
distorted. All this semi-sensical bullshit, if you can understand it,
goes a long way to explaining my dis-ease. <u>Enough.</u>

I have just finished talking with you ont' blower. Despite the
shock of hearing educated 'posh' – but actually not that posh (eg
'rarely' for 'really' doesn't 'appen) – I really (pronounced 'reeu-
ghleh') enjoy talking ~~to~~ with you – a delectable cocktail of warmth,

255

compassion, empathy, love (?!), didacticism with hardly a hint of
aristocratic austerity, dictatorial dominatrixdom (joke. – bad one)

It ends there.

Typing out his SESs, his stepwork, his grief, pain, fear and
courage, made me sad and angry, but typing out this letter I found
a big smile on my face, and my heart glowing.

As the Frenchman said, Happiness writes in white ink on a white
page. Here followed two years of smutched white-ink sober happiness – halcyon days! – when he was only a bit crippled, vulnerable,
but functioning, kind of normal. Happy. I think we were both
amazed about it. Cooking together. Working. Sitting there on the
sofa like a pair of Celia Johnsons saying, 'Happy, darling? Oh,
terribly.' My cold feet tucked under his skinny thighs. Dancing
together! He would put on Horace Silver, and stand, holding out
one elegant hand, about eye level. I would take it, and twirl and
jive around him as he stood there, one leg a little bent, leaning on
his stick and occasionally pulling me in. Collapsing in that laughter
which sometimes seems the whole point of human beings being
together. Resting our heads on each other and thinking oh thank
God, thank God. Him coming to pick me up from Luton airport
in a minicab, on his sticks, with flowers. Me trying to play the
piano. There was a Chopin nocturne I tried to learn for about a
year; I once played it all the way though, stumbling, counting,
restarting, forming each chord from scratch. It took me about two
hours, from beginning to end. 'Semi-quavers!' Robert would call
cheerfully down the stairs. I found little messages from him on the
sheet music: 'More regular here – otherwise sounding lovely! x'. It
didn't sound lovely at all. It didn't even sound like Chopin's descrip-
tion of how English ladies play his music – 'looking at their hands,
with great feeling, and many wrong notes'.

Happy! Yes. Two and a half years out of ten.

Chapter Twenty-Three

Happyland, March 2009

For his fiftieth birthday I gave him a signet ring. Lockhart is a clan, I thought – there'll be a crest. The jeweller had a vast two-volume book of all the crests for all the names. The Lockhart crest is, to Robert's amusement, a wild boar's head on a plate. I had a signet ring already, a present from my mother. I didn't have the Young family motto on it because the Young family motto is 'Be Right and Persist', and I didn't feel I should be encouraged in that. Also, as Baroness Alacrity pointed out, the sight of my whole family being right and persisting simultaneously would make strong men weep.

I knew something of the Lockhart clan. Robert, against whatever odds, and very indirectly, had cropped up in my *Book of the Heart*.

Robert the Bruce, 1274–1329, the King of Scotland who was famously saved by a spider, wanted his heart taken to Jerusalem after his death [by] Sir James Douglas, in a silver canister which he wore round his neck. On the way Douglas got caught up in the battle between the King of Castille and the Saracen King of Granada, during which, surrounded by the enemy and seeing that all was lost, he flung his precious necklace before him crying 'Onward as thou wert wont, I will follow or die!' Alas he died. The heart was found beneath his body, and taken up by Sir Simon Locard of Lee, who with others carried it back to Melrose Abbey in Scotland where after much dispute it was reburied in 1998. Locard changed his name in its honour – to Lockheart. He included in his coat of arms a fetterlock and a motto – *corda serrata pando*. It means 'I open locked hearts'.

Kathleen, my grandmother, was a Bruce. We used to have a sign up by the bath, typed long ago, wiggly from damp, and foxed: 'As this family is directly descended in two lines from Robert the Bruce, we should rescue spiders from a dreary end in the bath.' I liked to think of Robert's ancestor carrying my ancestor's heart across Europe.

'Did I open your locked heart, *darling*?' Robert says in his special affectionate piss-taking thespian voice, with a headtilt, and concerned eyebrows. '*Did* I?'

'Yes, *darling*,' I say. 'You did. And so did I.'

We had a party for that birthday at my parents' house. My nephew's band Penguin Café played, led by him on the Blüthner beneath which I used to read and eat almonds. There were speeches of a most gratifyingly sentimental kind. One of Robert's favourite exes, Beth, the one who broke his heart when he was twenty, sent a huge bunch of flowers but didn't come because she thought we were going to announce our engagement, and wasn't sure she could bear it. My dad had a lovely evening flirting with our friends, wondering whether or not they were his daughters, then went to bed at about midnight. Around one he got up again, dressed and came downstairs saying, 'Are we having a party? How wonderful, now who wants a drink? Robert? You haven't got one.'

Robert said, 'No thanks, Wayland, I'm still an alcoholic.'

'Doesn't that mean you want one all the more?' Dad said. This was not the first time they'd had this conversation. Robert did not forgot that he, for a while, had been the demented one.

Robert's present to me was a necklace made up of tiny multi-faceted Indian sapphires, all different colours. We had worked out a way whereby he could only buy me things I liked. We'd go to his friend Susan's shop. He'd sit in the cafe next door smoking, drinking quadruple espressos and reading the rugby league reports in the *Daily Telegraph*, drawing spectacles, moustaches, witty captions and speech bubbles on the photographs, while I went round the shop looking at the pretty things and choosing a small array at a variety of prices, which I left with Susan. Then I'd go to the cafe, drink a single cappuccino and laugh at the things he'd done to the newspaper while he went in and chose something from my selection.

His birthday card read: *'Ma Chere, je te souhaite une bonne anniversaire. Tu as achevé cinquante et un ans avec beaucoup de grace. Tu a un beauté, une intelligence et une poitrine (bleep) extrement idiosyncratique. Je t'aime* sans aucune condition. *Amour, Robert.'* (I wasn't fifty-one, by the way. He liked to indulge his morbidity by saying, for example, of a thirty-ninth birthday, 'now that you're entering your fortieth year'.) Another card involved my head being photoshopped on to the drum of a washing machine, alongside a version of the serenity prayer entreating me to accept the dirty socks that I cannot wash.

The party was a big, good, normal thing to do; an announcement to everyone that though battered and fragile, he was alive and well and available and cheerful, that we were together, that happiness was entirely achievable as long as you pay attention. Fifty years old; thirty-three years since we met, twenty-seven since we first shagged, seven we'd been together, and two that he had been sober. We felt like we'd only just begun.

Chapter Twenty-Four

A week after our birthday party, Kath rang. I woke Robert: John had collapsed dead on the bathroom floor. He'd been in pain and refused to see a doctor, and cracked jokes about more movements than a Beethoven symphony, and so forth, but nobody had expected him to die. It was bowel cancer.

Six weeks later I was asleep beside Robert when I got the midnight call: Wayland was dead in St Mary's. Really dead, this time.

I'd woken that morning on his hospital room floor; when I left he'd asked where I was off to. I said I was going to the library to work. 'Good,' he said. 'Work well.'

Robert and I went together to the Chapels of Rest. I was there with him in Wigan when he tapped his dead dad so sweetly and ruefully on the nose, and let out a sigh, so very slowly. He was waiting for me after I held my dead dad's hand till it was cold, and with me when I went back to mortuaries in London and Wiltshire, over and over, to hold his cold hand again. We walked together at their funerals. We blubbed like fools. We took photos of our dead dads to lunch with us, and propped them up against the salt and pepper. We were the Dead Dads Club. We listened to Horace Silver's 'Song for My Father', and designed a repertoire of duets that John and Wayland might be playing together in heaven: Schubert's Fantasia in F minor; Brahms's *Hungarian Dances*, and his Sonata in F minor if they were allowed a piano each, and their playing had improved on account of them being immortal now. I have no idea how I would have got through that loss without Robert sober and strong at my side.

The flirty Pleyel got shipped out to a friend in Camberwell to make room for the two-metre Bechstein after John died. It's as long as Rachmaninoff was tall. 'That's a big piano, for a house,' said the movers. We still can't open one of the doors.

I became obsessed with buying miniature grand pianos on eBay. I bought a little pale blue enamel Chinese one, a shining black one from which a ballerina springs up when you open the lid, to the tinkling strains of the *Moonlight Sonata*; an elegant brass 1930s piano-shaped powder compact, with collapsible legs, a velvet powder puff and a mirror in the lid. Another has a little wood-lined cavity, the proportions of a grave, in which to keep cigarettes; it plays Brahms' famous lullaby.

At John's funeral, Kath shoved John's tweed porkpie hat on Robert's head. It suited him very well. 'Do I look like a twat in a hat?' he said. 'Or a jazz cat?' Actually he looked like – imagine if Snufkin took a wrong turn, and turned louche. One thing he would never wear was a suit jacket with jeans. It meant something tragic to him: a failing attempt at respectability you can't afford; the poor man in court with nobody to speak for him and no decent trousers, lonely old blokes in basement flats trying to keep up appearances.

He looked like a jazz cat. He lost the hat within weeks. He professed not to mind. I did mind. I got him replacements (no sentimental value), and he would lose them too; the wind would blow them off and they'd go bowling down the Uxbridge Road and be squashed under a bus. He couldn't go after them, on his sticks. God knows where they all are. He could have re-hatted half the neighbourhood.

*

All through this period, Robert must have been doing the cool, relentless Steps.

'What does unmanageability mean to me?' the book made him ask himself. 'Unhealthy untrue belief systems,' he wrote, 'about ourselves, the world, and people. Such as: We're worthless. The world revolves around us – not that it *should*, but that it *does*. It isn't really our job to take care of ourselves. Responsibilities other people take on as a matter of course are just too large a burden for us to bear. We over- or under-react to events. Emotional volatility—'

'Do I accept responsibility for my life and my actions?' it continued. 'Yes,' he wrote, misunderstanding it a little. 'I am almost always able to carry out my daily responsibilities. This has given me self-esteem.'

'Do I treat every challenge as a personal insult?'

'Not at all.'

'Is there something I think I can't get through sober?'

'If I was diagnosed with a terminal illness I would seriously contemplate resuming my not so illustrious drinking career.'

I wondered why he didn't consider the effect this would have on everybody who had re-invested in him now he was sober. Such disregard too for the people who would look after him. Did he not care? But I suppose that is not what the question asks. And as it happened, when it came near it, this was not what he did.

'Do I ignore signs re my health, thinking things will work out somehow?'

'I try to ignore the fact that my heavy smoking may eventually kill me.'

'What convinces me that I can't drink successfully any more?'

'I don't want to die.'

I do think the vocabulary used in AA might have been better thought out. Like God, surrender is just not a good word for a lot of people. (It's good that a new translation, as it were, has appeared: *Recovery*, by Russell Brand, in which the first two steps are now: 1: Are you a bit fucked? 2: Could you not be fucked?)

'SURRENDER: If resignation is acceptance of the problem; surrender is accepting that recovery is the solution. What am I afraid of about the concept of surrender, if anything?'

'I'm not afraid,' Robert responds. 'Perhaps the "if anything" may be my arrogance in terms of losing my individuality.'

When the vocabulary becomes annoying, reading and meetings help: you can find out the nuance and the context, through actual human beings who have been there. AA really doesn't need to be religious. But perhaps one of the functions of the religious aspect of AA is precisely to deflate defiant addicts who consider themselves intellectually superior to simple religiosity. The message (which the self-destroying addict sorely needs to take on board) is along the lines of: You consider yourself more evolved than the poor saps who use this sort of language, but you are wrong and your talent for nuance and spontaneity is closely allied to your talent for lying, avoiding responsibility and fucking up your life. Your precious individuality means nothing here. You are an addict like all the other addicts. Get into line. Surrender. When you are securely sober, we can talk again about your distaste for this vocabulary. Until then, lay your ego down at the door, fall into step.

Or maybe they just need to update it.

*

'Have I stayed in touch with the reality of my disease?'

'Due to WKS,' Robert wrote, 'I sometimes forget I'm an alcoholic. But generally yes.'

He did tell me this. Both of us fell about laughing, until we cried.

*

'Do I believe I am a monster who has poisoned the whole world with my addiction?'

'I don't believe that I am a monster – I become one when I'm drunk.'

'Have I noticed that now I don't have to cover up my addiction, I no longer need to lie?'

'I appreciate the freedom,' he wrote. 'I love it.'

'Am I willing to give recovery my best effort?'

'I am willing to give recovery my best effort in every way esp. doing these bloody steps.'

'What is my understanding of Step One?'

'I don't know. Yet!'

*

We went up to Wigan to scatter John's ashes – some in the garden, some on the moors at White Coppice, where you could look out to the west and see the sea and Blackpool and the long, low coast where John had walked in the wind with Lily Glinka. Kath was bald and funny in dramatic ear-rings. She'd been so busy looking after John she hadn't noticed her own cancer. We gave her nice pyjamas and a red leather coat she'd liked, that I never wore. In John's painting shed I looked through stacks of his watercolour landscapes, and found among them a couple of sketches he'd done for cover designs for my books.

Kath gave Robert some of John's ashes in a little bag. He didn't know what to do with them so when we got back to London I put them in the cigarette box piano and closed it, and I put that in the bottom of the Bechstein, and kept the lid shut.

Chapter Twenty-Five

London, 2009–10

Robert's music was coming back all right. Jackie the violinist, who had always been a muse to him, would come over and play; I would loll on the sofa listening to them. I was singing again; so was Lola, and some of her friends. He wrote a tender, lush theme with violin and cornet for my First World War novel. With everything he did my heart grew because I completely loved both his glorious music and the fact that he made it.

He heard, somewhere, the phrase 'Dying with your music still in you', and it put the fear of God into him. He had always written to commission and didn't know how to write without it. He wanted to work, but he was having trouble starting. I said, Would you set this poem, 'i carry your heart' by ee cummings? I had read it at my father's funeral. Yes, he said. He would.

He wanted to get his hand in with some quartet arrangements. I fed him melodies; he chose the ones he liked: Cole Porter's 'Get Out of Town'; Giulio Caccini's '*Amarilli, Mia Bella*', and Dido's lament, 'When I Am Laid in Earth', from Henry Purcell's *Dido and Aeneas*. He wrote an extraordinary Elegy ('in a variety of keys') for

Wayland, to be played at his memorial service. He made notes and costings in his diary for a recording, a CD to include these pieces, and another, 'String Quartet, not in a specific key, 10–15m'. He never wrote it. Periodically I come across blank prepared manuscripts. 'Fantasy for Violin and Piano, for Jackie': sheets taped together into their long paper accordion, all the staves and clefs written in, but not one note written. An empty promise; a flower dead in the bud.

On the next page to where he wrote 'Dying with your music still in you', he had written: 'I haven't gone I'm just dead.

Just like that, leaving the quote marks open. I saw it for the first time in February 2016. I'd never seen it before.

Chapter Twenty-Six

Step Two is 'We came to believe that a Power greater than ourselves could restore us to sanity'. This too can keep people occupied for years, defining Power, defining sanity, and getting over themselves.

The book starts cheerfully: 'What do I have to hope about today?'

'That I will become more resourceful, kinder, more helpful,' Robert responds in kind. '+ more understanding of people (including myself), + more understanding of situations. That I will remain sober. That I will be able to write beautiful music that is listened to by many people in order to give intense pleasure to them which in turn gives intense pleasure to me courtesy of my considerable ego.'

And then the questions invite a litany describing appalling drunk behaviour, seen clearly now in sobriety and summarised, finally, thus: 'All good things had to be better. Good conversation – more booze. Good sex – more booze. Good food – more booze. Good music – more booze. Good travel – more booze. All bad sad shocking things had to be either glamourised or suppressed by booze. The most-feared state? – Mundanity. Drink to find something out of nothing, or drink to achieve oblivion. Mundanity was a dent, an insult to my supremely interesting character. Balance, normality, routine, rhythm: they are what I insanely labelled as mundanity.'

The early Romantics, the poetic, melancholic, tubercular ones, Chopin, Keats, Shelley, the Brontës, sought to rise above human mundanity by desiring, and desiring to desire, more than others do. Later Romantics became embittered and self-destructive; numbed, and tormented by their numbness. Robert and I were both susceptible to both of these. Both of us wanted more, suffered desperate ebbing and flowing, ended up numb.

I can't bear the idea that I was addicted to him. It seems so mean. Perhaps it is as futile to try to pin down what addiction is as to try to pin down what love is.

The book asks him if his insanity tells him that things outside himself – drinking, for example – can make him whole. He responds: 'Nothing outside myself can make me whole or solve my problems except for one thing. Love. Or the love is inside me. And I can inspire it in others.'

And does he have 'any fears about coming to believe'? He certainly had doubts. 'I can often feel the desire of many of the people in the meetings to stay sober and their desire for *me* to stay sober too. It is certainly a power greater than myself, but surely this is humanitarian not spiritual? My other higher power is my dead father. He was immensely proud of me getting sober. The pride that touched me is still and always will be alive. But is this spiritual?'

'In what do I believe?'

'The power of nature and the power of music.'

'Do I have problems accepting that there is a power or powers greater than myself?'

'No.'

268

'Can a power greater than myself help me to stay sober?'

'It is doing,' he wrote. 'The most inspiring aspects of sobriety are enjoyment, and experiencing pain, sorrow, hardship as constructive things from which I can learn.'

'What evidence do I have that a higher power is working?'

'I am not drinking.'

'What do I consider examples of sanity?'

'The ability to look at people, listen, take time to respond in a cogent, respectful way.

'Daily discipline and structure. Allowing structure to be flexible.

'Having the self-discipline to suppress obsessions with eating too much, working too much and fucking too much (if only the chance were there) . . .'

That pulled me up. Of course the chance was there. Or he was expressing a desire for sex with someone else? Had I had deceived myself in him again? Was trusting him insane of *me*? Do we all insist on believing the best about a lover, in the face of really quite incontrovertible evidence, because we *so* want a prince or princess to call our own? Do all lovers idealise each other in some personal and idiosyncratic way, then hate each other for not living up to the idealisation?

It left me unsettled, wondering about my own self-delusory ways. Humans do love a delusion. We lie, because we prefer good news. Is love an insanity, like the ancient Romans thought? I don't want to think that. I know it's irrational – but reader, I *loved* him. The point is not to make him out as a wonderful human being. He clearly wasn't – and was, like most of us. What makes a person special? Can we be unilaterally special? Or are we only special insofar as we are special to other, possibly deluded, people?

I wonder what would *I* consider examples of my own insanity? What changes in *my* thinking and behaviour would have been necessary?

Back to the orange notebook.

'In what areas of my life do I need sanity now?' persists the book.

'Trying to find an equilibrium in my relationship with Louisa,' he wrote. 'One minute she is beautiful, voluptuous, talented, sexy, loving, funny and kind; the next she is ugly, fat, opinionated, pompous and affected.'

Oh I know this wasn't written for my eyes. And yes I frequently found him charmless and revolting. I breathe carefully and take comfort in the fact he says much the same about his music: 'Certain passages of my music I think are wonderful then soon after the same passages seem to be below average. Basically, try to develop a more quasi-objective critique of my work.' I slot myself into this sentence, in music's place: 'Certain passages of my girlfriend I think are wonderful then soon after the same passages seem to be below average. Basically, try to develop a more quasi-objective critique of my girlfriend.'

Still, seven compliments to five insults, that's a win, isn't it?

No. I hate him, for a while.

And then the book suggests that finding ourselves able to act sanely in a situation with which we were never able to deal successfully before is evidence of sanity, and wants to know if Robert has had experiences like that. 'My father's death,' he wrote. 'Shocking, unexpected. The death of a man who I loved dearly. And Louisa's father's death. My thoughts were: I'm sober now – I can help her. This was the first time I could help the wounded instead of poor wounded me, the victim, needing help from her.'

And wasn't it just. It had been transformative for me – what I needed from him, and he knew it. During that hard time of loss when Wayland died, having Robert at my side gave me a peace I would not otherwise have achieved, and an experience with Robert of love as it should be.

'How is restoration a process?' asks the book.

'It is a life-long quest, the roots and the fertile soil of restoration,' Robert replies. 'Many aspects are storing for the first time: an exhilarating mental process.' I am seeing the book now as a therapist; Robert lying on the couch, dimly lit.

'How am I demonstrating open-mindedness in my life today?' she asks (she's a woman, certainly. Her voice has become slightly sing-song).

'I listen and try to take in what is being said before responding,' he says. 'Not that often, I have to say, but it's improving.'

I want to interrupt. I was there on the end of the couch, diving in with such detail, analysing, overanalysing, trying to be with him. Was he saying he had *never* listened? That he responded without listening? I recalled the sessions at Clouds, when his ears first opened.

Christ, this was exhausting.

'Is there something that I am willing to do now that I was previously unwilling to do?'

'Tell the truth. Bathe and shave. Communicate in a civilised fashion with my ex-wife. Develop a relationship with Louisa's daughter. It's happening, slowly. I'm making no direct amends yet but she can see that I'm making her mother happier, I invite her out occasionally and she knows that if she needs to discuss with me the damage I caused to her, I am ready.'

Gosh. I wonder if she did know that.

Much later, it was pointed out to me that Robert reserved a particular kind of wariness towards those who he saw as gatekeepers to the people whose love he needed: his wife, re his son; Kath, re John; Lola, re me.

*

Kath died in January 2010. The funeral was in the same church as John's; the wake at the same hotel. Robert, who was shaken and upset by the death of the stepmother he had at last been able to love, noted her good qualities from the funeral address: 'Letter writing, very good at choosing presents, hostess, hospitable to a varied range of guests, always spoke her mind, ruthless honesty, dealing with two awkward Lockharts who to quote Robert were never wrong.'

Friends of Robert from his AA meeting came; they and I looked at each other with that curious distant intimacy that comes with knowing you share a great deal, much of it embodied in the man there beside you, and yet you don't know each other at all. We exchanged the AA smile. Later we sat with Kath's sister Chris in a cafe, and Chris gave me a beautiful little ring of Kath's, with a tiny ruby, and I felt like family, bonded in with Kath and John just as they left. We went to where the rest of John's ashes were buried with Auntie Sybil, and then up to Pat's grave on the moor, and Robert stared at it and laid flowers. I'd said in the florist on the roundabout, we need flowers for three graves.

That night Robert and I stayed at his childhood home. We sat on the floor and went through boxes of his old toys. We built his grey plastic castle, and read to each other from his *Beano* annuals, and packed up four galloping plastic horses from his *Bonanza* covered-wagon playset, to bring home. In the freezer we found lasagne that Kath had made, and we had that for supper, as if she had cooked for us. We slept in his boyhood bed.

*

'What fears are getting in the way of my trust?'

'My increasing fantasies about being able to drink normally. Quite rare, but disturbing. My increasing desire for a drink – 2–3 times a week, almost always in bed after midnight. That the whole concept of trust is a pile of crap invented by pissheads for pissheads – the sardonic cynic still lurks in my darker areas.'

'Have I sought help from a power greater than myself?'

'Yes. People who care for me, indeed the majority of AA members, don't want me to have a drink. And, when my girlfriend was shockingly aggressive and critical and unnecessarily so. Deep breaths and first line of the serenity prayer. I apologised. I thought, even knew, that I was not out of order. But so what. In her eyes I was.'

His offence had been wanting to chat about the menopause with a mutual male friend, and using me and my body – which wasn't anyway menopausal – as a rather graphic example. I didn't feel that the physical intimacy he had as my boyfriend was something for him to use in public chat. But shockingly aggressive? In the grand scheme of things I really don't think so – I was asking him not to embarrass me. But to tender, newly unanaesthetised Robert? Evidently. An unfortunate aspect of all this was that he remained more sensitive to his own issues, and to those of other addicts, than to those of others in general. He had become more patient: 'There are usually good reasons for why someone behaves like a cunt,' as he observed. He once made me chase a drunken down-and-out man down Queensway in order to give him a note he had scribbled, with his phone number and an offer of support. I loved that he wanted to do this. But I was still waiting for him to do something, *anything,* for me. It was too difficult for him. Again, he did not like me being upset about anything to do with him. It scared him, because I was always the strong one, and that brought back guilt, which made him want to drink. All of which, simply, meant I had to suppress the considerable concerns and fears and anger and above all the massive desire for reassurance that I was carrying. He couldn't handle it. So, in general, I held them in. How could he 'know' that he was not 'out of order'? He hurt my feelings and embarrassed me. Fact. And, right or wrong, I did feel that if a ledger had been kept from the very beginning, I was so stratospherically in credit that perhaps now a tiny bit of the benefit of the doubt might have come my way. But the addict in recovery remains vulnerable, sensitive and self-obsessed. Those who love an addict basically have to put up with it. Even at the expense of their own feelings. It is an emotionally expensive kind of love.

Charlotte, my friend in Italy, asked me recently if I would have gone through with it, if I'd known in advance. Ah, but only by going through it do we find out. And, at risk of repeating myself: that is why I am writing this book: I can tell how it was for me. And, a bit, he can tell you how it was for him.

Here is the end of Robert's step work, on the penultimate page of Step Two, with this ironic heading:

MOVING ON

– just what John advised him to do, years before.

*

I was very glad to finish transcribing the papers. Rereading them in this impersonal font, I take a more distanced look. And I see more clearly how addiction at every stage, whether it is active (i.e. the sufferer is using their drug or drinking the alcohol) or in recovery, is of its nature a most self-absorbed condition. There is something in the idea that in AA the obsession is transferred: all the energy that previously went into drinking now goes into actively not drinking. Doing the Steps, as Robert observed, is not an exercise you tick off; meetings are not something you can ever go to enough of. It is a way of life, serious and demanding in unexpected ways. I looked ahead in the Step Working Guide to the further ten and a half steps and questions. It takes time, courage and emotional graft to make the 'searching and fearless moral inventory of ourselves' required by Step Four, to answer the eighty-two questions involved. Step Eight asks for a 'list of all persons we have harmed', and the willingness to make amends to them all. I don't know if I could do that. I'm bloody delighted that I don't have to.

Life in recovery is a thousand times better, because the alcoholic is no longer killing himself, no longer locked away incommunicado, and no longer a drunken arsehole. But it would be folly for the one who loves the alcoholic to think this new stage will make everything OK. The alcoholic does not just become a non-alcoholic when they get sober.

When addiction has its hands on the controls, it is never going to steer its person towards healing, because healing threatens the addiction's existence. The addict has to wrest control of the vehicle, the brain and body, from that dark pilot and then shout it down, over and over, till it is a heap in the corner. Every time the addiction even shivers the addict has to shout it down again. And when addiction is down the addict has to keep it there, by constant vigilance – while also steering the vehicle safely and also beginning to learn how to deal with the ancient fears, damages, sorrows and angers which admitted the addiction in the first place. Just because you've got the beast in a corner now doesn't mean your initial issues are dealt with. And meanwhile, everyday life still has to be maintained. It's quite a multitask.

The person who loves the alcoholic needs to get on board with the world of recovery. I went to meetings – AA open meetings with Robert, as well as Al-Anon meetings. I read the literature. I talked to friends also in recovery, and to the people who love them. It is something of a full-time job. But it brings understanding, without which love is empty, a self-indulgent fantasy. And isn't love, anyway, always, a full-time job?

Part Five

2010–12

Chapter Twenty-Seven

Paris, London, Spring 2010

There's a photograph of him, taken on the Paris Métro in the 1980s, huddled up in his overcoat, wearing a balaclava Kath had knitted for him. He's grinning evilly up at the photographer, his friend Richard, who, Robert said, 'named this item *Mutilé de Guerre*', after the signs they used to have reserving seats on the Métro for wounded soldiers. I had it above my desk as I wrote about my soldier, Riley, who lost his jaw in the trenches. Next to it was a photo of Robert's great-grandfather Jack Ainsworth, in uniform, and another, of Jack's grave in France.

Robert was a very commendable cripple; patient, generous, helpful in letting others know how to treat him, utterly without self-pity, determined. And he was a fine recovering alcoholic: straight, open, devoted. Yes, he could have given up smoking, and done some exercise. But he had been sober three years. The future was thinkable about. The music he'd been writing, what happens when Lola leaves home. Fantasies about a place outside Wigan, on the moors, or by the sea. We liked the look of our future. It seemed ours. I had another book out (*Halo*, a children's novel set in Ancient Greece) and I had a real, aware human man to love, a relief and a pleasure beyond words. In many ways he was like a fifteen-year-old, learning things as if for the first time. 'All that time you lot spent learning to be normal,' he said, 'I was perfecting my left-hand trills.' Now, he was working towards balance. After he left Camden, despite his disabilities in walking and piano playing, and despite us having been triply bereaved within a year, there was a real spring of the soul. We joked about Steps Eight and Nine, and what amends exactly he'd make to me, when he came to it. Sobriety and gratitude, sex and proximity, worked their magic. It's not called making love for nothing. Him living half in Wigan, half in London, worked very well, for both us: mutually independent. Happy. Normal. Slightly dazed by the quiet miracle of there not being much wrong.

It's difficult to recognise when a damaged person is unwell in a new way. But in 2010 he was not well enough. He'd had a sore throat all winter. He was tired. He'd seen five GPs over the past two months. 'Pharyngitis,' said the first. Then, 'It'll go away of its own accord.' In March we were in Italy, me working on *My Dear I Wanted to Tell You*; Robert writing music in my old ankle-length white fake-fur coat, stern-eyed. The doctor in Grosseto said he needed tests: go and see the doctor in London. All of us were sad and unnerved because my friend Charlotte's beloved Great Dane, Messalina, was sick; her breath stank and she was exhausted, and the vet sat in the courtyard looking miserable, saying she wasn't sick enough yet to put down. The Icelandic volcano delayed our departure, over and over. We drove back across the Alps in a friend's white van full of mozzarella and tomatoes.

The GP says, but you were referred to Charing Cross. Robert hadn't had a letter. He didn't realise he'd been referred. She looks down his throat. She says, 'You could go to the Royal National Throat, Nose and Ear. They have a clinic today. I'll make a call. Two o'clock?'

We could have gone six weeks ago. Robert says, 'There's no point thinking about what we could have done.' Undertone: he could have given up smoking. He could have got into rehab earlier. Alongside that, the GPs could have seen what they were looking at: his history, and so on. He ticks many boxes.

There *is* no point. Here is now.

An overworked young doctor who introduces himself as Mishi jumps up and down to get things. Two students and a nurse stand by, a Greek chorus at the beginning of our drama. I was about to put, our tragedy. But we know better than to assume. Robert and his many lives.

Mishi puts a tube up Robert's nose, and Robert 'poorly tolerates a fibre-optic laryngoscopy', it says in the notes. Someone else peers round the door. Mishi says, 'Take a look. He says: 'There's something there.'

Robert looks at me, I at him. Genuinely, in that moment, we both know. We know what it is, and we know what we will do about it: an eye-joining moment of perfect understanding. The rising to the occasion.

Am I going to rise to the occasion? Is he? Ha – as usual, he *is* the occasion.

It is first names all round. Everyone is incredibly nice to us. I sense a rising of levels, shoulders going back, pores tightening, the soft swish of everything irrelevant sloughing away. Adrenaline, low-level, controlled, to be paced because we're going to need it. Fight or flight. Fight.

Robert's only direct experience of cancer is his mother dying of it when he was twenty-four; and then John, and then Kath.

Back home he says would I please not *look* at him.

He goes to bed early; I sit beside him hiding the webpages as I look up all the things it might be.

The next morning after taking Lola to school I just get back into bed beside him and read. He sleeps till about one. We go for lunch at an Italian restaurant near my sister's, where the guys know us.

A comfort place. I take some photos of him. He looks lean, tough and terribly handsome. We flirt like billy-oh and are quite in love. He eats tortelli in tomato sauce. Soft.

I go to my mother's to make her dinner. We get on worse than usual. Three of my sisters call by while I'm there, which I resent, unreasonably, thinking, 'If you were coming over anyway why do I have to be here, when I am needed at home?' As I leave, my mother's carer, coming in, says: 'Are you all right? You look tired.'

'I *am* tired,' I say, after a tiny pause. I am both sad and relieved that no member of my family saw it and asked. I haven't said anything to anyone. I don't want any reactions.

He has been referred to UCLH, Rosenheim Building (now demolished), a Victorian redbrick hospital wing of the most formerly prosperous sort, with a view out the back of the spot where I was born. I am standing in the street in the rain looking for the entrance, and there is Robert in a minicab, also looking for it. The magnetic pull between us is back, very very strong. I feel us conjoining across the tarmac.

Joyce the clinic receptionist has wide-apart eyes, a long neck and straight carriage. Robert dubs her the Pulchritudinous Gazelle. A man in the waiting room has what Swift calls the Hendon Rasp: the hoarse voice of old-fashioned London cabbies. Another has a voice-box voice. 'Maybe I'll get one of those,' says Robert.

The registrar is about twenty-five. He looks like a prince from a miniature, with smooth, beautiful hands. Robert thinks his trousers (pale, mottled wool) are too tight, and with his weakness for doe-eyed Asian beauty rather fancies him. He is very kind and gentle. The fibre-optic laryngoscopy is again poorly tolerated.

'The septum is twisted,' the Princeling says. 'That's why it's difficult to get it up there.'

I recall the bloodied face at the door, the broken noses. I look out of the window at the backlot graffiti. There is something almost unnoticeable in the Princeling's tone of voice when he pulls the tube back out, and he says 'OK'.

We are to be saved by heroes from Mughal miniatures. I shall buy them all white silk pyjamas embroidered with lotuses. The Princeling says, 'Well, there's something going on in the right tonsil area.'

Robert says, 'Is that a euphemism for cancer?'

The Princeling says, 'Yes.'

Robert says, 'Be brutally honest.'

The Princeling says, 'I will be, as soon as I know anything.'

At the end he says, 'Don't worry, we can do something about this. There is treatment.'

Robert says, 'Ah, so you're not just going to put me in the incinerator?'

The Princeling, very at home with gallows humour, arranges for triple scanning.

Scan one is ultrasound: the one you have when you're pregnant. The cloudy billowing landscapes it displays could be a baby for all I can tell. Then a CT scan, and then an MRI. Each reveals, from its own point of view, what is going on inside Robert's head. His lymph glands are apparently clear. The scan-meister, kind, with a brother-in-law who is also a film composer, tells us this with visible relief. Even we know that this is good. He takes a biopsy from each gland as well. His is a shoulder-clasping kind of kindness, and he is careful to include me. Lots of eye contact, and coming over to tell us what he's doing now and that he'll be back in a few minutes. We are to return next week for results, and a biopsy of the – thing.

A redhead is kneeling at Robert's feet, doing something necessary.

The Princeling registrar is called Jagi. Francis Vaz, head and neck, is the consultant. We haven't met him yet. Ring his secretary with any problems.

Later, in the follow-up letter, it said 'ulcerating mass'.

I like the letters.

'Why?' asks Robert, who doesn't read them.

Because things written down are under control. I like that they say 'Many thanks for referring this 51-year-old composer to the

Head and Neck service at UCLH . . .' and 'I saw this pleasant gentleman in clinic today'. This pleasant gentleman.

*

Robert came up very late, bathed, shaved and fragrant. Around five the pain woke him. He went off down the stairs, and didn't put the light on. He couldn't find his spray. I got it, and made him a hot-water bottle, and he moaned a little at the relief as he had moaned with the pain. He cried. I lay chanting, even in my sleep, *Please God, let it be small, let it be local, let them fix it. Please God, let it be small, let it be local, let them fix it.* It was getting light by then. Spring mornings. Glorious, as they say.

I was working out how I was going to be with it. For two days I was full of tears – jog me and they would have spilled over. Then I was marvellous – calm, gentle, kind, efficient. I was lovely. He said so, a lot, and thanked me, as if I might have done anything different. I had a tendency (unexpressed) to race straight to the very worst it could be – it's already in his lungs, he has three months – while tripping on moments of 'But it could be tiny, and benign!' The AA training kicked in, the Serenity Prayer. We don't know; be calm.

He said, 'I'm not going to fucking die.' And that seemed reasonable. He looked terribly rock'n'roll in his hat, like a Fifties trombonist, or Ian Dury. I was falling in love with him again, despite already being in love with him. I hadn't known that could happen. Why was it? Because he needed me? He always needed me. Because I thought I might lose him? I came over very Dusty Springfield: I only want to be with him.

I was planning not to tell Lola until after her exams in June. I genuinely, madly, thought that was something I could do.

Obviously, it was necessary to carry on. We knew that. So I went to a party for a book about a wife-murderer, where I saw Swift. I could not-tell anyone, except her. I had already not-told Lola (who had asked if I was all right, on Monday evening), and Charlotte (who enquired). But I knew Swift would ask, and I would tell.

I told. Put my hand on her arm. She said, among other things, 'You knew this was going to happen.' But I didn't know. Nobody knew at this stage.

I went to the library and read John Diamond's book about his cancer (*C: Because Cowards Get Cancer Too*) in one sitting, and surmised that Robert would die and I would marry Charles Saatchi. I was stepping into yet another new territory I never wanted to enter – led, again, by Robert. I was glad, in some ways, to have been in addictland, or rather recoveryland. It had taught me perspective, and how to recognise happiness. It had taught me to take as long to enjoy the relief of a problem's being solved as I had taken to fret about the problem in the first place. But now I was returning to living with a very unclear future. I had minded that a lot the previous time. Now, though, it was different: we were on the same side. We had both known that things could go very wrong again. We had not expected this kind of wrong. But still: an unclear future was something we were familiar with. I was fairly sure that what I was thinking then I would give a hollow laugh at later on.

*

They rang. He had an advanced cancer in his throat. He needed to go in for a biopsy to reveal what kind. His lungs and lymph nodes were confirmed clear. This was good. It was quite big but only in one place. Primary. This was good too. Amazing how many things were good!

*

There is delay, in the waiting room. A humorous nurse comes in, wide hips, West African accent. She coughs, and says, loudly, 'Good afternoon, everyone! The clinic is running late. We are very sorry. Mr [miss the name] is not here but everyone is working hard to catch up. We love you all and we care about you. Thank you for being patient.' Two minutes later she appears with a box of chocolate seashells, and takes them around. I refuse, thinking there won't be enough for everyone, for the people who really need one. At the end she brings them back, and says, with a steely look, 'My friend, my darling, you didn't take one. Take one.' I take one. It is delicious. I become aware that I am one of the ones who really need one, and wonder how fat Robert's illness is going to make me.

I fill my bag with booklets and leaflets in pale green and mauve, about sex and money and work in relation to cancer. Robert doesn't look at them. He says: 'I'm not that interested.'

There is a huge rabbi there; a youth in a wheelchair, with an eyepatch; a handsome man reading a book about Bowie in Berlin; some strange and interesting voices, a sunken, shattered chin. I think about Riley Purefoy, the hero of *My Dear I Wanted to Tell You*, and his jaw shot off at Passchendaele, and the irony. Robert says he'd quite like a voice-box. I imagine him smoking through a tracheostomy.

Then in to see Mishi with his beautiful smile, and the angelic, dry-humoured clinical nurse specialist, Lynn.

I write in my notebook: *large. single. advanced. hasn't spread. tongue palate neck tonsil ecg + bloods Monday: in 11 May for biopsy on 12th Clinic 19 May to decide treatment.* The pain team is mentioned: codeine phosphate for the time being. Robert is worried because codeine-based painkillers can be risky for addicts. The drug and alcohol team is mentioned. I enquire whether Wernicke-Korsakoff Syndrome will make things difficult, and they don't know. Perhaps for the anaesthetic. They need to check kidney function and be sure his liver is up to it anyway. We learn a new word: iatrogenesis. Damage caused by the cure.

The tea and coffee, though the kind with thin petrol-coloured bubbles on the surface, is free.

In the corridor afterwards, Robert says: 'Oi. You promised you'd dump me if I ever got cancer.'

'So I did.'

'Well then?'

So I say, 'OK, I'm leaving you.'

He says, 'Thank God, at last I'm rid of her.'

Then I say, 'Now you have to beg me to come back to you.'

He says, 'Darling, please come back to me. I love you. You're adorable. Come back to me.'

We have hysterics because yesterday he described David Hockney as an adorable man, and I just found that very funny.

I am happy because nobody, let alone him, has ever begged me to come back to them before. I say: 'Maybe. If you make it worth my while and stand up straight *all the time*.'

When I say I love him he says: 'Still? Amazing.' Or: 'A woman of taste . . .'

Like last week, after the doctor, we go straight to bed. It seems right. His mouth smells different. He is still smoking. About four a day.

I say, 'Am I to ignore the fact that you're still smoking?'

He says: 'I'm on it. I'm cutting right down.' (He always says this.)

I say, 'Because it's what I hate most about this whole thing.'

He says: 'I was going to not smoke in front of you, for that reason, but I decided against because I'm not going to deceive you again.'

His breath smells burned, metallic, and of decay.

*

I wrote to Charlotte:

I should tell you Robert has a cancer in his throat. It's primary, i.e. it hasn't spread, and is apparently unlikely to as his lymph system is clear. I'd decided as a protective measure that he had three months to live, so I am oddly enough terribly relieved, though it does seem unkind of fate to crown his past seven years' experience with this.

He's sober and cheerful, and gets up early saying: 'I'm going to work on my Four Last Songs . . .' I find I love him beyond measure.

So I may be a bit odd over the next however long it takes. At the moment I haven't really told anyone, because though I feel I can deal with *it*, I'm not sure I can deal with people's reactions.

But you already know, don't you? So I'm confirming it.

It's the anniversary of Dad's death today.

It was also the day that Messalina was put down. The irony of the beautiful giant dog, the black velvet dinosaur, having the same thing as Robert, at the same time, and getting iller and smellier, and being put down, does not escape us. But it's too sad. It's just too sad. That beautiful dog.

*

A few days later, I was in Wiltshire for the setting of our father's gravestone. I went alone, with no feelings at all. I didn't go to the grave – I didn't want to think of him being in there, in any sense, on any level. At lunch my siblings were discussing issues relating to our mother's carer's upcoming holiday and how it was to be covered. One needed to know why I was reluctant to take on a particular duty. I had to take her aside and tell her that I was going to be available for nothing, and why. I didn't want to tell them – anyone – about Robert's illness. I felt bullied, though not by them. By circumstance. My hand was forced but how could it not be? Any of us would happily never tell anyone this news. I actually was pretending it wasn't happening, and it made perfect sense.

I practised telling on my sister-in-law: she was affectionate, sympathetic, and not over the top. 'It is always so tough,' she said. 'What are we meant to do? How to feel? Time seems so slippery slidey suddenly.' And then I told my brother. He was cool, in the good way. Before I had left that morning I had told Lola. A-levels or no A-levels, I really wasn't going to get away with not mentioning this. I acknowledged the strangeness of having a person you felt ambivalent about having a deadly illness in your house. When I got back she nearly didn't tell me about her own odd day, which included calling an ambulance for a man who collapsed in the street in front of her.

I said, 'You know you were thinking of not telling me because I have enough on my plate already?'

She smiled sheepishly, and I said, 'Yes, well, NO. That's not how it's going to be.'

I hadn't yet told her about Messalina. The hierarchy of sad things is an odd one.

Because I had told Lola, I told Louis. This is how I became an experienced teller.

By the way, if you're wondering what to say in response to news like this, I recommend the following:

If you're willing to help, say, 'Is Tuesday a good day to bring soup?'

If you're not, say, 'I am very sorry to hear this.'

*

I took to listing my fears in a blue notebook, alongside possible outcomes of the fear proving true. I had the blue notebook for questions and meetings and so on, and my normal notebook for feelings, and a white plastic folder into which pieces of paper went. Systems comfort me.

Fear of the Day:

That he will not be (a) physically fit for general anaesthetic. And thus (b) ditto for radiotherapy and chemotherapy

But if he's not, perhaps they could do something under local, or do something else I've never heard of.

And we cannot know about fear 1) (b) till May 19th. So no point thinking about it. Though asking ahead calms me. And him?

*

Robert and I went to an oddly scruffy Japanese place on Camden Parkway, which smelt sweet and damp the particular way some old places in Los Angeles do, as if things would peel off the walls, very unJapanese. It was cramped and comforting. Then I dropped him back at the hospital for his biopsy the next day. Mr Shah had said that in the process of the endoscopy they might possibly chip his teeth, because they have to get the jaw pretty far open to have a good look around. And he said the liver and kidneys are fine; fully up to the job of being anaesthetised, or irradiated, or chemoed.

Robert was smoking. 'It's my last one,' he said.

'What, ever?'

'Well I was thinking that.'

*

That evening I ran into an old friend, Joe, all upright and alive years after *his* throat cancer. I was so pleased to see him. He told me he had been in love almost with his surgeon. Besotted.

When I got home I found Robert had created a person out of a triangular Mongolian fur hat, my bra and a belt, and left him (or her) on the bed, to keep me company.

*

The following day I went in at 6.30, taking ice cream. Robert was in good spirits, on a drip. The day after that I raced out of the British Library Reading Room to take his call. It was much bigger than they had foreseen. They will operate. They need to remove part of his jaw.

290

I wept in the loos.

I longed for Joe's result; I feared John Diamond's. I emailed my family:

Some of you know that Robert has been ill:

Well, he's had a load of scans and a biopsy, and he has cancer in his throat.

It hasn't metastasised, and his lymph system is clear, so that's good, and he's in the care of splendid team at UCH, who will tell us in detail next week exactly what it is and what they are going to do about it. Surgery, radiotherapy, chemotherapy are all on the cards, with treatment starting in the next couple of weeks, and he's living with me and Lola for the duration. I'll keep you posted.

Er – so that's that. He's tough, as we know. Wish us luck.

I emailed them again, sending a jpeg of the military field post-card which gave me the inspiration and the title for my novel, which said:

'My dear_____

I want to tell you, before any telegram arrives, that I was admitted to 36 Casualty Clearing Station B.E.F. on ____ with a slight/serious wound in my _____ .

I am now comfortably in bed with the best of surgeons and sisters to do all that is necessary for me. I will write and tell you how I get on . . .'

Thank you for your kind messages. You are a lovely family to be in at such a time.

xxx Lou

My mother wrote back:

Oh darlings, how boring, how boring. LOVE LOVE – . . .

    I couldn't get up the field postcard because ADOBE wanted me to accept God knows what before letting me see it. XXXE

And one sister wrote:

UCH are known for bringing forth wonders like **you**.

*

Fear of the Day: I fear his voice will go.

Chapter Twenty-Eight

UCLH, Summer 2010
It is an oropharyngeal squamous cell carcinoma. It is T4. T in this context stands for primary tumour; the number classifies extent. In throat cancers T4(a) means the tumour has grown further than the mouth or oropharynx into nearby tissues such as bone (yes), tongue (yes), the sinuses (no) or the skin (no). At least it's not T4b.

The Princeling had said, 'throat, neck, tonsil and palate'. It took a while for the concept of one cancer at the junction of four places to make sense to Robert. It became one of those things he couldn't get, like where his socks were kept. I wondered if it was because of the WKS. But socks don't matter, and this did. He was telling people he had cancer in four places, i.e. that he was dying, when he wasn't. 'Actually,' they said, 'he has a more than fifty per cent chance of living for more than five years.'

Personally I see percentages as always fifty–fifty – either he does, or he doesn't. It doesn't make any difference what happens to everybody else. The David Bowie song became my earworm: 'Five years, that all we've got . . .'

I was going to work as usual: writing and researching in the British Library. It is handy for UCLH, and has plenty of open spaces for taking phone calls about appointments for more scans, blood tests, heart tests, kidney-function tests, liver-function tests, lung-function tests, hearing tests, biopsies and echocardiograms. It has large clean lavatory cubicles with quality loo paper: good for crying in. Robert did not cry. He rested and worked at home, and at the end of each day I briefed him on his upcoming engagements. He was bad at these things; I am good at them. I went upstairs to cry on my blue velvet bed. He clumped up after me and said, 'Are you weeping? There'll be no sneaky weeping. You want to weep, you weep on me.'

*

Fear of the Day:
   I fear he will die and it will take a long time.

*

I emailed Swift:

Hey honey –

I can't actually bring myself to say this in person now; but I'll talk to you tomorrow.

   They want to operate, pretty soon; take out a section of his jawbone and replace it with a bit of fibula. They'd do it all at once. It's a twelve-hour operation, with up to five surgeons. He'll be two weeks in hospital; feeding through tubes etc, then six weeks recovery at home, if all goes well. Maybe some radiotherapy, afterwards. They seem to think this has a pretty good chance of working. He is between aghast and very cheerful, and claims to be most upset about having to give up smoking. I now have a giant bottle of liquid morphine for pain emergencies, which we could have done with at three this morning. I had to show my driving licence, as it's a controlled substance. I am finding it very tempting already. Robert has asked me to hide it.

I spent £400 in Paul Costello in Amersham. And left a dress to be altered and sent on. Hmm. Grandiose and bankrupting.

Love you. Please stop smoking.

xxxx

sswift wrote:

oh god. I will just keep reading the part that says they think this has a pretty good chance of working.
X

louisayoung wrote:

Good plan. I am feeling quietly optimistic, in a mad way. For how else could one possibly feel? Just mad. Which I don't fancy.
xxx L

sswift wrote:

That made me laugh.

*

Comfort of the Day: friends. Beth coming round with fish pie. Richard. Jackie. Will. Swift. Deborah. Louis. John, Judi, David, Michelle, Simon. All of you. The delicacy with which the hard times other people had been through equipped them to comfort, help and cheer Robert and me up now.

*

I crashed the car, went to the Library with Lola's laptop and no phone, and stuck my finger in the blender making soup for him. Spinach & watercress with blood. 'Extra iron!' I thought. He couldn't get solid food past the pain. I put ground almonds and olive oil and cream in everything to fatten him up. I prepared chicken broth and ordered special green nutrition powder from California. I was so scared. I knew I was doing the right things but I still felt I didn't know what to do. In his pain at night he beat the mattress with his fist – then a few hours later, tough, biting it, he walked into the kitchen smiling and told Lola she looked beautiful.

Once, for a few minutes, I was very angry with him. All the things that could have been different if he had made some different decisions. He continued to smoke. There was no point saying anything.

Fear of the Day: I fear I will shout at him.

*

At each stage it turned out to be worse than they had thought.

His old self-destructive self was still hurtling along its physical trajectory even though – except smoking – he has stopped doing what set it off. The cause was clear: neat spirits and smoking combined; far more dangerous in combination than the sum of their parts. Who knew? He saw a hypnotist (I cried in the car outside) and joined a programme at the chemist.

Haunted by cultural references – headlines, radio stories, lyrics – I earwormed the old country song 'Too Far Gone' all week, and spent one long wait at the clinic circling every positive word on the back page of the newspaper. Driving past the hospital that morning I passed a car with the bumper sticker *Miracles Happen*. So that was nice. That night on the web I found the Oral Cancer Foundation. They put their medical stats as a signature, so I just looked to see survivors, and take joy in the fact of them. Only later did I think: the dead don't post.

When you are a teenager adults can be invisible, irrelevant, not real. When you are pregnant everyone you notice is pregnant; push-chairs multiply and only families count. Now I look at strangers and think: do you have a cancerous beloved at home? And perhaps they do. The leaflet says two million live with it. Does that mean living with it inside them? Or as I am living, alongside in the same house?

If you remember all the stages of life and all the things that were important, you become a wise, kind and sympathetic person. But while learning, you are someone who crashes the car and bleeds in the soup.

*

Fears of the Day:
    1) It metastasises before the surgery
    2) He goes through all the treatment and it recurs anyway
    3) They won't be able to operate
    4) I'll drive into a tree.

*

The horror justified self-comfort. I became extravagant. I found myself in a restaurant eating duck while the Isley Brothers sang 'Summer Breeze'; buying flowers, and thanking God that Robert's PRS payments and royalties from his workaholic days continued, and that I was self-employed and solvent – I had a book contract with sympathetic publishers and no deadline. I have seen people get through cancer where work is inflexible and money scarce; and I am profoundly grateful that we were not put through that added hell. I was at that stage no stranger to retail therapy. Shopping was not safe. I bought a bed without measuring anything, knowing it probably wouldn't fit in the back room, and even if it did it wasn't big enough for anyone taller than me to sleep on. I thought: but

I mustn't get rid of the old daybed, because Robert may need to sleep on it when he's iller. I imagined one of those big hospital beds, out of place like a Tardis in the sitting room, with him dying on it, facing north so he can see people when they come in. I felt people should face south when they die, but if a bed faced south in the sitting room the door would be behind their head and people would have to go round . . . there's no space . . . I was wondering about how to arrange the furniture if he died.

I resolved not to take my card around with me. I put the old Ikea daybed on Freecycle, to prove I was not ruled by fear.

*

I genuinely felt I would wake up and it will have been a nightmare. How could it be happening? The roses were beautiful. Days came and went. Lola was revising upstairs, and Robert snoozing on the sofa. I gave him morphine in a spoon. I counted out his drugs, filled a little partitioned box with the doses for when he went out. Diclofenac, paracetamol, vitamin B, thiamine, codeine phosphate. MST – strong morphine, twice daily. Various sprays for his throat. Movicol, laxative to counteract the morphine. Drugs because of drugs. They found a home in a blue straw box Louis gave me that before, I used to keep tea-lights in.

The cancer and its treatment would quite possibly, probably definitely, maybe, leave him unable to eat, or talk, ever again. Him, the piano-playing, food-loving, chain-smoking, heavy-drinking, always-talking runaround who can already no longer run around, drink or play the piano. The word 'compromised' came up. Unpredictable, they said. 'It's not that simple.' They didn't know. And sometimes he moaned, and said: 'Jesus, even my eye is hurting.' Or, 'my tongue'. They would be removing part of his tongue, down the back, the talking and swallowing part, not the sticking-out part. So many things being taken away from him.

I spilt sticky liquid morphine, on the sheets, the floor. There was a drip-stand with bags of liquid food in my house. These were strange new things. The world was changing around me.

For example – there seemed to be nothing in the world now that was not to do with food. Advertisements for food, magazines about food, photographs of food, and food itself. Gleaming tomatoes lounging in piles outside the shops on Uxbridge Road, ranks of chocolate bars in the corner shops, stacks of oranges, little plastic dishes of baklava, tubs of pickle and salad, skewers of fat-dripping kebab. Bunches of herbs waved at him; he tripped over food wrappers in the street; the smells of curry and monosodium glutamate and bakeries and frying chicken dawdled after him as he hobbled down the road. On the radio, entire programmes talked about food; its growing, its cooking, its eating. In the papers, complex descriptions of meals consumed, mouthful by mouthful, thrilling taste by delicious detail. A tormenting ubiquity.

'How about oysters?' I said. 'Easy to eat? Nutritious?'

'They remind me of what's going on in my mouth,' he said. He added cream and chocolate ice cream to a fortified reinforced milkshake-style meal replacement drink, and was sick.

There was a supermarket in the Uxbridge Road called Supreme Food and Wine, which he nicknamed (after it was taken over by a religious family who didn't sell alcohol) Crap Food and No Wine. This was not so funny a joke any more. Maybe in a week, I thought, I will never hear his voice again. I wondered if there were particular conversations he might like to have, now while he could, and how to suggest it. He became *very* one-day-at-a-time. He sat happy on the sofa, belly full of soup, looking at the paper, preparing for a bit of composing, working up a song I had admired when he was doodling it on the piano. And he did stop smoking! And Jesus if it was that easy, why the hell did he leave it so late? It seemed that yet again he left it too late to come back whole. Maybe he won't come back at all, I thought.

But standing on the front doorstep, he smelt the roses, ten feet away. 'Sort of peppery!' he said, and he smiled like a kid. He never smelled the roses before. They were Madame Grégoire Staechelin, pink and bounteous, flurries of them tumbling in slow motion. The ones we had piled on to Wayland's coffin the year before.

His hands no longer smelt of fags and his fingers were less yellow. Already. He said the hypnosis was a load of hippy crap. But he wasn't complaining about not smoking. That week I earwormed George Jones: 'Good Year for the Roses'.

One gets used to things very quickly.

*

Fear of the Day: I fear he will live forever dumb and in pain, moaning softly.

Chapter Twenty-Nine

Home, 12 June 2010

I was on the new daybed, which had to come in through the window because no, it didn't even fit through the front door, let alone up the stairs and into the back room. I was haranguing Robert about how insulting it was that he couldn't even be arsed to propose to me, after everything I'd done for him, even though he knew *perfectly well* that I'd never ever say yes because although I am a hopeless romantic we all know I am also a rabid feminist who will never marry a man etc etc. He was rolling his eyes at me, lurching to his unsteady feet and hobbling over to the piano. I continued my rant, along the lines that even if I were ever to marry anybody which I wouldn't I certainly wouldn't marry *him*, not with a bargepole, as he was an ingrate and a pig. He hobbled back, saying, 'Oh for fuck sake. I *was* going to take you up to Hampstead Heath and be *romantic* but as you're being such a fuckin' cow, fuckin' *hell fire*—'

And then he's down on one cranky knee, flinging away his sticks as if in receipt of an unlikely miracle, and he's presenting a tiny octagonal box with tucked into its satin slit a little Victorian diamond ring. 'Will you fuckin' marry me then?'

I burst into tears. FUCK FUCK FUCK, I yell. YES, I say, covering my mouth with my hand like a lady on a chaise longue who has just been proposed to. Of course, I say. Oh my God yes. Jesus I love you so much.

We went for lunch at the Italian restaurant, and I put the ring on the tail of a prawn on my spaghetti. It sparkled joyously in the sunlight, among the bits of tomato and parsley.

He had asked Jackie to get the ring for him. I remember her asking, 'So if you were to have an engagement ring, what kind would you like?' and me not twigging. Not the tiniest little bit. I remember her saying, 'You will get married, you two, I'm sure of it' – and me just not twigging.

*

I made a little film on my phone of him being really pleased with himself. And me. We couldn't stop laughing. We were going to get married when he felt better. So he had only got round to proposing because of the illness: so what? It was a glory to be snatched from the teeth of . . . other possibilities. We would have a proper wedding in the country, at the church where my dad was buried: we'd invite everyone and they would all come, all the people we'd known over the past thirty-three years. We'd have the tent, dress, frock-coat, sunshine, all the champagne in the world, heart-stopping love and loveliness. We'd have 'Come Down, O Love Divine'. I tried on a vaguely traditional wedding dress or two and thought oh no way, it'll have to be Vivienne Westwood, and gold. Or green. I could go as a superannuated mermaid. He agreed he would shave. Word got round. Cards and flowers arrived. Everybody loves a midlife romance. An ex of his was reported as saying, 'Well they're perfect for each other: he'd have anyone, and no one else would have her' – and we laughed. My mother said, 'Do it now. Sooner the better.'

*

His CPEX (Cardio-Pulmonary Exercise Testing) improved, but even so because of his existing health problems – the complex, systematic, imaginative and thorough way that alcohol had dismantled him – Robert was deemed potentially too weak to undergo the microsurgery which was the normal thing. The anaesthesia required for an operation of the necessary duration might be too much for him. They spent weeks testing him to see if he'd be strong enough; every test was borderline.

'Everything about you is difficult,' the anaesthetist in the floral tea-dress told him, and didn't know why I laughed. Also, were they all good-looking? Or did they just look good to me, because they were helping?

Because they didn't think he'd be strong enough for more than four or five hours of anaesthetic, they were thinking of giving him a replacement jaw of titanium chain – in links like a bicycle chain – instead of a section of his own fibula. This way would be quicker and simpler; the jaw replacement would be ready, waiting, rather than their having to extract it from the patient's own body. He had, they said, a twenty per cent chance of 'mortality'.

'Eighty per cent chance of survival!' he'd said.

One in five of dying, I thought.

So, he was to have, instead, the old-fashioned surgery. 'This involves something called a pedicle,' the surgeon explained.

Oh for God's sake.

I knew all about pedicles. I had encountered them twenty years before in my biography of my grandmother the sculptor, who had worked with the pioneering reconstructive surgeon Major Harold Gillies, making plaster casts of soldiers' wounded faces, on which he would then plan out his surgery. And I had spent the past three years intensively with them: *My Dear I Wanted to Tell You* was all about pedicles. In the novel, Riley Purefoy's face was rebuilt by Gillies. In 1916, surgeons weren't able to cut a flap of flesh from one limb and take it to another and sew it in place vein by vein, artery by artery, capillary by capillary, as the tall blond surgeon had done for Robert at Charing Cross in 2004. They hadn't the time, the anaesthesia, the techniques. Instead, they would cut the flap, but keep it attached to where it came from by a long strip of skin and blood vessels. This strip would naturally roll inwards, so the surgeon would loosely stitch it into a tube, to protect the blood vessels, and keep it all clean. This way, the flap could be moved to wherever it was needed – the longer the tube, the more topographical flexibility there was – and take with it its own blood supply, off which it would live while it settled into place. Then, when by the miracles of nature the network of capillaries from the flap and those from its new site had found each other and joined up, the pedicle – the tube – could be cut free again at the new site end, and split open again to make a strip, and carefully laid and stitched back in place where it had come from. At the Queen's Hospital (now Queen Mary's) at Sidcup, where Gillies perfected this surgery on the facially injured of the trenches of the First World War, flaps would be moved along in stages, healing up and being moved on again, bit by bit. The tube pedicle ward was known as Burma, because the men's faces were hung about with loops of pedicles looking like lianas in a tropical jungle. All this I had written about.

So Robert was to have a pedicle and a flap, just like Riley Purefoy; like a First World War soldier. The right side of his jawbone, from the temporo-mandibular joint to the centre, was to be removed and replaced with the section of titanium chain, and a flap was to be brought up on a pedicle from his back, to rebuild inside his throat. Riley had a vulcanite jaw, and a double pedicle flap cut from his scalp and swung down like a hammock to cover it. I said, 'Have pedicles improved since Gillies' day?' Surgeons don't expect you to know very much. I resolved to send everybody a copy of the book.

I have form when it comes to what I write appearing later in my actual life. I once wrote a novel about a former-motorcyclist single mother with a bad leg who was living in Shepherd's Bush and going out with a policeman. When I started it I was none of those things; by the time it was finished I was all of them. I resolved to start work immediately on a novel about someone surviving cancer in the most magnificent way possible. Or at least to give Riley a very happy ending. As it turned out, people tended to assume that Robert's cancer came before the World War One novel, and was why I had written it. But no – though it's true to say that like almost everything I've ever written, this too was about him. (In the Egyptian Trilogy: Harry. In *Lionboy*: Sergei the manky cat. In *Lee Raven Boy Thief*: Lee. In *Halo*: the darker bits of Leonidas. In *The Book of the Heart*: see above. In the *My Dear I Wanted to Tell You* series: Riley Purefoy's physical injury, and Peter Locke's mental ones). But I had already finished the book about the rebuilt face. It was well on its way out into the world. I had been thinking of a sequel . . .

. . . and this is the moment when the normal healthy, dull, everyday world fades away, the world that we had begun to love so much since Robert's sobriety kicked in,. I wasn't thinking about a sequel (later I wrote two, *The Heroes' Welcome* and *Devotion*, and I'm writing a third), or about my work at all. There were other things on my mind. I knew a sequel would of necessity be informed by what Robert was about to go through. Thinking about how to respect those grey areas where somebody else's story overlaps and entwines with our own stories could take up a novelist's entire life – and here Robert's life was entwining with both my life, and my fictional characters' lives. Without thinking, I put fiction away. All that concerned a world in which Robert and I no longer lived. Cancer turned out to be another of those diseases which doesn't only happen to the person who has it, but to everybody around them too.

A major difference now that cancer, rather than addiction, was the issue, was the shift in how we were seen. The addictions caused the cancer, and they were both going on in the same body, but there was none of the ambivalence we had seen before 2007. On the cancer ward, you receive the full symphony of sympathy, in all its unrestrained magnificence – I even got free aromatherapy massages – or would have, if I'd had time to take them up. No longer the demon alcoholic; instead the angelic cancer patient. No longer the co-dependent fool, instead, the beloved carer. To be honest, it was a long drink of water. People bring you cake. You can talk about it to anybody. They might suggest some stupid herb that they think can cure it, but nobody says, 'I don't actually think cancer is an illness?'

The sixteen pamphlets I brought home this time included 'Life After Cancer Treatment', 'Help with the Cost of Cancer', 'Sexuality and Cancer', 'Coping with Hair Loss', etc. I did a little reality shift, and imagined: 'Sexuality and Alcoholism', 'Help with the Cost of Alcoholism', 'A Guide for Enablers by Enablers', 'Coping with Co-dependency'.

Compare and Despair, as the wise person said. But – cancer and addiction are both illnesses. They both kill you. With cancer, Robert and I were united against the illness. With addiction, for a long time, the illness and Robert were united against Robert, and I was – oh yes, I was chopped liver. Robert said, later, that he would rather go through the cancer and its treatment again, than return to life as an active alcoholic. I've heard others echo this. With cancer, you know what the enemy is. It's clear and identifiable. With addiction, the enemy is you.

*

He was working like a loon through the period before his surgery. He'd written most of the planned CD: quartet arrangements, including the drop-dead gorgeous theme tune for *My Dear I Wanted to Tell You* with Jackie on violin and his cousin Diane on cornet, which he recorded in time for it to be used on the audiobook, which was read by Dan Stevens.

In those days I kept trying to take little films of him on my phone – 'Because you think I'm going to die,' he said, and I pretended fairly ineffectively that that wasn't why. 'God,' he said, irritated. 'You're at it again. Why don't you just *become* the item? I can just see yer . . .' warming to his theme '. . . a mobile phone with long blond hair – and little legs . . .' he's smiling now, pleased with himself, making little legs with his fingers '. . . hm . . . I married an iPhone . . . I-*podded* her all night long . . .' He falls about laughing at his own joke.

Days before the operation he recorded his setting of the ee cummings poem, 'i carry your heart'. He read it aloud, as a guide track for the singer. The beautiful music, and Robert speaking the beautiful words, in his beautiful deep honey-gravel Lancashire voice, days before that voice disappeared. Him saying: I fear no fate, for you are my fate, my sweet.

Chapter Thirty

University College London Hospital, 09 June 2010

Dear Robert

I hope that this will clarify matters and put a few things into perspective. There is no international consensus for the treatment of oro-pharyngeal cancers but in the UK a significant proportion are treated with chemo/radiotherapy or radiotherapy alone. There are exceptions to this and one of the contra indications to single modality treatment with chemo/radiotherapy is the involvement of bone. Your cancer is large and appears to involve the underlying bone. There is no absolute means of determining bone involvement. The determination [is] based on a combination of clinical appearance and radiology. In this context we feel that combined modality treatment with surgery first followed by radiotherapy or chemo/radiotherapy is most likely to afford the best chance of cure. Surgery is however likely to have a permanent and significant impact on your function on speech and swallow. We cannot ascertain with certainty if bone is involved. We do however have a very high index of clinical suspicion. I have done a literature search. When bone is involved, complete response to radiotherapy is very low . . .

Surgery of this magnitude, which would include a tracheostomy, splitting the jaw to access the tumour, resection of the cancer, neck dissection for removal of involved neck glands and reconstruction, is undertaken on an almost weekly basis. We attempt to stratify risk and anticipate any complications by putting a person who is being planned for surgery through a CPEX test. Unfortunately your CPEX tests translate to a very low score and this equates to 18 per cent peri-operative mortality. You are presently undergoing tests to ascertain whether there is a heart or lung component that has contributed to this low CPEX score. This will also inform us as to whether any of the contributing factors can be addressed and optimised.

If your risk of peri-operative mortality is high, it is likely that the post-operative period will be prolonged and complicated by issues such as wound infection and healing, chest infection and long convalescence.

This will obviously have significant impact on your ability to have the follow-on radiotherapy. If you do not have the post-operative radiotherapy this may negate the surgery and significantly compromise the chances of a curative treatment. Clearly these are statistical figures and there is still a good chance that you will do well after surgery especially if we can optimise your management.

If you are deemed not fit for surgery then we will discuss radiotherapy with you. The outcome of radiotherapy is less certain depending on the extent of the cancer and particularly the involvement of underlying bone. As iterated before we cannot ascertain this with certainty. I apologise that I cannot be more specific with numbers and figures and this unfortunately is the nature of the cancer disease itself.

If you proceed with surgery we anticipate you will be in hospital three to four weeks. The major risks with the surgery are peri-operative death, chest infection which occurs in one in five patients, wound infections about one in twenty, return to theatre one in fifty and failure of flap one in twenty. Clearly these are risks that apply to a fitter person and we have to assume that our risks are higher than this.

I hope that this is useful.

Kind regards

Yours sincerely

Chapter Thirty-One

Home, June 2010

When you're not going to be able to eat solid food because half your throat has been removed and replaced with a pad of flesh from your back, and you can't really swallow liquid food either because of the risk, if it goes down the wrong way, that either you choke, or a bit of food gets into your lung, festers there and gives you pneumonia (one in five), you can get a tube up your nose. Or if they think it's all going to go on for a long time, you can get a PEG. It's an oddly appropriate name: it sounds like a tap in a beer barrel. Short and practical; opening and closing. But it's just an acronym: percutaneous endoscopic gastrostomy. Robert had his put in on 18 June. They punch a hole in your left side, half-way between nipple and sacroiliac crest, direct into the stomach, and feed the very fine clear flexible tube in through the mouth and down down down and then back out into the world. About five inches of it comes out of the small pink puncture just below the rib. Inside the wall of his flesh there is a bumper which holds it in place, and another, a white triangle, on the outside. You need to keep the site clean. It always looks a little sore. I feared the worst about this but a few months into this regime the kind nutritionist who looked like Barack Obama said he'd never seen a better peg site. This sort of thing can make your day.

On the end of the peg tube is a small screwy tap type arrangement, with a cap you screw up or unscrew, white plastic, attached by an inbuilt little noose around the tube, so you can't lose it. You unscrew the cap – well, actually you don't start there. You start with the plastic bottle of Jevity, the size of a large bottle of cleaning fluid, but squishier and thicker. Jevity is beige, nutritionally balanced, made in the Netherlands, and smells of melted ice cream. It arrives every few weeks in big cardboard boxes. The list of ingredients looks like everything you wouldn't want to eat even if you were well. It's clinically approved.

You take a Giving Set from its plastic wrapper: some lengths of clear plastic tubing, with a big purple screw fitting at one end which goes over the mouth of the bottle of Jevity. There is another plastic fitting in the middle which you plug into the feeding pump, and a pleated bellows arrangement, with attachments and little levers, open here for this and there for that. You open the bottle, screw the purple screw over the opening, hang it up upside down on the special hook. Press press press on the bellows bit to bring the liquid as far as the other end of the tube ('Shall I do it, darling?' 'Would you? Thanks, I'm a bit tired'), press till the tube is nearly full, then plug the bellows into the pump (bit fiddly), make sure the pointy bit is up on the purple plastic thingy; then you unscrew the peg's cap, the ridges where the feed leaks and lodges and dries on, and screw the end of the tube on to the peg, and then turn the pump on, so it can heave and sigh, all through the nights, pumping measured doses of gunk straight into his belly. When it blocks, which it does, it bleeps, and Robert, full of morphine, sleeps through that so I am soon sleeping again like the mother of a small child. In the morning, if it has worked properly, it needs detaching from the pump, and flushing through. If it hasn't, it needs swearing at, and I need to try to inject a can of Ensure through it with the big purple plastic syringe, to make up for the overnight feed not working. I loathe and detest the term 'feed' in this context. He's not livestock.

Medicine also goes through the peg. He takes a lot. He is well ahead on the list of things you have to take to counteract the side effects of the things you have to take, and some of those have their own side effects too. Much of it is not liquid, so there is pounding to be done, in a pestle and mortar. His idea of taking medicine is, 'Ah I must take my medicine' – find some medicine – take some. As the new medicine involves morphine this is not so good. So I am in charge of the medicine. I become an alchemist.

He has realised that the liquid morphine, the oromorph, contains alcohol, and must be refused. He is firm on this. The powdered morphine is powdered in with everything else. We have a small grey stone mortar from his stepmother's kitchen. One pill – the gabapentin? – leaves a pink residue which sticks to the stone. Capsules can be emptied out, but little flakes of the coating that holds tablets together refuse to be ground, and float around, perilous to the passage of fine granules through the minute eyes of the peg system. The amount of water required to get everything in sometimes makes him sick, which becomes difficult, later, without a throat.

I hum a little tune: Voltarol, Voltarol, to the tune of 'Spiderman, Spiderman'.

Jackie came over and we recorded him reading Dylan Thomas and Yeats, and they chatted. I found I couldn't really talk.

Chapter Thirty-Two

UCLH, Midsummer's Day 2010

I dropped him off the night before. Sunday night. He didn't want me to come up to the ward, so I drew up in the ambulance bay out the front. Off he hobbled with his sticks and his shoulder-bag. The last thing he said was, 'Everything is going to be all right.' As was my habit, I believed him – both his intention, and his capacity to know. I had been waiting for him to say something which was worthy of being the last thing I would hear in his real voice, so after he said that, I dashed off.

Surgery day was 21 June. He went to theatre at 8 a.m. Lola and I decided to give blood – her first time. She got a badge, and I took a photo of her grinning and pointing at the needle into her arm. They gave me a badge too because it turned out it was my twenty-fifth time. Or because when they said, 'How's your day going then?', we told them. The nurse said, 'Congratulations – you saved a life today.' I said, 'Can I choose which one?'

Lola loved it. They loved her. We ate our biscuits and drank our tea and kind of enjoyed the symbolism.

I invited everyone who had enquired about him or expressed

goodwill over to ours and by 5 p.m. they began to arrive. We ate and drank and played the piano and talked till later than I had been prepared for. Eight, nine in the evening – still light, and me in the garden ringing the Head & Neck Ward, being told he was still in theatre.

Is that good?

Yes, they said. Probably.

The operation involving microsurgery, for which he had been deemed too weak, which would have taken too long, was usually eight or nine hours. This had already taken twelve.

He came out at ten thirty. 'Oh he's fine,' they said, 'in the ICU, settled in for the night, it all went well.' I burst into tears and at that moment my brother came in the garden gate and I howled all over him.

*

The next morning I was up there first thing. Robert in his green robe was superb – illuminated! He had a face like a car crash and big metal staples where they'd cut his throat, twice, to get his jaw out, and a tracheostomy and scarlet railways tracks down his side where they'd pushed the flesh and veins up under the skin to rebuild inside his mouth, but his eyes were flashing, intense, merry. He was strong, after all. He had been under for fourteen hours. It went very well. He reacted enormously to everything that was said, pulling on sleeves, demanding to be heard though he could not speak. The tracheostomy plug in his throat looked like the bastard child of a washing machine dial and a baby's dummy, and made disgusting bubbly snorting noises. The trackline down his side reached almost to his arse. He was battered and swollen, yellow and mauve where he had been painted. They thought he'd need to be in the ICU for two to three days, but he was well enough to leave in twenty-four hours. Record time – he told me so several times, in writing.

'It went impeccably,' said the anaesthetist.

Surgeon Grumpy as Robert called him (as opposed to Surgeon Happy, the other one), came by the next day on the ward, and smiled, and relief was written on him, it was true.

Impeccably.

Robert, meanwhile, was brilliant, incandescent, trying to get up and do physiotherapy.

I had been concerned about the pedicle. In 1917 they hung about, like streamers. I had half thought it would be looping about over his chest, and then in due course they'd cut it away. But no – things *had* advanced since Gillies' time: Robert's was under his skin, lying over his collarbone, looking as if it might pulse, like a hose or a snake. It immediately began to annoy me, like an errant cable left the wrong side of a table leg. I was going to spend the rest of my life wishing they'd threaded it tidily underneath the clavicle.

I had written of Riley after his surgery, based on contemporary photographs, that his face looked like no man's land, like sandbags held together with barbed wire. In this too, things were different now. Robert really didn't look that bad.

That he couldn't talk at all was because of the tracheostomy. It was not possible to tell how things would be when that was closed up; meanwhile there was a revolting contraption for sucking phlegm out through it. They'd given him a wipe-off screen device to write on. He wouldn't shut up. He wrote TELL HER I LOVE HER, and gave it to a nurse, and pointed at me. He was writing a list of things you could do without being able to talk: WALKS BIRDWATCHING MUSIC SHAGGING – WITH YOU. I told him how unbelievably proud and happy I was. He cried, and he wrote I'M ONLY CRYING BECAUSE I MADE YOU HAPPY, and I took a photograph of it, because of believing things more when they are written down. Now I believed that he wanted to make me happy, and for the first time I could see that he always had wanted that, and that shame about not being able to do so was among the many shames which had fuelled his terrible carousel.

In the following weeks he used notebooks to talk. I think he threw them away. I wish he hadn't. I would have got them out of the rubbish but I was trying to be respectful. He knew that.

I did find one, later, under a piano. (It's reproduced on p. 397.) He wrote at random on different pages. There isn't much order, and I don't know who things were addressed to. They make a peculiar and specific kind of poetry, an account of his rollercoaster of agonised despair and buoyant optimism, his humour, his fear and his irrepressible need to communicate and be playful.

Chapter Thirty-Three

My Car, Summer 2010

I was at the lights on the Marylebone Road heading to the Euston Hilton, as he called it, when my phone rang. Seeing his nickname come up (The Genius), I answered. I thought it was a nurse or someone ringing for him, like waiters and Australians in the past. But it was him. And he said hello. Croaky and weird and nasal, as if goblins had nailed down his tongue. But him. I nearly crashed.

He was talking talking talking. He got the hang of it quickly. It wasn't that bad! I mean, it was awful, and hard work, for him and for the listener, but it wasn't that bad. It was a miracle and a fountain of joy. We talked on speaker for the rest of my journey towards him, and while I parked, and across the car park and the lobby, until we got cut off in the lift.

'Doing brilliantly,' they said. On 14 July he was out of hospital and I posted the Raveonettes' 'My Boyfriend's Back' on Facebook.

At home, I looked in his mouth. His tongue – the remains of it – lay sideways. At the back his epiglottis hung awry, like a chandelier in a bombed-out ballroom. It was clean and strange. I could kiss him. He could kiss me.

That summer was, seriously, all right. He healed up. His face was not so much scarred as odd and pulled about a bit. His mouth took on a humorous, slightly bitter sideways twist, Buster Keatonish and not inappropriate. The stitchwork had been immaculate.

I started to get the hang of his speech. Pillow-talk suffered, and it drove me mad when he talked to me while I was driving, because I had to look at him to properly understand and hear him. 'Wait till the lights!' became my cry. He got the eating back up too – he was on shepherd's pie after only a month or so. We went to Rousham, we went to concerts, we went to speech therapy and the nutritionist and clinic every week and the dental hospital, he swallowed little boluses of things that showed up on the X-ray film they made and I photographed it, his bicycle-chain jaw hanging there, his swallow improving. He had a kidney blood test, a mask-fitting. He had an eye test. Jackie played at the Wigmore. Lola sat her A-levels, and got her results. We didn't go on holiday.

'Thank you,' he said, 'for all this.'

'You'd do the same for me,' I replied.

A beat, then we both started laughing.

'Tell you what,' he said. 'I'll get you health insurance.'

*

Something hasn't come up very much for a while. One day at a time; one disease at a time? It's not that his alcoholism ceased to exist, or to matter, but recovery from cancer and cancer surgery was a more immediate requirement. And I really was leaving it to him. Of course the voice issue made meetings harder. I actually can't remember if he was going to meetings now. I also can't remember anything about the breast cancer my mother developed during this time. I don't know what year she had her mastectomy. I know she didn't like the tamoxifen, and chose not to continue with it. I know that she and my family dealt with this without my contributing a damn thing. I understand how that happened, but I'm sorry.

*

I was waiting for one of my sisters in my car on a yellow line near Holborn, using the time to apply cream to my hands, putting my rings on the dashboard. A parking warden approached. I saw her in my rear-view mirror and pulled out, thinking to find somewhere safer. When I pulled in again the engagement ring was nowhere. I searched my lap, I stood up, I searched the seat. I lifted the little rug in the footwell, and the other footwell in case it had jumped. I looked in the door pockets, under the seat, down my shirt, everywhere. I knew it had gone down the ventilation vent under the windscreen. There was nowhere else it could have gone.

Back home, Robert said in his goblin voice, 'Oh good, does that mean I'm off the hook?'

David, the Buddhist Saab specialist (The Karma-chanic, oh how we laughed) came round, and searched, and unscrewed things and took them to bits, and said, 'It's in there somewhere. It can't have got out.' He said, 'When the car's had it, call me and we'll find the ring.'

Chapter Thirty-Four

UCLH Radiotherapy Dept, September 2010

I hadn't quite got the point about radiotherapy and chemo. Though it wasn't actually chemo. It had been going to be cisplatin; it was in the end a biological therapy called cetuximab: more expensive, potentially better, less likely to cause deafness which they recognised as an issue for a musician. 'It will also,' said Dawn the oncologist, with a wry smile, 'involve complexion-related side-effects that are, hm . . . a test of love.'

Test of love? Bring it on! I thought. Vainglorious romantic idiot that I was.

From 13 September, once a week for seven weeks, he sat for hours in a big, well-worn, blue puffy armchair, cannula in his arm, being poisoned, while I read him the paper, or wandered the neighbourhood getting in the groceries at Sainsbury's on Tottenham Court Road, or drinking coffee. I had a Chinese massage one time.

The radiotherapy started a week later, five days a week for six weeks. We took cheesecake in to the unit staff. The red-faced Northern girl; the beautiful sunshine smiley girl, God I've forgotten her name already – Marie? no – and the carroty redhead; the camp man, the Indian girl, Polish Beata. Val who did little dancing steps with her tiny feet. Dr Asad with the pretty shoes, who never smiled. They worked in the depths of the hospital, the second basement down, in corridors which extend under Tottenham Court Road. Robert's machine (LinacE – linear accelerator E) was, apparently, right next to the tube platform, only the wall between them.

In *Doctor Who* when the new scary thing appears, you don't know to start with if it's going to be good or bad. LinacE is like that: a great swan of a machine, a vast Kenwood mixer, a 1970s telephone, a spaceship, strong and unnerving.

I watch on computer screens from a different room, two of them giving different angles on the scene. In front of LinacE is a gurney to which Robert is led by white-coated radiotherapy handmaidens. They assist him out of his shirt – the long scar down his back is red and livid – and lay him down on his back. They bring to him his turquoise mask: this has been made and moulded to fit precisely to his face, head, throat and shoulders, of a light but firm plastic mesh. The colour glows rather. They place it carefully over him and screw it down with little metal slots and bolts to the block on which he lies, so he can't move. It is scratchy and claustrophobic, a torture implement in primary-school blue. It is vital that he does not move. They check repeatedly. It takes time. There are holes melted into it for his nostrils, and a hole for his mouth which looks like the mouth of Munch's *Scream*. (Robert's long-term plan for it is to spray it gold and hang it on the wall: make a medal out of it.)

The handmaidens move away, the table rises to the machine, offering him up, back arched, bare-torsoed in jeans and boots, his knees falling sideways. It is impossible not to think of altars and sacrifices. LinacE starts to move. It leans in, turning, turning, so gentle and curious, looking at him from various angles, circling him, sort of enfolding him, over and over. The Swan photographs him for fifteen, twenty minutes. The handmaidens come and check again. It has to be exactly right. After a while the beeps begin, and the handmaidens silently leave the screen.

The red and green sign lights up outside: Radiation On. Every day for six weeks, burning him. Every day I sit in the corridor. Every day I take him home.

During these weeks I develop a bad Facebook habit, watch all of *Mad Men*, and write a series of relentless, bitter villanelles.

*

By day twenty-four he was deaf in one ear. His saliva turned to snot in his mouth, a plague of acne burned on his face, and he was drooling constantly. He was so tired he collapsed reaching across the bed for a T-shirt. Just collapsed. Peeing in his food-product bottles like he used to pee in vodka bottles. Blood and mucus on the sheets every day. He slept, went to be burned and poisoned, he injected medicine into his stomach through his peg. He lost weight. We had to get it back up. If he took too much feed he was sick through his non-existent throat, and then what about his medicine? I had responsibility but no authority. Do I give him more? Or not? Or how much?

I dragged his wheelchair behind me because these UCLH wheelchairs don't work well being pushed. I tipped it over in the street from the main building to the Rosenheim, an unfortunate kerb. Everyone ran to help us. I used to say to him, in the bad old days: if you end up in a wheelchair because of this I'm not going to be pushing you around. And now because you have to mean what you say and not make empty threats, I was glad that the chairs were crap and the small print let me off. I wasn't pushing him, I was pulling him. So I was keeping my word.

I slept in the back room, to give him peace and quiet and because I didn't like the gurgling at night. I thought he was about to die or vomit.

*

They said that 'a week or so' after the end of the treatments, he would start feeling better. I latched on to the 'week'. Then the 'or so'. How long is 'or so'? Four weeks later he was not physically capable of getting to meetings.

'How are you today?'

'Worse,' he'd say. 'Worse than ever.'

And he was depressed. Clinically. He did the 'Can you move and do you want to kill yourself?' Patient Health Questionnaire #9 Quick Depression Assessment. He scored more than five ticks in the blue section which means Major Depressive Disorder. I stole the Instructions (*for doctor or healthcare professional use only*). He didn't want to kill himself but he'd thought about it. He ticked the box to say so. They said: it's normal at this stage.

The low winter sun was strong in our room, shining right at him all the short day, so he moved into the back room, where he slept twenty-one hours a day. He wouldn't feed (feed! Well, I can't say eat) or take his drugs if I didn't make him. He was running on empty. He hadn't had a bath since July. I was again running that line between making sure what needs to be done is done, controlling, bossing, nagging, saving him – again—

For a while, I had been taking him in a hot wet flannel every morning, to ease open his caked-up bloody burned mouth. I mentioned it, in a 'thank God we don't have to do that any more' way. Looking for good news as usual. God perhaps I am unbearable. And he said, 'What?' He'd forgotten. 'Write it down,' he said. So I wrote it down.

'Good things: His ear hasn't fallen off. The hole which was developing behind it has I think healed up, after six weeks of injecting splurges of amorphous anti-bacterial gunk into it. It's hard to look to check. His hair is only falling out round the back, so he hasn't noticed. A lot is gone. It looks like an outdated tonsure on an ancient monk. He is passive rather than concerned or interested. I feel that I am inflicting healing on him. His neck burns are very dry and shiny and a bit scaly, but the scabs are gone. He is so cold he won't undress, so I peer down his collar. The light is never good. To be honest I don't know what is going on. His mouth stinks. Cheesy, bad breath-y – dog breath. It falls to me to clean it, dragging out sticky yellow gob with the pink sponges on sticks. He retches. It smells. Sometimes it is caked thick like a scab against the very back of his throat and I use the long flat-headed tweezers to ease it off. There is a satisfaction to this, and afterwards his voice is clearer. The rest of him smells of nothing at all. Presumably because of the blandness of the feed? He doesn't change his clothes – his pyjama/clothes combo. I suggest washing; he says, 'tomorrow'. He's too tired. It's cold. Beautiful bright frosty days, full of sun, sparkly. I hear his hollow cough upstairs, coughing through a throat that half isn't there. He doesn't shave. He's had enough removed from his face. No sharp knives. As a result he has half a beard. An entire little slightly Spanish-looking moustache, but no beard where he has been irradiated. He doesn't eat, drink, walk, talk, read, laugh, smoke, play, fuck . . . who is Robert, if he doesn't do these things?'

He has exercises for his tongue, to be done every two to three hours, with a mirror: Start at one corner of your mouth and lick all the way around. Touch the corner of your mouth with the tip of your tongue. Then the other corner. Lift the tip of your tongue and try and touch the back of your top teeth . . . and so on. Hourly: Use the pink sponges; dip them in water, gently sponge over the tongue, and roof of the mouth. Practise swallowing your saliva. After you have cleaned your mouth, repeat the following: Place a teaspoon in a cup of ice, or use frozen swabs. Use the back of the teaspoon or frozen swab, rub on the roof of the mouth, and back of the mouth (left side, avoiding the flap on the right). Remove the spoon, swallow immediately. Repeat five to ten times. Dip a clean sponge in lemon juice, gently rub along the back left side of the mouth, and along the tongue, then swallow. Dip the sponge in lemon juice, gently suck the lemon juice from the sponge, and swallow. Repeat five to ten times.

For the tongue tip: tea toe two tar top team time tip tea time day time tea pot detail table mat day out top hat and tails day and night . . .

For the back of the tongue: key car kay core got goat gate game carpet counter kitchen cacti good gorgeous grumpy grandad . . .

He didn't do them. He was nil by mouth: nil going in and not much coming out. 'You all right?' I say.

'Half left,' he says.

*

He is prescribed Ondansetron. Ondansetron! It sounds like an intergalactic disco . . .

*

I felt madly extravagant, and fantasised about buying a 1920s velvet coat for £850, a thirty-year-old camellia for £300, a rug for £4,000. Rugs cost a lot, especially big ones. Lola sussed me – I wanted a big rug to keep the sitting room warm because then it would be warm for Robert and he would get better.

*

In April 2011 *My Dear I Wanted to Tell You* was published, though I hardly noticed. I was 'working' on the sequel, *The Heroes' Welcome*, but at that stage it was no more than a painful diversionary tactic which failed to divert.

I absconded occasionally. The district nurses would come by, and Jackie would stay the night. There were a couple of brief foreign book tours for *My Dear I Wanted to Tell You*, and once when a friend was singing her final night as Eliza in *My Fair Lady* at the Châtelet in Paris, Lola and I went on the train – an attack of spontaneity, a last-minute overnighter. We went backstage to congratulate her, and Sarah invited Lola out on to the stage, and let her wear her massively long white fur cloak from the ball scene, and swan about in it. Then we went and ate very late, coupe de champagne and steak tartare, and it was magical and almost a shock to see how enjoyable things could be.

On the train back there were calls, the feeding tube was blocked, when was I getting in?

*

It was an obsessive existence. I emailed Jackie the instructions:

Jackie –

Could you make sure

at night, that he has his evening meds and sets up his feed – sometimes he goes to bed for a nap, sleeps through and forgets to do it.

in the morning, that he doesn't sleep through his feed finishing (it beeps loudly), and therefore neglect to flush the tube through with water. It usually finishes between 7.30 and 9ish, depending when he started it. It's OK to leave a bit of feed unfinished in the bottle; important not to leave tube unflushed because that's when it blocks.

His medicine is on the kitchen table. I usually bring up the morning meds and give them to him when turning off the feed and flushing. There is chicken broth and fruit smoothies/juice in the fridge, and the jars of Ensure. He needs to get as much in as he can . . .

His appointments are in his diary (sitting room, table). Monday Helen the speech therapist is coming at 9.30; cd you leave keys?

Also on Monday he has an eye test at Charing Cross Hospital at 2 p.m. Letter on the mantelpiece. He might want you to book a cab for him: he gets special cheap ones from the council (phone number here); ref number HF648042. On Thursday Josephine the Physio is coming at 11 a.m. – same key arrangement. Also probably (but he needs to confirm with her – phone number here) he needs to go to Gaynor the Counsellor at 1 p.m. Disabled parking pass is on the kitchen table. I'm back last thing on Thursday.

There followed a list of seven more emergency phone numbers, from Louis to the district nurses, and the thirteen medications he was on, and the mouth exercises and cleaning routines he should be doing.

He did get a chest infection – from food going down the wrong way due to lack of swallowing capacity). They gave him amoxicillin for it, to which he was allergic, so there was diarrhoea and he was back in hospital, but on a different floor, oh the excitement. He was in isolation, in case it was some terrible infectious diarrhoea rather than an allergy.

What do you actually do with shit-covered sheets? Four times in one night? But the shit smelt of nothing. It was as bland as the beige feed.

*

Robert and I once sat down with a friend, an NHS doctor, and ran through all the treatments he had had, and their cost. It was an estimatory kind of maths to set that against the tax he had paid over thirty-five years of drinking and smoking, but there was no question about it: 'You've paid for it,' the doctor told him. 'Every treatment, every investigation, every visit to hospital, every drug, every surgery. And more.'

*

I became obsessed with the questionnaire in the *Guardian Weekend Magazine*. Answering the questions each week was a way of taking my emotional temperature.

When were you happiest?

Robert Lockhart

What is your greatest fear?

Robert Lockhart

What is the trait you most deplore in yourself?

Robert Lockhart

What or who is the romantic love of your life?

Robert Lockhart

What was your most embarrassing moment?

Robert Lockhart

How do you relax?

Robert Lockhart

What is the worst thing anyone's said to you?

Robert Lockhart

Who would play you in the film of your life?

Robert Lockhart

What would your super power be?

Robert Lockhart

What did you want to be when you were growing up?

Robert Lockhart

What does love feel like?

Robert Lockhart

Who would you invite to your dream dinner party?

Robert Lockhart

If you could edit your past, what would you change?

Robert Lockhart

What single thing would improve the quality of your life?

Robert Lockhart

What is the closest you've come to death?

Robert Lockhart

What song would you like played at your funeral?

Robert Lockhart
What is the most important lesson life has taught you?
Robert Lockhart

*

I woke to his misery; I slept alongside it at night. If I said nothing, was I neglecting him? If I said something, was I taking on his responsibility? If he didn't do the exercises he wouldn't improve. He didn't do them. He'd been asleep. They said, get up, have structure. He couldn't. I couldn't make him. I couldn't help him. (I was helping him. Not enough.) So I left him alone. That's all. As with the alcoholism, he had to sort it out himself. The echoes were unbearable and I had no preparation for that.

The moment Lola left the house I cried. He tried to comfort me.

The district nurse said, My, you're looking so much better.

I didn't know – still don't – if it was the Swan, or the drug that was better than the other drug, which did this to him.

Chapter Thirty-Five

My Street, Spring and Summer 2011

I am always happy when I see now a little red metal lid from a vodka miniature, sharp-edged and shiny, lying in the street, because each little red lid I see tells me that not every little red lid I saw in the street back in the day was one of his, which tells me that perhaps sometimes when I saw them and thought, my stomach collapsing, *Fuck, fuck, he's drinking again*, he might not have been. Then I feel bad about letting it make me happy, because each little red lid still denotes somebody drinking a vodka miniature in the street, and that is never going to be a happy story. But Robert was particular about litter. He didn't like the idea of birds eating things that might damage them.

2011 was a very shrunken year. The burden of hope remained heavy – they said things would improve and yet things did not improve, so I stopped expecting, and I hoped only very quietly. I think this made things easier for both of us. I was gentler with him. I got over my fear and dislike of the word carer. The last thing he or I had wanted me to be was his carer. I was his girlfriend, he was my boyfriend; it was important to both of us that he wasn't redefined by his illness as being dependent on me. (My hospital technique was just to swan around as if I owned the place, and if anyone questioned I'd smile vastly and gesture vaguely and say, 'I'm with him.') But now, minding about a word was a luxurious detail, no longer relevant in our limited lives. This was a different universe of romance. He needed looking after; I looked after him. He dragged himself the two hundred yards up the road to Paolo's – he had to sit on a neighbour's low wall halfway, for a rest – and texted me later saying could I pick him up. The subsidised cab service couldn't understand his speech when he rang. He missed appointment after appointment through sheer exhaustion. It was an immense effort to get to the hospital. For months he was having fittings for a plate to be made for his mouth. It would make his speech clearer. He wanted this.

In spring he started smoking again. He said it was his only pleasure, and I poured a bottle of Jevity over him, in fury, as he lay in the bed. My logic – if he was going to continue to sabotage himself, even now, then so would I. Not my proudest moment.

The roses were out again. He'd managed a year.

In late summer he was sitting on the neighbour's wall when I unexpectedly came round the corner, and saw a flash of something red in his hand.

I took the empty quarter bottle physically from the pocket where he was trying to hide it; walked up the road.

*

He went back to Camden for six weeks. It was a horrible kind of flashback, only worse, because – because of everything. When I visited I'd lie down with him on his single bed and try not to say the wrong thing, just hold on to him, if he wanted.

I didn't know if he was engaging with it, and assumed that he wasn't, really. Couldn't. But he did! I have the papers (see p. 402).

It surprises me still to see the positivity and strength, the clarity and ambition in what he wrote. They ended with: 'I am still angry and even embarrassed about my relapse, but I have learnt from it. And finally, just something about my four and a half years of sobriety – it got better and better. Never again do I want to return to that hell.'

*

I had no idea whether or not he drank after he came back from Camden that time. It seemed impossible for me to have any opinion or feeling by then. Anything I did might cause him pain or shame. He seemed tiny, physically, mentally, emotionally, spiritually.

Him, at the door of the back bedroom: 'Lou?'

Me: 'I'm downstairs.'

Him: 'Oh good.'

He'd go about his business. Coughing, rumbling about. Pissing in the loo (not too bad a day). Lurching downstairs. Putting his coat (or mine) on over his pyjamas and going to sit on the doorstep. Drift of fag smoke (pretty good day).

Putting his coat (or mine) and jeans on over his pyjamas and saying, 'Where's me sticks, Lily?' (very good day).

'In the corner, love.'

'I've lost me specs, Lily.'

'Yer've not, Bert, they're on yer 'ead.'

Lily and Bert were longstanding hyper-Northern personae, for mocking our age and domesticity.

Step by careful step on his sticks he proceeded to Paolo's cafe, resting on the way.

Sometimes he would say: 'Are you going to the library?' And I would say, 'No.' And he would say, 'Hmph.'

I carried on making soup. I stopped and started the feed pump. I wished he'd never come off the morphine. I was afraid to have any emotion because I loved him and I was so angry.

Around this time *My Dear I Wanted to Tell You* was shortlisted for several prizes, and won the Galaxy Prize for the audiobook, with his music. I told him and he was proud.

The title became ever more ironic and multi-layered. Initially it had been about the phrase on the field postcard: 'My Dear, I wanted to tell you before any telegram arrives'; and the fact that facially injured soldiers often couldn't speak, physically, and about the old true cliché of returning soldiers never talking about the war. Now it incorporated everything about Robert too: Robert who used to love everything so much and be so brilliant, and could now do virtually nothing. Robert who had talked for England, until he no longer could. Robert who never asked, 'Why me?' He knew why him.

*

In December Jackie celebrated her birthday by having an all-day session of playing Beethoven Quartets at my mother's house. At New Year a great tree in our forest fell: Louis's beloved mother died, in Ghana. In early January, Jackie, Lola and I went for five days in Morocco: a break. Absconding. Comfort. Sometimes people assume I must have felt guilty about this, but I didn't. I was doing my best, and if you're doing your best there is no reason for guilt. (The problem with that, though, is that different people have different bests and it is tempting to compare them. Robert's self-loathing during his alcoholic years was partly because he felt he *was* doing his best, but that his best was far worse than other people's: mine, for example. This left him with two harsh inter-pretations: either this really *was* his best, in which case perhaps he should just remove his wretched toxic self from the sight of better humans, or he was lying to himself and others about it being his best, in which case he was a nasty manipulator stringing his victims along and should likewise remove his wretched toxic self etc.)

I had a realisation while I was away: that when someone I love is unhappy or angry I *too,* like Robert, take it personally. It's the same damn thing. Because I don't want them to be upset I become upset because I can't prevent it. Which makes it worse. And who am I to prevent it? It's not mine. It's just another way of being obsessed with someone else's behaviour at the expense of my own.

I remember being on the white Moroccan roof in clear cool sun, hot bitter coffee, long loving conversations, riding horses along the Atlantic beach with seven dogs. Taking a call on the back of a horse in the dunes from the district nurse who didn't know how to unblock the feeding tube. Pretending to Lola that wasn't what I was talking about.

But you know what? He'd been clear of cancer for fourteen months.

Part Six

2012—

Chapter Thirty-Six

A&E and ICU, 22-23 January 2012
On Sunday, 22 January 2012, I woke at the usual kind of time—
Can you tell this is the day he died? By the way I put it? Well, it
was and it wasn't.

I went in to check on him and his tube, as usual. I had a strong
urge to lie down beside him, like a young woman's longing, to just
shove him over and get in with him. But he wasn't in his bed –
which was like the budgie not being there and the cage door still
being closed.

He could only be at Paolo's. I dressed and went down there. He
was in the dingy little yard at the back, in his velvet-collared coat,
with double espresso, fag and the *Observer*, complaining about its
(lack of) classical music coverage. I ordered my coffee and went
through and sat with him. It was good to see him up but I still only
wanted to lie down with him. We chatted: his gurgling voice, my
concentration, his laboured sips at his coffee, my inured ignoring
of his cigarette. *My Dear I Wanted to Tell You* was starting on Radio
4 the next day. *Book at Bedtime.* He was proud about that.

He said he was hungry. There is a particular joy when the sick person shows even the tiniest enthusiasm, even – specially – for the most ordinary thing. I said, 'Good.'

'Why?' he asked.

'Sign of life,' I said. 'I'll make you soup.' His long-term plan that his first meal would be over-cooked tortellini with extra sauce at the Italian had recently seemed over-ambitious.

He wondered when Lola would be off. She had finished school, got into university and was about to go travelling.

'Ten days,' I said.

'Already?' he said, in his tongue-nailed-down voice. 'Don't worry, I'll be here. I'll look after you.' There was no jokey echo to this. Just kindness. I liked that.

I gave him a lift the eight hundred yards to his AA meeting. He said, 'Don't pick me up, love, I'll probably go for a coffee afterwards. What are you doing?'

'Seeing my mum,' I said.

'Send her my love.'

'She worries about you,' I said, out of the car window, as I dropped him off.

'Tell her I'm fine,' he called, and clumped off up the path to the church hall, where the survivors were gathering by the door, smoking. Sticks, skinny legs, overcoat, wintry lunchtime, London.

I went to see Mum, told her he was fine, and decided to stop in at the Coronet in Notting Hill to see *War Horse*. Cinema is escapism, isn't it? I quite liked it, thought as usual about how Robert could have done better music.

I came home afterwards and was settling in when there was a knock on the door: a stranger in a woolly hat – a young man, polite, agitated. He said something about Robert, the Princess Victoria, and Hospital. He was Will, a barman who'd known Robert for years. Robert had been having lunch and he'd had a fit. I should go there. Did I want him to come. No of course not, why would I?

I drove down the Fulham Palace Road thinking, 'Just another Robert emergency, you'll leave another bit of yourself that you can ill afford behind.' And, 'Having *lunch*?'

A&E. A long wait.

Why so long? They could just direct me to him.

They took me through and put me in a little beige room; a little beige room without him in it. I was puzzled. Was this going to be a bigger drama?

A further wait. I didn't like it. Whispering behind the door jamb.

A doctor came in. Two, actually. Young men. They said some things.

damage

oxygen

lack

twenty-two minutes—

and to each rational question I raised, they said

no

no

no

They said, brain damage.

I thought, well he's had that before, and anyway he has loads of brain. The doctors were looking significant. It seemed I needed to respond.

'How much brain damage?' I said. I said, 'Is he conscious?'

'No.'

I can't remember the other words they said. I asked what that meant in practical terms, and one of them said, 'His brain is not able to support his heartbeat, or his breathing.' It was something like that. 'There is not enough function.'

I had to circle it a couple of times before getting the full view of the landscape. He's unconscious. He won't be conscious again. He won't be conscious again? What—

No

I think I said, 'No more Robert?'

Like a three-year-old. No more Robert? Bewildered.

He's on a life-support machine. Without it, he can't breathe and his heart won't beat. 'You know what kind of person he was, what he would want.' I have no idea why they are saying this, though it seems urgent. There are more tests they need to run to confirm something which it seemed would make not the slightest difference but it had to be done and couldn't be done yet because there had to be a period of time between the first test and the—

Was?

Can I go to him?

Of course.

At what stage did I find out what had happened? Did the boy who came to the door tell me? Or someone at the hospital?

He'd ordered roast beef, Yorkshire pudding and broccoli, and he had tried to eat it, and he had choked.

The pub people didn't know his history; they didn't know he couldn't eat. Did anyone give him the Heimlich manoeuvre? It was Sunday lunch in a gastropub. Families in there. The dad of the neighbouring table had held him upright. Laura, the six-foot Aussie barmaid with the glamorous white streak of hair, had been with him. They'd called the ambulance.

He'd ordered roast beef, Yorkshire pudding and broccoli? He what the FUCK?

He is on a gurney in the back of A&E, in a gown. Numbers on a whiteboard; cardiac studs on his chest, cannulas. He's propped up, the sheet tenting over his knees very pale and smooth, all perfectly him, but his mouth is distorted, pulled about by the ventilator tube strapped uncomfortably tight with a small length of gauze.

'Can he feel that?'

No.

Too many nos.

He looks eight hundred years old. The plastic ID bracelet gives his name as unknown. 'He's not unknown,' I say in fury. 'I know him.' I hold his hand; he holds it back, tight, and my heart fills with joy. His eyes are closed.

He's in a coma. Boyfriend in a coma. He's been in comas before. Not like this. He's brain dead. Someone used the term. Perhaps me. His brain is dead.

And with a sudden swoosh, you are again in a new universe, dragged there in Robert Lockhart's slipstream. And you blink, and you start to adapt.

What do you do with a person in a coma? It is a panicky thought and I respond in a panicky way. You play them music. I've seen *The Diving Bell and the Butterfly*.

I decide I just won't tell Lola this is happening and that way she need never know or be upset about it. I had always wanted her to love him and now here he is causing more grief and trouble.

I have no headphones.

I open his eyelids with my fingers and stare at him. His eyes so blue and clear and empty. I can't position myself within his gaze to look him in the eye without climbing up on top of him and the gurney and everything. I think – Well, just do that then, Jesus, if ever you could just do anything you can just do anything now. But I don't.

Streams of black blood shit are coming out of him. They clean him up, over and over. They are called Michael, Richard and Greg. He is wearing the same kind of gown as when he was in intensive care after surgery, so lively, writing lists of everything he would do without speech or eating or walking or piano playing.

A child in the waiting room has a cough.

After an hour or two I ring Louis. Lola is at his. I tell him. I slip outside to the car park and ring Swift. I say, under the pollarded plane trees, 'Robert is dying.' She doesn't know what I mean. Finishing dinner with her children, Sunday night. I say, 'No, really. He really is.'

343

There is a young Italian doctor who seems to want to unplug him now. I think I stare at her. She fades away.

I want to hear what you have to say about all this, my love. I know what I think. I want you.

Louis and Lola appear. I have marzipan; Lola makes me eat it. She has brought headphones. I still just want to lie down in his arms; it's all I've wanted all day.

I can't get the headphones on him right because I can't get at him because he's entangled in hospital stuff. 'I can't get at it!' is one of his phrases. I put on Martha Argerich playing Chopin, from my phone. I don't know if it's starting at the beginning. I don't know if it's too loud or too quiet. I want him to tell me if it is how he wants it, perfectionist musician. I run down the battery on my phone.

Louis is behind me all evening, quiet, there. The medics line up. Swift appears.

I'm at the top of a stairwell ringing his ex-wife. There had been discussion recently of something bureaucratic about their son and when I say 'This is a difficult call' she thinks it's about that. I say, 'No, it's more difficult than that.'

He can't stay here. They don't want to take him upstairs because upstairs isn't open. They don't want to open it. Nobody actually says, just turn it off now, it'll save us a lot of trouble. Nobody is unkind. They take him upstairs. We follow in a separate lift. They open upstairs specially, and then bring in another person, a very old person with laboured breathing. There is a relatives' room. We are on the eleventh floor. It's the Intensive Care Unit.

Robert's son arrives, with his mother and stepfather. For a moment I think: he'll come back to life now, for Jim. I feel us all to be strong and loving for Robert, standing around him. I wish I had done better, all my life, so that his son did not have to be here now for this. It gets late. They leave.

He is in the middle of a vast empty ward. The stertorous lady – Evelyn – has had a diabetic collapse; she is far away. After a while a man is in a glass room at the end. The machinery – apart from Robert's – is silent, dark and watchful, waiting to save other lives, another time. The windows are wide and the sky and the lights of the city below are glorious. It is now night.

I sit. People bring me tea. Lola has taken hold of me and holds me to the earth. I feel her hand firm round my ankle when I start to float away like a balloon, drifting across landscapes, distant, high above. She stands by me, sits in the relatives' room, refuses to go home. She is eighteen now.

I have an idea. I say to the doctor: 'Can you marry someone who is brain dead?'

He says, 'It wouldn't be legally binding, but you can do whatever you want.'

Later on, as Louis leaves, I ask him to buy two wedding rings, the next morning. I don't have my purse with me. Lola gives him her bank card.

'What kind?' Louis says; I say, 'Ordinary.'

Lola dozes, fully dressed on the couch in the relatives' room.

I lean over Robert again and again, lifting his eyelids gently. He stares straight up. He would not meet my eye. Now, I move myself around above him so that my eyes are on the line of his staring, and our eyes can meet. Hello, I say, into the bluest vacuum I ever saw, clear and blue as an empty lake, a cloudless sky, a perfect flower. Forget me not, I say. Speedwell. Blue to blue. I lift his eyelids over and over, swearing each time not to do it again. The restful fall as they drift shut each time. Pretending, you see. Hoping.

His heart is beating, and his breath rises and falls.

Absolutely blue and absolutely empty. I have never seen anything so empty.

I sit down again, and talk to him all night. Lola brings me tea. There is a nurse, a man, a perfect companion. He brings me tea. Greg.

I go up the corridor, and down the corridor.

I brush my teeth and think about his mouth, his teeth, his

345

poor fucking battered bloodied mouth, massacred, surviving. So much work.

*

Before dawn a skein of Canada geese hurtle past the wide window against streaks of grey and pink: over the river, Hammersmith Bridge, banking round, heading for the gleaming reservoirs at Barn Elms, where we went that funny night with Truncheon, and many times since – or did we? Did we ever go anywhere? Or was it always going to be when things came right?

I had requested a chaplain. He comes at seven, and as the drab light rises he reads the bit about looking to the hills whence cometh my salvation. I lean over the top of the bed weeping and hugging Robert's head and crying all over him and thinking I hope you are dead, because you wouldn't like this – what if you witnessed it all, me signing you away? When I positioned myself so your dead stare seemed kind of to be looking in my eyes, did you see me? Feel me? How dead are you?

'All right,' you'd say. 'Half left.'

That dream you had, that you were in an improvisational theatre group and they said 'Are you coming out to dinner, Robert?' and you said, 'I don't know' – and you didn't know what it was about, and so I told you: it was about whether you were going to stay, to come with us, to live, to let yourself be nourished, to face having to make it all up as you go along, like we all do.

You had so little, and I dragged you on. 'I want you back,' I said, and you said, 'I'm coming back. Slowly.' And I said, 'Good.' But maybe you didn't want to come back.

*

People start to return. I do not want the night to be over. I wish they had not come because they are harbingers. We drink tea.

346

Louis arrives with two big white cyclamen flowers from the pot by the front door and two stems off the dark red geranium, still flowering in this warm weird January, tied in a green tartan ribbon left over from Christmas. And two little square leather boxes, which he puts on the relatives' coffee table.

Jim says, 'What are they?'

I say, 'Listen, Jim, I've got a sort of mad plan. You know how your dad and I were going to get married?' – Jesus, did he know?

'Yes,' he says.

'Well, I thought, let's just do it anyway.'

He smiles – a tiny twitch of a smile. He nods. I say, 'You can be best man. Lola could be the bridesmaid—' I feel myself about to go off on one, hysterically – Jim's mother as Matron of Honour, Louis as the vicar – I stop myself.

Louis shows Jim the rings.

Later, we are all around the bed, inside the pleated blue curtains. I pick up Robert's left hand, the one without the oxygen monitor clipped to a finger. It's not going to work to try to hold his fingers to the ring, so I just touch it to them. I'm not going to think about this or fumble it. I say, 'Well, I was always the practical one', and there's almost some laughter, and I put the ring on my own finger and I say, I do, darling I do, and I kiss him. And I put the other one on his finger, and remember a line from a Lyle Lovett song where the preacher asks her, and she says 'I do'; and the preacher asks him, and she says 'Yeah, he does too' – and maybe I say, yeah, he does too. The chaplain isn't there. That wouldn't have been right.

At one point I look at Jim across his father's body and say, 'Listen, anything. You know that, don't you? Anything in my power you ever need from me.'

At another point some people outside are making a racket and someone tells them to shut up and they do.

Greg comes in. He says they will turn off the heart machine, the noradrenaline; they'll turn the ventilator down bit by bit, it could take up to an hour. We all say um right. OK. But that fucking tube is still sticking out of his mouth with the tight bandage like a gag scarring his cheek, and I say, Can you not get rid of that, and Greg says yes he can. They pull the curtains round. I sit there, and Greg pulls the tube out and I am afraid it will pull up Robert's guts, but there is nothing.

We step back in. There he is, his own lovely face. I could kiss him now but this is not a fairy tale. There will be no waking up. I look across at Jim on the other side. I take Robert's hand, I think Jim has the other one, I put my palm flat on Robert's heart and it beats and I think oh, it beat on its own, and that was for me, my love, it was for me, and I take it into my body, and I hold it, yes, in my heart, through the palm of my hand flat on his breast.

And I think he is dead, but then there seems a small, small breath – and then Greg pops his head round the curtain and says: 'Robert's dead now.' And I say what? Because I can't hear him, and he has to say it again. And I look back and he is, and it is completely different: his lips are white and I want him back. I think, oh, no, I shouldn't have looked away, we should have kept you forever on the ventilator, breathing with help, heart supported, we should have – Or do I? Or do I look to Jim? The only moment of anger I have with Robert then is the sadness on Jim's face. My heart's blood floods away from me, pouring away across the hospital floor; there is no gravity, no sense. It is just an awful mistake. All of it.

I don't know what happened next.

Chapter Thirty-Seven

Home, January 2012

After he died it started to get cold.

He died twice! Once in the pub; once under my hand.

Christ, could he not stop being complicated and liminal even when he was dead?

The house was full of flowers. People were there to prop me up and hold me down – Lola, Louis, friends who knew grief and knew how to be, quietly, never left my side. I was living on champagne and marzipan; Lola directed the over-sympathetic to the off-licence to get more when she saw they were hugging me too much. Casseroles appeared on the doorstep. People came in their lunch hours. Funeral planning.

Grandma's funeral date was set in Accra. I could not miss her funeral. I could not leave Robert unburied in England. I was not talking, sleeping, eating, or actually breathing. The kitchen table was covered in notes in different writings: Swift's, from the initial call to the vicar: 'Could he be buried there before next Thursday?' Lola's: the coroner's phone number, and that of Laura, the barmaid in whose arms he died the first time. Mine: 'Hypoxic brain incident'.

A list of music: '"My Song is Love Unknown"? Joni Mitchell "Trouble Child"?' My sister's on the back of an envelope: '£22.80 per line inc VAT, min 3 lines' – the price of a death announcement in the paper.

Laura came by to tell me what had happened in the pub. She looks like a Modigliani. We talked about how she'd known him for years round the neighbourhood, how glad she was he had sobered up; how her co-worker Will had tracked down where I lived through a series of cafes and cab drivers who knew Robert, and had knocked on doors up and down the street. I told her I was jealous he had died in her arms, not mine. She said yes, she'd thought about that, and was sorry.

He was there; I was not. He was dying; I didn't know. I don't know if he was all right or in pain or what he was thinking. How could I not know these simple things about this, his irrevocable moment? If I'd been there he wouldn't have died. He asked them for food and they didn't know he shouldn't have it. Should, that word we banned. They couldn't understand him. They couldn't help him. I never thought he would die not in my arms.

The ambulance people cut off his clothes: his handsome coat, his soft green jumper, his father's shirt, his stripy thermals. The warm tweed trousers that he liked remain intact. The coat is lying on the piano now, shredded. Later, I made a cushion of the jumper.

Chapter Thirty-Eight

In the Kitchen, February 2012

Did I see it? How could they have let me see it?

I remember the telephone call. I was in the kitchen, in the evening, four or five days after his death(s). The handsome funeral director rang. She had buried my father, walking in front of his hearse in a top hat. She said something along the lines of, Why didn't you let us know he had a communicable disease?

I said, 'He didn't have a communicable disease.' Thinking – *Did he? Christ, he could have – No. He's spent the past four years pretty much in hospital. They'd have noticed.*

She said, 'Well, he's come labelled with . . . are you sure?' She's a nice woman.

'I really don't think so. I think I'd know.' I thought of all the things I've not known about him. 'What do you mean "labelled"?'

'Well,' she said, and she didn't want to say. I made her say. I pictured a big paper label with orange writing on, tied to his dead toe.

'Well,' she said. 'Contaminated.'

Contaminated?

She said, at last, that the details which came with him said he may have had hepatitis C.

What posthumous gift was this? Was he *still* causing trouble? Might I have hepatitis C now?

Part of me marvelled at him: how like him! I found myself laughing. Only not.

Because at various points throughout his illnesses information had been kept from me through spurious privacy or administrative correctness, I was thinking it might be possible that this *had* been diagnosed and I not told. But nothing had been kept from me since the cancer. Unless it had been diagnosed posthumously? Was that possible?

I recalled the label on his wrist, in A&E at Charing Cross: Unknown. My fury, because he *was* known. And loved. And now, contaminated. A fine insult.

Of course it was Charing Cross who had handled his death; who had sent him to the undertakers in Wiltshire. They didn't know him as well as UCLH did.

'Can you check?' I asked.

Not till the morning.

I googled hepatitis C. Phrases like sexual intercourse, intravenous drug use, no symptoms, cancer and death leapt out. I could not bring myself to read. I knew he did not have hepatitis C, but why was someone – who? – saying he did? Where did they get the idea? Did he have it years ago, before I became involved in his medical life, and never tell me? But he wasn't an injector. But he was a drinker and a maker of appalling decisions while drunk . . . And so, as usual, I ran with every possible iteration of every idea.

I had half expected ghouls to reveal themselves after his death. I feared women spouting of infidelity. I hadn't thought of past lies about drugs and contamination and communicable disease.

In the morning, the undertaker rang to tell me it was just that hepatitis C had not been ruled out –

352

Well did they rule out bubonic plague and leprosy and mad cow disease? I didn't say this.

– it was just that they hadn't had the chance to communicate properly with UCLH –

So they assumed he had it? What he did die of wasn't enough for them?

– and there are procedures, necessary for the protection of the staff, she said. She was really sorry. It wasn't her fault.

Why did I mind so much that it was hepatitis C? Why did I feel it as an accusation? Was it because it's the needle-sharing disease, and whatever he was, he wasn't a junkie? Maybe even, 'at least he wasn't a junkie'? Was I being as moralistic about drug addiction as I hated other people being about alcoholism?

At the time I think it was simply that it wasn't true; it was a horrid thing to pile on to his poor body in its helplessness, and it was an unnecessary and untimely fear to put on me, both physically for my own health and the potential effect on the health of others, and also emotionally – the fear of ancient lies or betrayals suddenly appearing, that I would never be able to talk to him about, to understand or clear up, undermining our past.

So they communicated properly with UCLH, and no, he didn't have hepatitis C.

I can picture that polythene sheet so clearly, with the tape with 'CONTAMINATED' written on it. I see it lying under and around his body in the special room at the undertakers, before I brought his coffin clothes. Or maybe the day I brought his clothes. That would make sense.

No! Beware of this phrase, which consolidates the possible from probable to manufactured memory.

Chapter Thirty-Nine

Driving, February 2012

We – Lola, Louis and I – were driving down the M4, from London to Wiltshire, taking my father's old green suit, which had become Robert's preferred suit during the cheerful period (post recovery, pre-cancer) when he was capable of wearing a suit and feeling happy about it. He wore it to our birthday party. It was a tiny bit dapper. Now it was his coffin outfit. I had with me Robert's share of John's ashes; I'd put them in a heart-shaped box to put it into Robert's coffin by his feet. That, the funeral directress told me, was the correct place. How pagan we are.

Louis was at the wheel – Lola had banned me from driving. Someone had only to look at me for me to collapse. My legs had no strings. I was not safe standing in my own sitting room, nor lying in my own bed. I was in the passenger seat, talking to Swift on the phone when, as we paused at the entrance to the round-about, we were rear-ended, by an airline pilot. 'Good God,' said my mother later when I told her. 'Was he in his aeroplane?' No, I said, a Volkswagen Golf. But he was in his one-piece camouflage flying suit, and didn't want to get the insurers involved. I tried to get out, and dropped the phone, Swift's voice calling my name. I fell over.

The car, it turned out, was – in that mysterious way which happens with cars which you can still drive and which look fine but for a dent in the back – written off. I was happy when they told me. I said to the insurance-company lady, OK, but you're not taking the car away. 'Well, madam,' she said, and I said, 'That car contains the engagement ring given to me by my dead fiancé and was rear-ended while I was bringing my dead dad's suit to the undertaker for my dead fiancé to wear in his coffin and David has to come and get it out—'

'OK,' said the insurance-company lady, overwhelmed. 'How much do we pay David?' I wept.

In the street outside the house David puts on his fine silicone gloves and begins to take the front of the car apart. He unscrews the dashboard and lays it to one side as best he can, because wires within are still attached and must not be pulled too tight. The steering wheel is leant up, askew. He moves round to the other side of the door and approaches the ventilation system from the other direction, through the high open bonnet. He shifts tubes and gently lays aside important things whose names I don't know. It is too redolent. I go inside and make tea.

Hours later he comes into the kitchen, holding the ring with the diamond as big as a very small Ritz delicately in his big car-grubby, silicone-gloved, Buddhist fingers.

I cry. He cries. I love David. I'm wearing the ring now.

Chapter Forty

Westbourne Grove, January 2012

At the glamorous florist I considered the roses available in January: striped ones, lush ones, elegant ones, pink, crimson, globe-shaped, petticoat-shaped, creamy white, purple, green-tinged, scented, all incredibly expensive and beautiful, stark and shivering in their chrome buckets in the cold on the street. The florist wondered what they were for, filled up with tears when I told him, showed me all his catalogues, ordered me a stupidly gorgeous amount of the loveliest there were, and pressed a big bunch of the ones I first admired into my arms as I left. I took them to the Italian restaurant where we had put my engagement ring on the prawn, cried, and texted three friends. Within half an hour they were all there. I hadn't even asked them to come.

You are stranded: all the love you had for your dead person has nowhere to go, and it backs up inside you as grief: terrible, rocking, draining, mad, unreadable grief. Love which has lost its object.

After a while – weeks, months, years – when grief's crazy pinball ricocheting has calmed a little, you begin to learn what to do with it. You redistribute it. The love that turned into grief becomes love again, and you spread it about, among whoever needs it. I needed a great deal, and I got it, and I learned a new territory of gratitude.

Chapter Forty-One

West London, February 2012

For a brief and peculiar period Steve the coroner became my friend. He called by on his motorbike, and told me over tea how he didn't really want to be a coroner any more. He used to be a policeman. Policemen like me, always have, I don't know why.

He had to consider suicide, though he didn't tell me that, not wanting to upset me. Will told me, after Steve had rung him about it. Steve wanted to know why Robert's throat had been stuffed with unchewed meat. I said: He just wanted his lunch. Having not had lunch for eighteen months. He was a greedy man, capable of sudden compulsive bad decisions. If Robert had any sense about what he put in his mouth he would never have been an alcoholic or had the bloody cancer in the first place. The friend who had found him with his foot off wrote: 'I gather the circumstances were typically bizarre and weirdly in character.' As Swift said, 'He died of being who he was.'

Steve recorded Robert's death as 'Accident'. I would have called it misadventure. There's a bit in *La Traviata*, where she sings '*ch'avvi una vittima della sventura*' – you've been a victim of – misfortune, misadventure, bad future – *avventura* being Italian for future, same root as advent. It's one of those bits where Robert would grab your leg, saying with rising excitement to match the rising notes, 'Oh, oh, she's off! She's off!!'

Of course I wondered about whether the whole thing had been a long, slow suicide by instalments. I couldn't swear it wasn't. In his triumph he was superb, he had fought and worked, his appetites were ferocious. I found him superb *all the time*, the streak of granite in him, his tenderness, his love. But I understand that he did not like not being as superb as he used to be.

But no. It was not suicide. He was happy that day, feeling up to a meeting, promising to look after me. And in a house full of morphine, would a kind man go out to a family pub and choke to death on purpose in front of children? Though – even when the kindness of a suicide is not in doubt, he or she has by definition reached a point where the desperation for release has become so clamorous that it drowns out all else.

I can't know if Robert intended to die. When I wonder what went through his mind as he ordered and then began to eat that meal, I wonder if he kind of 'forgot', fudged, that he mustn't eat solid food. I don't think he thought 'This may kill me, but fuck it, I don't care if I die', nor 'Haha I shall do what I'm not allowed to do.' But he may have thought along these lines: 'I have lost too much. The sheer density of loss in my life is unacceptable. I must reclaim at least one of the things I've lost. People have underestimated my capacity to defy the odds before. They say I cannot eat. What if I can? What if I order a proper meal, eat the fucking thing (maybe with the odd splutter and cough) and then tell Louisa and everyone else, to their amazement, *I had roast beef, Yorkshire pudding and broccoli. It was bloody gorgeous.* What's the worst that could happen? I'll have wasted a few quid, coughed up some beef, and been a bit embarrassed. I am Robert Lockhart. I have specialised in confounding people's expectations. I will confound them now.'

The following Sunday, I went, nervous, shaky, and alone, to his regular AA meeting. Two people spoke of doubts, of feeling undermined in their recovery. At the end I was allowed to speak: rather incoherently, I told them of Robert's death, and said that even if they didn't feel great about their own recovery today they had helped in his, even though he had died, and that through that they had helped me, and his son, and that there were thousands of us at home, who they probably never thought of, but who valued AA hugely, that their contribution was priceless, and I thanked them.

That this went down well was reported to me later, through people who'd heard it spoken of in other meetings.

When you crave the physicality of a dead person, what is it that's doing the craving? A physical person. A body, a heart. All of which will be dead itself soon enough. He looked very much deader after they had carved him up. When he was first dead he looked smooth, angelic, and empty; now he looked angry and 103. There was lots of extra scarring and stitching on him. I peeked, at the undertakers, at his chest and his scalp. This was not the exquisite needlework he had on his throat, his ankle, his thigh, his back. The Lady Undertaker said to me, 'Now why did you do that?'

Steve brought me round the autopsy report. I have it still: a huge file. I now know the size of Robert's lungs: one much bigger than the other – but this is normal. One is smaller to make space for the heart. And I know the weight of Robert's heart. I wanted to keep it, like Mary Shelley kept her husband's. I want to carry his heart with me literally. Keep it in a jar of wine on my desk. Lots of people have kept people's hearts. I felt Steve might have given it to me, if I'd asked.

And where was it now? Stuffed back in any which way among

a mess of organs? How could I know if his heart was in the right place? I needed it to be. I asked Sue Bullock, Robert's friend since the Royal Northern College of Music decades ago, to sing his setting of 'i carry your heart' at the funeral. That helped.

There was no alcohol in Robert's body when he died, and there was no cancer.

Chapter Forty-Two

Wiltshire: a graveyard, February 2012

Maria the vicar, a smiling Irish blonde, told me that as a young music student she had heard Robert play at the Wigmore Hall. She approved our choices for the music, and said: 'You'll need something not too tragic for the end when the coffin goes out because people will be in bits.'

We'd thought that, what with everything, we'd like Cole Porter's 'Why Can't You Behave?', sung by Ella Fitzgerald, if that was OK by her and the church.

'OK?' she said. 'Oh it'd be grand' – and she sang a few lines, and told me it was one of her favourites from when she'd been in cabaret. I marvelled again at Robert's ability to surround himself with fabulous women. I also made a note to clear the song with Jim – everybody else would get the joke and the love behind it, but Jim, although he knew perfectly well his father was capable of considerable naughtiness, *was* only twelve.

His funeral day was cold with bright bright sun. The handsome pallbearers, suited and booted, were crooked as children with sorrow. The coffin lay draped in roses and a cherry-red Wigan

Rugby League shirt: Robert Lockhart True Hero printed across it. Jackie was back from Australia, straight from the airport, wearing my clothes. The men of Wigan. Sue Bullock sang, her full soprano ringing across the little Gothic church and the bright February graveyard. His cousins Diane and Denise read Granny Annie's prayer together: 'Courage for the great sorrows . . .' The church heavenly full. Jim read the poem about don't be sad – 'He is Gone' by David Harkins. My mother and siblings walked where we had walked for Wayland, skirting the war memorial, Wayland's own grave, and his father's. Faces of friends we'd shared for thirty-five years; and unexpected people – his counsellor from Camden came, with her husband who had also counselled us. I wore my dashing Dalmatian print fake fur 1950s swing coat, and knelt by the grave until the funeral directress pulled me away, fearing I suspect that I might jump in. We threw earth and flowers on him. Would he think I was making a meal of it? Well I was, I bloody was. But running through it all was the thought: he should be here, taking the piss, enjoying the attention, a little drunk, flirting, moving on to the piano so someone could sing 'My Funny Valentine'.

'We're here,' Maria announced, 'to comfort each one who loved him, was infuriated by him and grieves his absence today . . . It falls to me today to say something of Robert's relationship with God – a hard task indeed . . God and Robert? The bon viveur, the lover of life, the passionate, deeply flawed genius who described himself as a decomposer . . .'

When she said this, in church, I heard his voice in my ear, as clear as it ever was: 'Well I fuckin' am now.'

'. . . the piano player at a party surrounded by dewy-eyed ladies? God, for Robert,' she said, and many hearts sank at the prospect of imminent misunderstanding, 'was a god of profound unending understanding, manifested in forgiveness and being forgiven, seen most strongly in nature, expressed in gratitude. In Love – for Jim and Louisa and all those sitting in this church today – in the discipline of sobriety – the gift of music and composition . . . he saw God in the arctic tern flying five thousand miles, and in the deep instincts of birds and creatures to return from whence they came.' And many hearts rose again, because that was exactly it.

'And God knew too that it was Robert's intention to marry Louisa, proposing to her in 2010 before the operation that was likely to cause him to lose the power of speech. Here in this church we discussed the possibility of a marriage service, even if it had to be in hospital, and sadly it was not to be. But Louisa shared with me their final moments together, an exchange of rings before Robert died . . . While the words of marriage . . . may not have been said in church, and there is no legally binding bit of paper to bear witness in law to their union, I believe the God that Robert honoured will honour the love they had for each other, the intention to marry shown in the exchange of rings as he died, and when at last Louisa stands reunited with Robert before their creator it will be God himself who welcomes them as husband and wife. For with God all things are possible. For God is love and those who live in love live in God and God lives in them . . .'

Fucking hell. You want romance?

Simon, his best friend from Oxford, Simon who had introduced us on the stairs, gave the address. 'Robert was a wonderful man. He had a unique and compelling personality, and a great gift for friendship. There was never any doubt in Robert's mind as to who he was or who he wanted to be. He was just himself and did not care one jot what people thought of him. He was wiry and extraordinarily energetic. He hated pretentiousness and sent up everybody he met. Most of all he was extraordinary fun, because what he really loved was misbehaving, in every way he could possibly think of . . . We looked on, fascinated, entranced and frequently appalled . . . He adored women, and women adored him. He left behind him a trail of broken hearts. Much time was spent persuading women to lie underneath a grand piano while he played Chopin. This was, he told them, so that they could appreciate the special acoustic qualities to be found there. He said that this had the most extraordinary effect on women . . .'

It is wrong to laugh during your fiancé's funeral. But it was so funny, so true.

'. . . His talent and his brain were such that he could do anything, and music was his passion. He also worked extraordinarily hard. At the same time he continued to live life as he liked to, to excess, but slowly the excess began to control him. He started a long and courageous fight against the illness of alcoholism . . . He did survive, and there started his greatest years. No longer drinking, he achieved all the qualities which he had had before: great humour, fun, generosity but now with one extra important one: great gentleness, that turned him as a person from the extraordinary to the sublime. There was no one, no one, anything like him. During this time Robert was deeply happy. His two great loves were Jim – of whom he was immensely proud – and who he called his 'unfeasibly handsome offspring', and Louisa. Without Louisa, Robert would undoubtedly have died years ago. Rob was devoted to her and adored her.

'Then one day he phoned. "Hello, Wilkie," he said. "This is the last time that you'll hear these dulcet tones." And he was right. And dulcet his tones certainly were.

'Sometimes I used to give him a lift to Somerset. On the way he would simply talk and talk and talk, for hours on end, about art, the landscape, music, everything under the sun, and he would do so with great knowledge and with a vocabulary all his own. Most of all he talked about people, with great affection and great humour. The journeys were punctuated by shouts of excitement from him every time we passed a bird, and tears of laughter from myself. At some point he would take from his pocket or his case a CD. There would be a great deal of faffing about trying to get the CD player to work – and then he would exhale, close his eyes, and lean back.

And simply, in complete silence and rapt concentration, relish the music.

'It was an extraordinary privilege to have been his friend. Although Robert might not have been a perfect man in some ways, to those of us who loved him he was just perfect as he was.'

Every funeral needs a speech by a person who is willing and able to speak of the dead person in a way not overburdened by tragedy, a speech that celebrates the happy qualities. Robert was a wonderful man – and one haunted by low self-esteem, shame, intense self-consciousness, tortured ambivalences, and all sorts of other darknesses that he strove to keep suppressed under the extravagant brilliance that so enchanted us all. We are all more than we know ourselves to be.

*

There was a banquet of ham and cake and tea and champagne, all sorted out by my loving siblings; wood fires inside and out, a tent, and the green eternal Dene with its trees and sarsen stones, the view he'd looked out on so often, with such pleasure. Photos of him were propped up on the piano, and a bird spotter's list he'd made, years ago, which included 'Great tits, blue tits, Lou's tits (one pair), Swift's tits (one pair)'. I couldn't find the speedometer he'd brought back from the woods for me twenty-five years ago, and that upset me. Someone over the years must have thought it a rusty old bit of rubbish – which it was – and chucked it.

We stayed up late. There was a great deal of crying, and some terribly funny moments. A woodwind player in trackies and a leather jacket pursuing me about the place wanting to talk to me about messages from beyond . . . Crying on Graham. I had a marvellous sense of moving through it all, wading. I had 'She Moved Through the Fair' on my mind:

The people were saying
No two e'er were wed
But one has a sorrow
That never was said
And she smiled as she passed me
With her goods and her gear
And that was the last
That I saw of my dear.
I dreamed it last night
That my true love came in
So softly she entered
Her feet made no din
She came close beside me
And this she did say:
'It will not be long, love,
Till our wedding day.'

*

The next day, in wellies and jeans, Jackie and I went back to the grave. The roses were frozen stiff on the great mossy hump. Really, it was vast. The funeral directress had said it was because I chose such a good-quality coffin – cheap ones, she said, collapse under the weight of the earth.

Kath's sister had brought some of her ashes to the funeral for them to go in with him too, but it was too late. He was sealed up already. So I just had the plastic bag. I put them in the hedgerow round the edge of the graveyard.

*

So many letters, cards, emails. So very welcome, so valued.

There was the odd idiot. A man I hardly know who said: 'I heard your partner popped off – still, at least it was expected.'

'Was it?' I replied. 'By who?' – And, if it had been, in what way would that make it better? But no, it wasn't expected. It was some long and debilitating illnesses, followed by a shockingly sudden accidental death. Which can be hard to get your head round.

My favourite was a drawing of him on crutches, a potato man with stick limbs, with written on it: 'I am very sad also I am sorry that robbet with the sticks is dead love from ruby.'

Chapter Forty-Three

Home, February 2012

I found it hard to think about how we might have been, and impossible not to. There was so very much for us. I expected too much from him. I was sorry. Where his talent and work might have taken him, without his addiction.

It was so quick.

My hands became aerated writing certain words: 'Wednesday was your funeral'. That electrical feeling like a skein of cramp under the skin.

When people said he would have died long before but for me, I thought perhaps I should have let him. But I wanted him. I wanted him still. I always wanted him.

How he died was quickly mythologised. I watched it happen, I did it myself, I couldn't stop it. I had wanted to keep his death new to keep him nearer life. He had been running away in slow motion – had he? Is that what he was doing?

I was so compelled by not losing his old voice – recordings of which I couldn't bear to listen to anyway – that I forgot his damaged voice. Writing him took him away again, farther. I stopped doing it. I'd be thinking: We'll make love again. We'll sit. I'm sorry I didn't get the telly fixed.

Truth: he had been drinking. Truth: he was smoking.

I texted Jim: 'These days probably feel a bit odd. They do for me.' He wrote: 'They do for me as well.'

Talking to the dead, I told Robert I'd do my best for Jim. Robert died at the same age as his mother did. I told him about his own funeral, how he's buried one row down, one grave along, from my father. Not in the north – I wanted him closer by, for Jim and for me to be able to visit. There is a grave-space next to Robert, at Wayland's feet. So that is my grave. There is a big R for Reserved on a square of terracotta among the mossy turf, and when I go to visit the gentlemen I walk on my own future grave and I always forget to see whether I shiver.

I tell him: 'I love you.' 'What, still?' he says, as so often.

I wanted a webcam on his grave to make sure he's OK, to see if he was under snow. I wanted to talk to him. How are you? What's happening? Tell me the funny little stories.

I wanted to go in with him. Ribs interlacing, skulls resting, pelvises slotting together.

GFW texted: he was at the rugby, and told me to put on the Wigan shirt from the funeral. Wigan scored: 6-8 to Huddersfield. I would have gone to the rugby with you, would have done all the things. All the things we couldn't do. I want to dream of doing them, starting with the lost things: kissing, talking, eating, walking. Can we?

*

They came to take away the feeding stuff.

*

I said to grief: I capitulate. I salute you. You are the emperor of your craft.

Like grief cared.

*

I had his phone. He wasn't good with technology. Technology was for sound engineers and producers, not for composers and musicians. There were several texts on it, to me, that he hadn't sent. I sent them to myself.

One said, 'I'm waiting for you; I'm at the back.'

One said, 'Where are you darling? I'm not worried I just want to know you're OK'.

One, presumably in response to similar query from me, said, 'In heaven, thanks to blackbird'.

*

It became The Year of Saying Yes, because the alternative was inconceivable. Oh it tumbled out, that year. We went to Accra for Grandma's funeral; weeping all night, the Harmattan wind blowing fine dust twenty-four hours; many days of ceremonies and drummers and dancers, relatives, special black-and-white outfits for each occasion, shake hands, shake hands, cold beer, hot food, endless church, leopardskin masks, gold wands, dirge-like hymns, dancing undertakers, the lead one like Baron Samedi in kente waistcoat, red bow-tie, top hat and cockade. Loving comfort from Osei's widow and children, all of us together, so close and kind. The Ashanti do good funerals. Then Ireland on horses with my twin friends who had lost their mother two years before, for what came to be known as the My Lovely Horse Holiday. Do not underestimate the capacity of a really big animal to give comfort. The Outer Hebrides with Jackie; mist, jewel-clear turquoise water, silvery distant streaks of light, St Kilda a smudge on the horizon, clarity and a feeling of your head and heart being washed in purity. The Kings Lynn festival, where I was booked to appear and didn't want to cancel, almost breaking down on stage and running away with milk chocolate and chips in the open car with the twins.

To Wigan, to try to sort things out. There was a storage unit. Driving back down the M1 in tears with a heavy car-load of John's records and CDs and Robert's thirty-five-years overdue library books, I found myself writing a song: '83 Miles the Wrong Side of Birmingham'. Suddenly, songs came thick and fast – about him, about me, about death, about drink, about love. To the Wigmore Hall, over and over, to sit alone at the back and cry. 'Weeping at the Wigmore' became a thing; my hobby. I wept all through Mark Padmore singing Jonathan Dove's setting of 'The End' by Mark Strand, not noticing till later, when he was hugging Padmore, who sang like several angels, that the composer had been sitting in front of me (tall and clean and handsome and pleased, alive). I hope that he took my tears as a compliment, when in fact they were the overflow of my loss, my envy, my hurt fury, at composers who were alive and listening to beautiful performances of their beautiful music about death, and how not every man knows what he shall sing at the end.

I spent money like water, and fled: to Croatia with Simon where, between diving into the sea and coming up for air, I had an idea from which I wrote a novel in three months based on the folksong 'The Unquiet Grave', where the corpse tells his weeping lover to piss off, she's disturbing him. To festivals in Norfolk and Scotland as part of a country & western musical puppet adaptation of Truman Capote's *In Cold Blood*, in which a friend had involved me, making me sing and play the guitar, and write songs. To Barcelona, babysitting for a friend, thinking of possible titles for the book I would write about him one day: *Bloody Robert; The Clothes He Died In; 34 Items Representing Love*. To Italy. Lola, who had put off her travels to hold me in place, was finally away. I could weep now, and throw furniture around and stand in Tesco's staring for as long as I wanted. My sister lent me her kind dog, to stroke and lean on.

In airports and stations, I missed the benefit of the special little wagon disabled people and their girlfriends get to ride in. It was no longer mine, though I was wheeling his ghost around which was just as hard as wheeling him. And nobody knew. You lose a role overnight. You become carer against your will and inclination, and then as you learn to appreciate its few blessings they are whisked away. I really missed his parking permit. You are, in grief, yourself disabled.

What was I to do with all this love?

I was living with someone who wasn't there.

How I missed him; his big heart, his curiosity, his wisdom. He was all over that year like a Sixties pop song, whispering, lurking, his tunes in my head, coming out under my breath without me noticing till someone said, 'Lou, you're singing . . .' I had streaks of obsession about loss: the ring, before it came back. His brain – did they replace it? There's a sign in a shop on the Weind in Wigan that says: 'We Frame Anything': I thought of getting his clothes framed, with his hat and sticks, laid out to form him like those characters he used to leave on my bed. I wrote my dreams out obsessively; and tried to do the 'three things to be grateful for' exercise that stops people losing their mind. It was always the same: 1) Lola, 2) my bed, 3) having had him.

There's a sign in a shop on Uxbridge Road saying 'Everything Must Go'. Well yes. Thanks, sign, for your timely reminder.

I rang his old college to talk about his library books, in a flurry of 'I have to do something about death, even if the only thing I can do about death is pretend I am capable of taking these books back'.

So many other things were alive, and him not. Together, and us not. Why *should* a dog, a horse, a rat have life, and thou no breath at all?

I was furious.

I wrote long long letters to him: 'I have spent so much time trying to put you right – I have, I shouldn't lie – that now there are so many adjusted versions of you lying around my mind that I am having trouble locating unadulterated you, you untouched by my idealising. You a little cleaner, a little more forthcoming with your monumental gifts, a lot more sober, more inclined not to smoke, healthier, less DEAD – these false yous, in my mind, warp and block the actual you – who I cannot begin to record, because you surprised and delighted me over and over. I couldn't begin to make you up. I can't believe that you are not with me.'

I felt that if wrote about him I would rewrite him and so lose him. My version would replace the original version.

'Do you want to replace the original version?' asked the computer screen. 'The original version no longer exists in this location.'

*

I went to a mouse taxidermy class. Because I am a teachers' pet, fast and over-achieving in lessons, I stuffed two mice. I didn't mind the chemicals and the peeling and stuffing, but then I had to pull their tiny translucent tongues out with tweezers, and that made me sick, the delicacy and vulnerability. I gave one of the taxidermied mice – the man, I decided – a little tiny hat and a tiny dolls-house, old-fashioned telephone, and put him on the stool of the cigarette-case piano. I tucked the other one up and put her in the little wooden grave cavity meant for cigarettes. I wanted Robert to ring me. I wanted to sleep.

'Why the hell are you doing that?' people asked, and years later I realise: I was afraid writing about him would be taxidermy. I did it to show myself what not to do in writing about him. Don't slough out his innards; don't pluck out his tongue.

At the end of the first year, we had a Memorial Concert for him at Bush Hall. Grief is meant to give way somewhat after a year. That's when the earth of the grave settles and the headstone can be set. (It was made by my nephew Louis, the one who liked wrestling stickers when he was eight.) It's when the corpse starts objecting in 'The Unquiet Grave'.

We printed huge photos of him; the Brindisi Quartet reconvened to play his quartets and Wayland's Elegy. Susan Bullock sang 'i carry your heart' again; Catherine Bott sang some of the French songs; John Parricelli did a gorgeous jazz guitar version of 'My Funny Valentine'; Jackie played an elegy she had written for Robert, and Peter Donohoe played the too-shiny piano of Robert's that had moved there years before. We recorded it for a CD and raised money for a music scholarship at Magdalen and for the rehab in Camden, and it was bloody marvellous.

I made a tiny speech. It started with 'He was the best of men, he was the worst of men' and ended with 'I never expect – nor indeed want – to meet anyone like him again.'

Chapter Forty-Four

Home, 2015

I liked having his things around. His DMs. His green jumper sewn into a cushion. His wild-boar signet ring. Some dead roses. Using his manuscript paper for my songs. Playing his tunes on his piano. Three years on, I still hadn't used up half the plastic lighters. In 2014 there was a stage adaptation of *My Dear I Wanted to Tell You* in London: it used Granny Annie's prayer as lyrics for a nightclub blues number, sung by my character Mabel, an enigmatic African American woman in a gold sequin dress. I wrote that scene into the third book of the series, *Devotion*. What we have lost remains, and comes round again to feed us in unexpected ways. I felt the gap where he used to be very strongly beside me that night.

A widowed friend photographs his wife's empty shoes in places she would have liked to go, and sends me a poem he has written about a jar of tamarind in the back of the kitchen cupboard. Another has his wife's make-up in the bathroom, ten years on. The curiously quotidian legacies they leave us, jars of stuff that dries up though the thoughts and feelings that our dead beloveds left us still continue to flow and feed our living conversations.

Bottles of vodka upset me, but alcohol itself wasn't a problem for me. I like it. So many flavours and strengths, so much control one can have over exactly how one can change one's mood. So legal, too, and safe, compared with other chemical means people use to alter reality. At least you know what it is. People being drunk wasn't a problem for me either, not if they were drunk sweetly and not that often, maybe with extra singing and declarations of love, but without violence and unkindness. If they were drunk every time I saw them, I found that extremely difficult, especially if they were younger, and sad, because I wanted to help them, and when the idea of helping a drunk enters my mind I start to shake and have to go away.

But my glass of pink wine on a garden bench was not Robert's bottles of vodka delivered daily to his flat by cab because he could no longer walk; it's not my friend's two bottles of cheap rioja that she brings with her *every time* she visits; it's not the couple of beers that used to make Boots imagine that scoring some heroin was a really good idea.

People used to say to Robert, 'Is it all right if I have a drink though?' and he would reply, 'Why, are you an alcoholic too?' Not drinking because someone else is an alcoholic is as illogical as it sounds. If they had cancer, would you go for their chemotherapy? An addict friend used to try to control his (non-addict) wife's drinking by ordering tiny splits of wine – two glasses per bottle – until his shrink told him stop, his wife wasn't him and he was projecting.

Robert thought that he and I got on best when he was stone-cold long-term sober and I was two thirds of the way down a second glass of wine. He was right. It would stop me from staring at him in fear about what the fuck was going to happen with him next.

*

A minicab driver picked me up at home. He said, 'That is the house of Mr Robert – how is he?' I said, 'He died, I'm afraid.' The driver pulled over, and wept. He said he was very sorry, he had liked Mr Robert very much, he talked a lot and was a very nice gentleman.

*

I have thrown away his hair gel, and taken the books back. Three and a half years longer wasn't much, given how long they'd been out. I wasn't fined. I looked for the staircase where we met, and couldn't decide which one it was. I left a rose on the piano in the chapel.

Riding my bicycle a few days later, doing a mental checklist of who was where and how things were, I found myself using the phrase: '. . . and Robert's safely dead.'

Chapter Forty-Five

Home, 2017

There's a sound in this house. I don't know what it is. Wind in the chimney? Something to do with heating? When I heard it during the awful times, I thought it was him, moaning low in his sleep, turning over, up in the back bedroom where he lay, day in day out, face to the wall, face to the room, attached to his feeding pump, unattached, lines clogged, lines clear, pissing in the bottle, pissing on the floor. It was a comfort to me. It meant that he was alive, maybe dreaming, maybe recovering. His breaths were always much quicker than mine. Someone said that we are all allocated the same number of breaths, and the slower we breathe them the longer we live. Rubbish, but I thought about it, late at night.

I hear the noise still, often. It still is a comfort to me.

Now Louis has come in. He's been watching the rugby in the other room. It is a comfort to me to hear Louis talking to the match as Robert used to, so involved, so passionate, in the other room.

He was helping me take things away the other day, and found the turquoise mask in the garden. I've been getting rid of it by instalments. It had caught my eye the night before, when the light

of the streetlamp fell on it in the dark: a phosphorescent *Scream*.
Louis said, 'Is this something that's being kept?'

I said, 'Do you know what it is?'

'I can guess,' he said.

'Take it,' I said.

'Sure?'

'Take it.'

*

I finish this six years after Robert's death. I still hum his tunes
every day, still cry at what I've been writing. I see what we went
through a bit more clearly, and hope that what I've written may
make these experiences clearer for some others too.

The nature of our tragedy may seem obvious. But on closer look,
it was simply this: we didn't have the time, the sickness-free time,
to be what we should have been together. And the comfort is that
within that stricture, we did have some absolutely glorious times.
In this way, this it is not a typical cautionary/instructive tale about
loving an alcoholic. A more usual misery memoir dynamic would
be: *I fell in love with an alcoholic, he fucked up my life and destroyed
our family because I didn't understand that his primary relationship
was with alcohol, behold my catastrophe all ye women and steer clear
of such men.* But Robert destroyed, in the end, nothing but himself.

I have thought so much about what put him so out of balance,
and one part of it is this. A price was paid by that socially mobile
generation. At sixteen, Robert's talent hijacked him. It tore him out
of his childhood's familiar society, offering him new, distant, dazzling
intellectual and emotional adventures. What did Robert lose, by
taking on what he was offered? His family security. His home. His
hometown. His friends and peers. Playing rugby. His mother, and
his father. It left him perpetually out of kilter, and he lost faith in
his judgement, and clung to the wrong straws. And that, in turn,
took from him everything else.

For others close to him, I regret a lot, but for myself, heartbroken as I have been, *je ne regrette rien.* My life so far has largely been a pretty good adventure, conducted on my own individual, idiosyncratic even, terms. Above all, I was able to maintain my social and financial independence, and this alone has protected me from the wider veil of destruction which alcoholism so often spreads. Robert funded his own addiction; there were no children going hungry, no mortgage failing because Dad drank the wages. He wasn't a nasty drunk, crashing cars, hitting people, terrorising neighbours. He saved himself over and over, but in the end his condition destroyed him. And however much that hurt, it didn't destroy me.

There is a moment in any memoir of loss where the writer speaks movingly of, oh yes, moving on. I wasn't sure I would be able to come up with that bit. But perhaps I can.

Devotion, the third novel about Riley Purefoy, is published. Lola's a grown-up. Jim is two years older than Robert was when I first met him in 1976. I seem to have finished this memoir, and I have other things to write. I'm making an album of my songs. Lola's boyfriend is my collaborator. We're called Birds of Britain, and the album, like this book, is called *You Left Early*. The songs are about loss, death, addiction. Love. Robert.

And then there's this: three and a half years after I had stood grief-blasted on stage at a book festival, I sat in the audience at another one and heard another grief-blasted novelist read about his wife who had died, of cancer, two months before. I wrote and told him – Michel – to do nothing irreversible. He sent me a terribly bleak and funny poem he'd written about people who offer to help. Fellow widow, I could laugh where thousands couldn't. Grief-blasted novelists half in love with our dead true loves and without the sense to keep off stage in the immediate aftermath should stick together. He's published a volume of poems about his wife, called *Undying, A Love Story*. I've been writing this. 'His and hers grief memoirs,' he observed. He's out this afternoon; he'll be back later. They are dead; we are not.

I won't mislead you: grief and love entwine like roses, and never die. They remain with the old and encompass the new. This is what love is – what it was for us. Life does go on.

London 2018

Appendices

From ROBERT'S REHAB PAPERS

<u>The Life and Times of Robert Lockhart</u>

Clouds, Autumn 2005

Born Wigan, Lancs, 1959. Only child. My parents, John and Pat, were deemed to be a glamorous couple in their lower middle class (for want of a better term) milieu. He a travelling salesman with a souped-up Ford Anglia, she a hairdresser. Not quite Elizabeth Taylor and Richard Burton but never mind. Especially 'not quite' on the drinking front (ie no history of alcoholism in the family). I was a relatively happy child, successful academically and at sport, plenty friends . . . My father was having an affair by the time I was about six, with Lily Glinka, a Russian secretary who was afraid of the wind . . . and who was anorexic (sp?) I think he was attracted by the 'victim' syndrome. At that age obviously oblivious I didn't think it odd that he often got home from 'work' at ten pm. My mother found out, and when he was on his next affair I found out about that one too. About age eight I was frequently woken by my parents arguing in their bedroom late into the night. This went on for about four years. My mother's attitude was to protect me but eventually she succumbed to an affair herself. He died two years later of diabetes. The next man later became her second husband. My father lost his job. I had changed schools – going to the local grammar (later becoming a comprehensive) – and had the dilemma of whether to stay with my mother at home or go to my paternal grandparents with my father. I left with my father to live with my grandparents – sharing a single bed with him. Particularly unpleasant were his seemingly nicotine-stained elephant-tusk-like toenails. I became somewhat estranged from my mum. I think it was that my father and I had more in common, not necessarily that I loved him more. I went back to my mother but the presence of my future stepfather drove me back to my father and grandparents. This scenario happened again, which must have had an unsettling effect. On the surface things were OK – still good academically – made the under-13s 100m and triple jump and sufficiently advanced to go to music college junior school in Manchester on Saturday mornings. This coincided with an influx of rough lads who beat the shit out of us supposedly posh grammar-school boys. I escaped punishment despite being a prime target as a classical pianist (one is automatically a 'puffter') because I had played for Wigan Rugby League schoolboys which even at that age was a sport for hard lads – but because I was studying the piano sadly had to stop due to the high risk of breaking fingers.

At the junior music college I finally met some peers with whom I had more in common. Sport went downhill, I became more isolated except for Saturdays. This was a period of sexual awakening – not easy when you only see each other weekly. Later I met a senior student – a very mature lady – she was 19. I was deflowered. It lasted six weeks and was my first experience of being emotionally devastated.

My parents had divorced. Dad met my future stepmother,

later they got married on the same day as my mother (a total coincidence). My dad and Kath bought a house – I moved in. With one or two exceptions – a quick slug from a whisky bottle when I was young, drinking 1/2 bottle of repulsive sweet sherry on Christmas day when I was twelve and vomiting in the back seat of the car all over my grandmother's best hat – alcohol did not play a role in my life. Aged 15 there was the odd semi-drunken episode at the odd disco.

I didn't like my stepmother, but thinking back it must have been very difficult to deal with a precocious, wilful teenager. I met Alex, whose parents had emigrated to America, leaving her homeless. I wanted her to come and stay, my father's response being 'do you want a red light outside the house?' What a hypocritical bastard, pathetic unthinking double standards. After what I'd witnessed with his relationships, perhaps a touch more sympathy, a touch more understanding, might have been appropriate.

When I was 17 I went down south to college – Alex and I sort of sustained the relationship for a year and a half – with numerous infidelities along the way – and then she went to live in LA. I felt totally bereft.

College was very difficult at first, trying to fit in with largely posh people. But I began to make friends and in the end had a good time, despite developing what is now called compulsive-obsessive disorder. Alcohol played a bigger role socially but was not a major issue. I had two relationships there, one with Beth – now a good friend. She was my first real love but I couldn't stand her one infidelity and like a typical male hypocrite dumped her. Biggest mistake of my life.

I went to London to study piano as a postgraduate for three years – and later took it up professionally. I taught at my first college and played cocktail jazz in wine-bars to support myself. I looked after myself, I was very busy. Still alcohol did not play a significant role. I worked hard, had a lovely new girlfriend, life was good – until my mother from whom I had become estranged died when I was 25. She was 52. She'd had breast cancer before but this time it was the liver. They didn't spot it soon enough, thinking it to be hepatitis. Seeing her dying – looking aged 80, deaf, blind, incontinent – was probably the most disturbing moment of my life. Professionals always focus on this event as pivotal in terms of the beginning of my alcoholism. Admittedly I did drink 1/2 a bottle of whisky before the funeral, but it's not as if I continued like that. Thankfully I didn't embarrass myself but I think that might have been the pivotal moment of change.

Then on it was a gradual, imperceptible, sneaky evolution I think – more pronounced in my early thirties onwards. By this time I had retired prematurely from playing the piano and started writing music for radio and TV, later also in theatre, films and jingles. Big pressure, scary deadlines, but I didn't have to be on stage so therefore I could drink. That world was brimming with booze and it became a habit. I could write whilst drinking – at first not drinking before 6 or 7 pm, later the odd one at lunch and later (about five years ago) a straightener – a brandy in my coffee – in the morning – then more in the morning (about two years ago). Sometimes I had to drink to get rid of writers block. It worked. That's the alarming and frightening thing. I was now a full-blown functioning alcoholic.

In the early 80s I lived with Lisette for 7 years – we split up 4 times. By this time, still thinking that booze was a laugh, I was overdoing it. Sex became a preoccupation, fuelled by booze. Alcohol was the mainstay. I gained a reputation as a party boy, late nights or rather early mornings, one-night-stands, short affairs, telephone sex, any sex. Low stuff. Stuff that embarrasses me now. Stuff that I could never contemplate doing. Ever. I eventually got involved with someone a lot younger in Notting Hill. We both drank a lot, with her on drugs also. I went to work in Dublin – not great for a budding alcoholic – but at least away from west London temptations. I met Emer, who was an editor on a doc for which I wrote the music. Funny, bright, talented, good skydiver and beautiful. She was an entirely different proposition. She didn't smoke or drink, hated drugs. I wanted her to come to London where she frequently worked. She wanted me to stay in Dublin where I infrequently worked. I went back to London, she stayed in Dublin. Very sad.

This stage was getting heavyish: 1/4 bottle of vodka a day + lots of booze with lunch and dinner. So trust me to marry. [NB His marriage was a few years after breaking up with Emer.] I got married pissed and got divorced very sober. The good thing to come out of this was a beautiful son, who is now nearly 7. I was less than perfect. I did love her. I didn't see my son for a while due to being pissed all the time but recently have seen him a lot. I go to their house to pick him up; kiss her on the cheek, shake her husband's hand. I think she finds this perplexing! – I take a deep breath. I'm doing it for my son. He's more important.

A year later I moved in with Anna. Most time was spent in the pub. Naturally my career deteriorated. Alcohol destroyed us. She would criticise my drinking while drunk which is no way to conduct a relationship.

On arriving back in London I stayed with an old friend Louisa [then] found a one-bed flat to rent. Louisa I can never thank enough for her support. I drank less and less and we got together, have now been for 3 1/2 years and we still sort of are, but the odd three-hour visit here cannot resolve much.

I have caused trouble courtesy of the booze. I would go to the shops for supposedly fags and newspaper but in a phone-box would pour a 1/4 of vodka into a half-full bottle of 7-up, fully equipped with the tools of the trade: extra strong mints, chewing gum, toothbrush, toothpaste. It must have been a strange sight seeing someone clean their teeth whilst pretending to listen to someone on the phone. However an equally big problem was Louisa's daughter, then aged 9. Things have improved but the young woman she is now rapidly and alarmingly becoming resents me for taking her mother away and seeing me never aggressive or violent but palpably pissed.

The booze antics I got away with for a while but when I broke my ankle in 3 places – the leg was nearly amputated below the knee – Louisa got keys to my flat which she had never visited. This was no bachelor pad. It was a disgusting shit-hole littered with fag-ends and 1/2 bottles of vodka most of which I had peed in.

After 3 weeks of no booze no fags and lots of morphine in hospital I stupidly went back to my old habits. I really should have grasped that opportunity to stop, but I didn't.

Eventually after several home detoxes I went to hospital for a two-week detox having had a severe alcohol-induced fit. Not the best place to be when crack was brought into the clinic.

Louisa said if I started again that was it. I started again. It is now semi or a third it – the relationship I mean. She is a fantastic woman, one of those annoying individuals who will occasionally have a fag or the odd glass of wine with her dinner. I'd love to be able to do that but all of us know we can't, we have a different nature. Louisa led me to Clouds. She initiated the whole thing.

This year started with a heavy long weekend which became a week, a month, a season, etc.

I miss my dad. He has a phobia about travelling – he has never been to see me since I moved south when I was 17. I don't go up there much, mainly due to the insensitivity of my stepmother. She perhaps wisely prefers her cat (ironically an unaffectionate one) to humans.

I've got a brilliant agent who nearly died twice this year of an MRSA-induced mixture of double pneumonia and septicaemia. Seeing him with three computers each side of his bed and innumerable tubes stuck into him really made me think. I was killing myself – knowingly. Something else was killing him which was not of his own doing. He weighed 3 stone. Thankfully, remarkably, he is back to normal so I'll get back my career when I am normal as well, whatever normal is.

On his career

I was relatively successful, but I suspect that I could have been a lot more so. I had two potential breaks in the States, the Dustin Hoffman Merchant of Venice on Broadway, and in LA with John Schlesinger's film, Cold Comfort Farm, for which I'd written the score, but due to being inert courtesy of alcohol I preferred to sit chatting to boring alcoholics in a rough Shepherds Bush pub rather than getting in touch with John and Dustin Hoffman, both of whom had admired my music. The boring alcoholics (myself included) were the salt of the earth, I was doing social research, proving that the Oxford University tutor could mix it with the dustman. I was the new George Orwell. What a hero. In the States they want to know what you did yesterday, not years ago. I became so alcoholic that I stopped working entirely. I've not spoken to my agent for months. I made myself unemployable.

Under the influence of alcohol I've taken things too far with people both socially and professionally. I've ended up in hospital after being beaten up. It all started pretty well – me being a slightly over-the-top risqué party animal, but ended up in a self-parody – empty, pathetic, repetitive, formulaic. I've spent nights at her majesty's pleasure. I've had death threats, one after a sarcastic remark to someone in front of his mates in a pub, after beating him at darts; one after going to bed with someone who told her psychotically jealous possessive violent fiancé. People I know have avoided me at parties . . . and I'm sure avoidance has extended into professional areas. In the music area, London is a village. People talk. The obvious hazards are my exaggerated reactions – Dutch courage, being over-ambitious creatively speaking, misjudging what musicians are capable of in the tense studio environment. Asking musicians to do another take when not really necessary, pressurising and potentially embarrassing them. This can lead to a stiff atmosphere, especially when I'm not exerting the necessary control to achieve the result in the allotted time, due to inebriation. When mixing music, spending hours – exaggerating detail when not necessary. Drunk in front of directors and producers. Very destructive to my career. I always turned up, always reached deadlines, but presentation was distinctly lacking. I told a reputable director at the National Theatre to fuck off. It's hard to get rid of a bad reputation. One gets labelled.

I thought that I was a better film, theatre + T.V. composer than most. In terms of sheer amount and consistency, this is pure arrogance. I have written, I still think, some very good film scores. Cold Comfort Farm stands out. But to assume it was one of <u>the</u> great film scores is, to say the least, a slight exaggeration. I'm deeply bitter about having destroyed my career. Jealousy of lesser talent, of what that talent has achieved, is a sad state of affairs. If I hear great work I feel nothing but admiration. The main reason I'm not there is very simple: I'm an ~~fucking~~ alcoholic. [The handwriting shows that having deleted 'fucking', he went back and put in the 'n' to make 'an'. He is putting a small but important thing to rights. He is taking care.] And I involved alcohol in everything I did, and persuaded everyone I was with to drink as much as me. This used to be known as 'Rob Duty'. And I convinced myself and tried to convince others that something was their fault when it was often obviously mine. I assumed I was clever and sexy when I most probably came over as a drunk arrogant wanker.

'He was a very talented musician/composer,' a fellow composer said, 'who never achieved the recognition he should have. It looked like self-destruct. He gained a reputation for being very difficult to work with – I don't think he suffered fools and unfortunately in TV there are plenty of those. I remember being asked to replace him composing for the second series of a TV show. I asked them why they would replace him when his music was so great and memorable – it was because he was too difficult.'

But this cut both ways. A colleague wrote this, years later: 'When

I worked with him he was one of the last (but best) people to score (in hand) his compositions for an orchestra piece. One of our first trips to Paris was for four days (the dreaded Jif commercial – oh the ignominy!! – he took an instant dislike to them – I can attest they were actually tossers). I built in an extra hour to get him to Heathrow and arrived at his Shepherds Bush emporium with a bottle of brandy to coax him into the cab. We drank it before it arrived. I checked to make sure he had packed (he'd just gotten out of bed) and he assured me he was ready. The cab came, he put on his leather jacket and walked out the door with nothing except a paperback of Jeeves and Wooster. We had to unlock the door again for him to get his passport. And that was it. Nothing, not a change of clothes, no bag, no nothing. I bought him a toothbrush which he lost somewhere between de Gaulle and the hotel. Checking us in, I went for a well-deserved pass out. Waking up, Robert was nowhere to be found. I spent my weekend tracking him down through various cafes. Luckily he left a recognisable wake and I usually managed to find him within a bar or two. But he had that orchestra in the palm of his hand. They all came in ready to toss off a 40-second arrangement; by the afternoon he had taken over musical direction, told the agency to leave but to come back and take us to dinner (we ditched them when we found we had the same tolerance for calvados and the same intolerance for wanky French advertising midgets) and the following day the musicians all showed up on time and hung on his every direction. They were looking for *him*, the reason why they learned the cello or the oboe or the violin. He played the piano at lunchtime and they stayed instead of having lunch.'

On Compulsion

Camden Town, Summer 2007

In the late 1980s with Lisette, both drunk at a party, I stripped naked, danced, annoyed everybody by biting their feet under the table, and damaged the newly decorated house – just the usual. Then the attention-seeking/compulsive-obsessive disorder came into play. I climbed on to a window-ledge and then <u>had</u> to jump to the other (50ft drop). Everyone was amused except for Lisette who was hysterical with fear. We went home to bed – 2am – furious row. I wanted to have sex. She was too tired and drunk. I left on my bike suddenly getting the idea that because I had to recreate an arrangement for a guest artiste and my friend Nina had her CD I had to go round there. And to have sex with Nina. She was asleep but her first floor balcony window was open. I shinned 20 feet up, nearly made it but then slipped and fell 20 feet landing on the (despiked) railings – bouncing on to the pavement. If those spikes had been there I would have been impaled, or, had I bounced into the basement, dead or severely crippled. I managed to ring on her bell, by now bleeding profusely from the anus. She answered, I sat on her bed, blood seeping through my jeans. She hates the sight of blood. I cycled home. Lisette took one look, vomited and cried. Straight to A+E. The wound was so close to the anal passage that they couldn't stitch it. Jokes were made: not Coriol-anus but Corialbinus. I was working as a music associate at ITV. Playing the piano on the Monday, people were concerned by the special chair with three pillows I had erected. I explained that I had been pushed over the balcony at a party by a jealous guy who thought, wrongly, that I had been chatting up his girlfriend.

<u>Significant Events Sheet</u>

An inexplicable emotional revelation. I have become resolute. This is kindergarten, possible flash in the pan, early days, self delusion, self deception, etc. Got to work out how to hang on to it when out of here. I know it's not really started yet.

    1) Realising that saying 'good morning' to someone <u>first</u> is important.

    2) excellent lunch

3) good new AA meeting

4) God-daughter's piano lesson

5) Speaking at AA with my speech impediment (decided to take it with me)

6) Chronic lasciviousness – very unusual

7) AA Beginners – a guy 4 years sober saying he was fine for 3 1/2 years thought he'd cracked it – last 6 months absolute hell!!??? Thanks. Good or bad to hear? A sobering thought. Ha ha.

8) Not being able to get to the prom (significant non-event). Pleased that I didn't lose it when realising I couldn't get to see one of the greatest musicians on the planet (Daniel Barenboim) conduct one of the great orchestras. Resigned, philosophical. Feelings far too many to process. I'm not a pea . . . yet.

From Robert's Stepwork

London and Wigan, 2009–2010

How does the self-centred part of my disease affect my life + the lives of those around me?

The problem I now face, sober, is differentiating between self-centredness and self-protectiveness. My principle criterion is not having a drink today. Nothing or nobody will get in the way of that today. Yes, in a way this is self-centred, but without my treasured sobriety I would be incapable of helping others, loving others, loving anything.

Did I believe I could control my drinking?

Trying to avoid the off licence before going to the pub late morning. Only successful if I got a taxi to the pub. After my siesta at my flat, ordering a cab straight to Louisa's, avoiding the off-licence en route. On the few occasions I managed this, I would later have to leave Louisa's to go and 'buy cigarettes', hiding my existing cigarettes in an inside pocket.

What things did I do that I can hardly believe I did when I look back at them?

The balcony-window-arse-impaling-on-the-railing occasion. When I went to stay in Prague with my then-girlfriend's closest friend. After one night on the sofa I complained that it had not been comfortable. Next day, after an alcohol-fuelled party, we returned to share her bed, obviously, as just good friends. Not.

Insisting to x that she had an abortion. Contraception had been used, therefore the pregnancy was not my responsibility. I did not want the child and told her so. I did not tell her that my becoming a father would get in the way of my work and of my drinking, although at the time I was not consciously aware of the latter. A vivid memory of her sobbing in the cab to the clinic, a vivid memory of her sobbing in the clinic and most painful of all a vivid memory of her after the operation, a grey pallor, her eyes dead, looking down and then looking through me. 'I've forgotten my hip flask,' I thought. I bought flowers, I bought videos, I looked after her lovingly, but drowned any feelings of guilt or remorse in vodka. 'It'll be all right,' I thought. It never was.

Did I behave in ways of which I'm now ashamed?

Relentlessly deceiving Louisa into believing that I was not drinking. A sense of relief, a sense of the naughty schoolboy getting away with it, and risibly a sense of nobility, of decadent heroism. Infidelity on an irregular basis to x, whilst she was away, sleeping with someone in the flat and not bothering to change the sheets. Not bothering to come home at all, sleeping in the West End with an actress with whom I was working. I said I had been working late, then had got drunk and wrenched my back; I couldn't get home + had to stay in a hotel. Again, heroic, bohemian, entirely justifiable. Any niggling doubts quelled by workaholism and a few drinks.

A lovely old lady, mother of a friend. For years (1980–85) I would to go round, to practise the piano and be fed, and for holidays with her family. When she died c2002, I was asked to the funeral. Apparently I was one of her favourites. I didn't turn up. I never bothered to apologise. Never sent a note. What was it like? I didn't fucking care.

I was divorced by my ex-wife, dumped by Anna and thrown out by Louisa. My drinking came first. It was *their* fault for not understanding the complex sensitive artist. I existed on a higher, more esoteric plane and anyway now these less-talented mortals, who couldn't be expected to understand my idiosyncratic genius, would no longer get in the way of my drinking. In other words I was a self-obsessed deluded wanker.

Did I make insane decisions as a result of my addiction?
[He did, and listed them, but I've been asked not to include them, so I won't.]

Did I ever physically injure myself?
One cracked tooth, one tooth knocked out. I told Louisa I'd been mugged. I had in fact been mugged by a garden wall. Facial injury – bad cuts, bad bruises, one cut near the eye socket. I had been mugged again by some evil bastard. Two evil bastards actually – a lamppost and a shop doorknob. Breaking my foot off. Getting into fights.

Have I over- and under-reacted to things?
Over-reacting: I interpreted criticism as personal slight meant to undermine me, professionally or emotionally. That much of this criticism was constructive eluded me. Or it was immediately dismissed. People were insensitive, jealous, small-minded. No further thought given. I had a chronic, painful infatuation in 96–97. I was, in retrospect, infatuated with the infatuation. She smoked spliff and listened to pop music; I drank alcohol and listened to classical music. I didn't like her friends; she didn't like mine. I smoked more spliff; she drank more booze. This was the solution,

I thought. A few weeks after I was dumped I saw her at a party – she didn't know who I was.

Under-reacting: only after my father's demise have I begun to genuinely grieve for my mother. I drank 1/2 a bottle of whisky before the funeral. then on, it was a gradual sneaky evolution – more pronounced from my early thirties.

Over and under: On being told I was scruffy + smelly I would rush out and buy a lot of new clothes and bathe scrupulously all in one day. The rest of the time I would wallow in what I styled as modish and bohemian – ie scruffy and smelly.

In what ways has my life changed since I've been in recovery?

I am no longer the most sensitive, vulnerable hard-done-by person on the planet. The formerly alien concept of gratitude plays a crucial role. Despite my formerly huge ego + massively extrovert personality (invite Rob round, he's guaranteed to initially entertain then surprise, shock and humiliate) I was in fact a shy, fearful person. Alcohol provided the antidote. Now I can approach people without wanting to dominate + manipulate them. A great gift.

What action have I been taking that demonstrates my faith?

Regular attendance at meetings. Writing more and better music. Sane music, hopefully devoid of effect, devoid of sensationalism. Not just doing the steps but infusing my life with what I have learnt. Despite my deeply faulted character I am becoming a more considerate person, mentally and physically more agile despite suffering from incurable illnesses.

Do I believe more change is possible?

Yes.

*

Hospital Notebook

London, Summer 2010

~~Particularly~~

(<u>upside</u> down)

Thanks so much for that elongated effort!
<u>Breathing</u> struggle fear of choking
CHOKING
from CATARRH

I thought 'This is it'

I will probably <u>never</u> speak properly
– <u>fact</u>
I've gone a bit tone deaf
temp – I'm a fucking musician
– composer

a much bigger medical shock
will be trying to get the TV to work
and watch England lose.

What are you doing tonight
New one: Lachrymose hiccup

Dear L.
Thank you
and I still
love you.
(even more.
in fact).
R X X

I think you should have a day off.
– a break from this
do something else.
It'll be good for you.
X

could you be so kind as to charge
my mobile?
Thank

BOWELGROIN AGONY <u>PAIN</u>

I'M NOT SOFT <u>NOT</u> A COWARD
THIS IS
BAD

I'm from Wigan
where are you
from?

Sorry! Didn't realise!

T.V. too loud
but don't say it's me

What is nebuliser?
I've had
enough pain.
Is it painful?

What is the noise NOISE

Dear _____
Did you mention cathata?
The nurse in the other
ward gave me such pain
(like the tube was stood on)
more pain than my neck! (haha)
I'm sure you'll be very
delicate
Thanks so much.

MY FIANCÉ HAS
GOOD TASTE IN MEN

CHEST PAIN
– BREATHING INV BAD
BIT PANICKY
– FRIGHTENED

IS DOC COMING?
THANKS
– YOU'RE GOOD THOUGH

You know what Hockney's
boyfriend said when he
met WH Auden?

I was giving Louisa the book

Will never speak normally
never fuckin' did
haha
My future wife !

has been phenomenal

Not had a drink
lose dad
Louisa's dad
Kath
now this reward!

Another northern humourist
N Wales   Barry Manilow

Not at first
but it grows
good woman

Class A drug   morphine pure
there is a limit 5-10-15

How's Lisette?
weirdest fantasies
Surreal stuff
very real

Mark Almond?
Sax
send regards
still married
These surgeons are amazing
so complex
ask Louisa she likes detail!

I probably can't eat again
either

I feel scared. I <u>have</u> been v. tough
Everyone impressed. But now –

Mouth physio!?

hurts when I
breathe in
I've not tried moving
on my own yet

I'm thinking of guys
in world war one
before! . . . ?

I'm in the Paris Hilton

Dominic
– you are strong + gentle
perfect combo.

silly ~~fucker~~ man

PARANOID about F-ing
CATHETAand I'm getting
married soon!!
[Two willy cartoons: one pointing
high, the other (with the word
NOT written by it) broken.]

<u>Hard</u> to
breath

<u>NOT</u>
too painful
tho
I
can't get
enough

there's a lot worse
than this
mild case

Did you study medics
at Univ? Where?

NO
BOOZE
3 1/2 yrs
<u>DAY AT A TIME</u>

I NEED <u>HELP</u>
<u>UNDERSTANDING</u>
WORSE PAIN
NO SLEEP

How are you?
It's not quite
all about me
but nearly
I had a dog called
Fella – dead
Robert – alive

comfortable
sleep
position?

back very uncomfort

do you know about
blood explosion
sickness
here earlier

old blood
swallowed in stomach

Now I can feel more gums
afraid of biting
plus hard bits

Also my
lovely future wife
left earlier

Like many men I am a soft
coward
How are you?

post op trauma
FEAR PANIC
SADNESS
TRAUM
FEAR PANIC
PAIN PHYSICAL YES
BUT MORE

manual cheek jaw behind eye

I'm really sorry!
I have great respect for you!!
My light has been on for 20
mins . . .your colleague didn't
come back please accept my
apology! I just wanted a little
favour? Could you find BBC4
for me? I'd really appreciate
that
I know you're dealing with
much more urgent things
THANKS
Robert
also bad pain left neck
area + nose

How's work?
[*He's drawn a section of
musical stave, with treble
clef, 4/4 time signature, and
the first bar of Mozart's
Minuet in G, one of the
classic first pieces that
young piano beginners
are given to learn*]

pseudo 'classical'
do you know Siegfried Idyll
overture to Parsifal
melancholic trumpet

What opera

lunch darling?
oysters sashimi
2-4 wee

I booked rooms in Magdalen
to show her.
– yes
she occasionally smiles
and she is older. 1 day 4 hrs

Jackie has been <u>amazing</u>
She's had cancer
Now close to Louisa
they're both a bit

~~Jackie + me love each other~~
both sides of her!
but nothing of that with us..

Now my main language
will be music so perhaps
I will write some
good stuff
better
what is iPod
Too emotional ie Rachma—

I've done so well
with the booze,
the best thing I've
ever done

and now
fucking fags
neat vodka

years of throat damage
I feel guilty about what I've
put Louisa thru'

32H[6]
her new adult novel
is going to be a great success
then film
music by ? <u>me</u>
~~Michael Nyman~~
Have you heard the theme
tune
sampled orchestra
cornet my cousin <u>Diane</u>
Violin

I've not complained
AT ALL for a month
– my future wife (!)
has been <u>impressed!</u>

But now

---

[6] This is my bra size. For god's sake.

<u>Camden Town, second time round:</u>

Winter 2011

What can I use from my four-plus years sober to reactivate my recovery today?

Leaving here four and a half years ago, I took with me a wealth of knowledge, and endeavoured to put it into practice. An old friend, an alcoholic/drug addict who had been sober and clean for twelve years, offered to be my sponsor. I was very fortunate. Talking to him everyday became a useful discipline. It was a matter of sticking to basics, going to regular meetings and speaking to Will, regular meals and a good diet (sadly not available to me any more) and lots of regular sleep. When I had my relapse I had not been leading a regular life.

I was now able to see my twelve year old son, look him in the eye and have a good laugh. He doesn't know about my condition – that's for when he's older. I can now approach his mother. I was able to see my father. He said he was more proud of my sobriety than anything else I had achieved. In sobriety I can now recognise and appreciate my love for others and their love for me. Gratitude, also. I owe so much to Will, my sponsor, my landlord Patrick in the North and most of all to my fiancee Louisa.

Prior to my lapse, I had not spoken with Will for a number of days, which says it all. When I did speak to him, I didn't admit to having had a drink, basically abusing the intimacy that had been forged. Our sponsors will be personally familiar with most of what we reveal; we do them good by reminding them of the pitfalls of our condition. And for a while before my lapse I hadn't attended AA. I think I used my disability and my cancer as an excuse.

I find it difficult to express the amount of freedom and simple enjoyment that my four and a half years gave me. Sobriety allowed me to rid myself of complications, neuroses and obsessions. Clarity of thought and the ability to take time making decisions made a huge difference. The impulsiveness fuelled by the alcoholic mind had disappeared almost totally.

[Louisa and I had] a somewhat tempestuous ten-year relationship. Sobriety has rid me of many of the frustrations I once felt. Despite her faults, the main fault in the relationship was my drunkenness.

Louisa's father died just after mine and she asked me to write a piece of music for his memorial service. The music flowed from my pencil – I experienced none of the creative blocks of yesteryear, therefore not needing a drink to unblock them. Music is, or was, my career; sobriety will be essential for any advances in this crucial area of my life. I am still angry and even embarrassed about my relapse, but I have learnt from it. And finally, just something about my four and a half years of sobriety – it got better and better. Never again do I want to return to that hell.

*

Further Reading

Obituary by Will Self
https://www.theguardian.com/music/2012/jan/27/robert-lockhart

Valediction by Nicholas Lezard
https://www.newstatesman.com/node/187357

Discography

Prelude in G Op. 32 No. 5, (Rachmaninoff), Rachmaninoff
La Bohème, (Puccini), Jose Carreras and Barbara Hendricks
'Here Comes the Rainbow Again', (Kristofferson), Johnny Cash
'It Hurts Me Too', (Red/James), Karen Dalton
'I'd Rather Go Blind', (Jordan/Foster), Etta James
'I'll Be Seeing You', (Fain/Kahal), Billie Holliday
'*Les Feuilles Mortes*', (Kosma/Prevert), Yves Montand

'Song for My Father', Horace Silver
'O Waly Waly', (anon./Britten), Roderick Williams
'The Salley Gardens', (anon./Britten or Ireland)
Hungarian Dances, Brahms
Sonata in F minor, Brahms
'Cantaloupe Island', Herbie Hancock
Sonata in A, Schubert
'Wild Is the Wind', (Tiomkin/Washington), Nina Simone, or David Bowie
La Fille au Cheveux de Lin, Debussy
'Hotel', (Francis Poulenc), Regine Crespin
'*Après un Reve*', (Gabriel Fauré), Regine Crespin
Clair de Lune, (Gabriel Fauré), Regine Crespin
'When I Was Young', (Merill) Eddie Fisher
'Trouble Child', Joni Mitchell
'Re-Hab', Stew & the Negro Problem
'Pale Blue Eyes', Velvet Underground
'*Leiermann*', from the *Winterreise*, Schubert
'Good Year for the Roses', (Chesnut), George Jones
'The End', (Strand/Dove), Mark Padmore
'Don't Fence Me In', (Porter), Ella Fitzgerald
'Why Can't You Behave?' (Porter), Ella Fitzgerald
'Anything Goes', (Porter), Ella Fitzgerald
'My Funny Valentine', (Rodgers/Hart), Chet Baker
'Get Out of Town', (Porter), Ella Fitzgerald
'Reason to Believe', (Hardin), Rod Stewart
'Don't Explain', (Holiday/Herzog), Billie Holiday
'Cry Me a River', (Hamilton), Julie London
'Only Him or Me', Townes Van Zandt
'Too Far Gone', (Sherill), Elvis Costello and the Attractions
'She's No Lady', Lyle Lovett
Four Last Songs, (Strauss), Jessye Norman
'Five Years', David Bowie
'The Unquiet Grave', (anon.), Joan Baez

Robert Lockhart's music can be found on YouTube, http://www.bmgproductionmusic.co.uk, or please contact Richard.Paine@faber-music.com

'83 Miles the Wrong Side of Birmingham', 'You Left Early' and 'Goldhawk Road' are tracks on the album *You Left Early* by Birds of Britain; released in June 2018. Birds of Britain are Louisa Young and Alex Mackenzie. Birds of Britain music can be found on Spotify, iTunes and in all the old familiar places.

www.louisayoung.co.uk

You Left Early

You waltzed in, your coat tails flying
Cool as an angel, without trying
You took the piano knowing every song
Billie and Cole, All night long.

You played for all the prettiest women,
Stole their fags, admired their singing
They could never leave you alone
You stayed so late and we played along

We all knew that you drank twice your share in half the time
You had it blazoned all around your soul like a neon sign
You lit the night, I'm not lying
When you stayed late and we played along

Wanted to be your silver lining
Strong and bold, bright and shining
I was going to bring you safely home

But you left early and you left alone
Yeah you left early and you left alone

You played for all the prettiest women
You broke their hearts, left them swimming
In lakes of their own tears at your heart of stone
When after all, you left alone

We all knew you drank, twice your share in half the time
You had it hanging heavy round your life like a ball and chain
Night and day, I'm not lying
And you left early and you left alone
You left early and you left alone

Oh, oh, your silver lining, strong and bright, both of us shining
We were going to bring each other home
But you left early and you left alone
You left early and you left alone
You left early and you left alone

Acknowledgements

For their faith, encouragement, patience and understanding, I thank my daughter; her father; Susan Swift; Charlotte Horton; Derek Johns; Michel Faber; my publishers especially Suzie Dooré and Ann Bissell, and all Robert's friends and family who understood what I was trying to do and let me do it; trusted me and by doing so helped me immeasurably.